Jubilation

A Celebration of Favourite Recipes

The Sustainers are grateful to the
Active Members of The Junior League
of Toronto who have shared with us
their resources and expertise.

We are deeply indebted to the
Corporations which have given us
financial assistance.

ALLIED VAN LINES
CARA OPERATIONS LIMITED
ESSO PETROLEUM
FORD MOTOR COMPANY OF CANADA, LIMITED
NABISCO BRANDS LTD
ROYAL LEPAGE REAL ESTATE SERVICES LTD.
THE BANK OF NOVA SCOTIA
THE CONSUMERS' GAS COMPANY LTD.
TRANSCANADA PIPELINES

The Junior League of Toronto

Volunteers
Vision
and
Commitment

Jubilation

The Junior League of Toronto, a member of an international organization, trains committed volunteers to serve their community.

The proceeds realized from the sale of **Jubilation** will be returned to the community through projects of The Junior League of Toronto.

Additional copies may be obtained by addressing:

JUBILATION

The Junior League of Toronto
P.O. Box 1986
Don Mills, Ontario
M3C 2E0

For your convenience, order blanks are included in the back of the book.

The Jubilation Committee members wish to extend their grateful appreciation to the patrons who so generously supported the first printing of this cookbook.

PATRONS

Mrs. Hugh Allan
Mrs. C. Robert Allen
Mrs. Gerry Anthony
Mrs. Johny Armstrong
Mrs. William R. Barber
Mr. Douglas G. Bassett
Mrs. Douglas G. Bassett
Mr. J. Douglas Bryden
Mrs. John S. Carruthers
Mrs. R. Ian Cartwright
Mrs. John Clark
Mrs. J. Gordon Coleman
Mrs. Gordon S. Currie
Mrs. John T. DesBrisay
Mrs. William A. Dimma
Mrs. W.T. Erskine Duncan
Mrs. Paul A. Eide
Mrs. William S. Eplett
Mrs. John Farquharson
Mrs. James Flintoff
Mrs. A. Harry Galley
Mrs. A. Elliot Gardiner
Mrs. James G. Gibson
Mrs. James M. Gilchrist
Mrs. Cedric G.E. Gyles
Mrs. David Hackett
Mrs. W. David Hargraft
Mrs. Peter B. Hatcher III
Mrs. Kingsley G. Hicks
Mrs. John M. Hodgson
Mrs. Ann Hogarth
Mrs. Michael B. Hutchinson
Mrs. Paul G. Jeffrey
Mrs. Michael Johnston
Mrs. John M. Judson
Miss Dayna C.B. Kenner
Mrs. Susan Kilbourne
Mrs. E. George Kneider
Mrs. Henry Knowles
Mrs. Douglas E. Knox
Mrs. George K. Laidlaw
Mrs. Allen T. Lambert

Mrs. Lee W. Larkin
Mrs. Bryan Leggett
Mrs. Robert G. Long
Mrs. P. Douglas Lougheed
Mrs. Ronald S. Lougheed
Mrs. Ian McLean Macdonnell
Mrs. Philip G. MacDonnell
Mrs. Garfield A. MacInnis
Mrs. George Mara
Mrs. Edward W. Martin
Mrs. Donald C. Matheson
Mrs. Richard H. McCoy
Mrs. James W. McCutcheon
Mrs. C. Michael McKeown
Mrs. John Douglas McVittie
Mrs. Douglas H. Mitchell
Mrs. William G. Munro
Mrs. John R. Nash
Mrs. W. Rankine Nesbitt
Mrs. James Omand
Mrs. Robert S. Parsons
Mrs. William E. Paterson
Mrs. John D. Pattison
Mrs. Edward M. Peacock
Mrs. Richard Perry
Mrs. Dorothy B. Peterson
Mrs. Frank V. Reddy
Mrs. H. Grenville Rolph
Mrs. H. David Ross
Mrs. Arthur R.A. Scace
Mrs. Robert Shaw
Mrs. William P. Somers
Mrs. Donald R. Steele
Mrs. Margaret S. Stewart
Mrs. James S. Tait
Mrs. John H. Taylor
Mr. John H. Taylor
Mrs. John B. Tinker
Mrs. John A. Tory
Mrs. Nancy E.D. Watt
Mrs. Donald Wilson
Mrs. Robert P. Wright
Mrs. David Yule

Jubilation

The Jubilation Committee would like to thank the members of the Junior League of Toronto and their friends who have supported this book by contributing and testing more than 850 recipes, and proof-reading our selections. Each recipe has been tested for accuracy and excellence. We do not claim that all recipes are original, only that they are our favourites.

Robbie Anderson
Elsiedale Armstrong
Mary Armstrong
Marilyn Ashby
Marjory Austin
Marg Baines
Jane Barber
Nancy Barber
Rosemary Barclay
Judy Benson
Pat Benson
Barb Besse
Marg Blaine
Nancy Bongard
Barbara Bowlby
Marilyn Braaten
Gerri Bradfield
Heather Brodeur
Doreen Bruce
Fran Brunton
Lynda Bryden
Deanne Burch
Judy Burgess
Joan Callahan
Ann Cameron
Sue Carlisle
Jane Carruthers
Nancy Carter
Barb Cartwright
Pat Catalano
Ann Cathers
Sue Cavell
Pat Christie
Eleanor Clayton
Margo Coleman
Jill Colley

Ann Collombin
Toni Conroy
Maggie Corcoran
Mary Couke
Joan Crocker
Joan Crossen
Cathy Crossgrove
Bev Cryer
Sally Cuddy
Gail Dalglish
Jennifer Dattels
Anne Dawkins
Candis Dickie
Louise Dimma
Barbara Donaldson
Denise Dorfman
Dawn Drayton
Felicity Duncan
Anne Dupré
Fran Edgar
Connie Eide
Carol Eplett
Ginger Farquhar
Amelia Farquharson
Marlo Finlayson
Judy Fleming
Judy Fletcher
Carla Foster-Speck
Joan Frederick
Bev Gaby
Mary Galley
Lee Gardiner
Willa Gauthier
Anne Gibson
Dyanne Gibson
Janet Gould

Frances Grant
Julie Gray
Tina Gray
Fiona Gunn
Sue Gustavison
Ellen Haberer
Jean Hackett
Bev Hargraft
Judy Hatcher
Marilyn Hawtin
Mary Ann Healy
Elaine Heinsar
Joan Hepburn
Diane Hewitt
Mary Hicks
Chris Hindson
Joyce Hodge
Christopher Holdroyd
Sandy Hore
Joy Housser
Ann Hull
Pug Hunter
Kit Huycke
Jane Irwin
Penny Jacob
Judy James
Ginny Jarvis
Sue Jenkins
Vivian Johnson
Bette Johnston
Irene Johnston
Karen Johnston
Virginia Johnston
Ann Judson
Esther Kemp
Jean Kemp

Nancy Kennedy
Janet Kennish
Heather Kerr
Ann Kerwin
Sue Kime
Marilyn King
Ruth Kitchen
Marilyn Knowles
Mary Knowles
Judy Knox
Bev Labatt
Wendy Labbett
Marion Lambert
Sally Lambert
Ann Lang
Bev Larkin
Diane Leggett
Sheila Legon
Gig Leitch
Libby Leon
Fern Lougheed
Marg Ann Lougheed
Sue Macaulay
Nancy MacDonnell
Sheila Mackay
Mandy Macrae
Janet MacInnis
Donald MacIntosh
Laurie MacIntosh
Vanessa Magee
Ross Magill
Lee Magwood
Janet Marsh
Bette Martin
Nancy Martin
Gladys Massey
Arlene Matheson
Kae Matthews
Mary Jane McAskile
Sue McCoy
Diane McKee
Joan McKinney
Jeryn McKeown
Gaylan McLeish

Peggy McLeish
Chris McMeans
Judy McMurray
Jo Anne Menzies
Barb Mercer
Rianne Merry
Barb Morris
Anne Moseley
Lani Moses
Sheila Munro
Ann Nichols
Jane Omand
Desmond O'Rorke
Pam O'Rorke
Margie Pacini
Mary Park
Penny Pashby
Marg Paterson
Susan Pattillo
Margaret Ann Pattison
Eileen Paulsen
Marlit Peirce
Marg Peacock
Nan Percival
Penny Perry
Dorothy Peterson
June Phelps
Sue Pielsticker
Ann-Marie Piton
Wendy Porritt
Maida Pugh
Elaine Quinn
Sue Reid
Eunice Richards
Debby Riley
Sharon Ritchie
Elaine Rosebrugh
Cathy Ross
Gretchen Ross
Judy Ross
Lynn Ross
Marsha Ross
Rosemary Ross
Mary Roy

Martie Russel
Donna Rygiel
Joy Saul
Louise Saunders
Sue Scace
Marie Schatz
Judie Scott
Nancy Scott
Janet Seagram
Rosemary Seagram
Ann Shaw
Cathy Shea
Kathie Sherrard
Ginger Silva
Lois Smallman
Sally Somers
Linda Sparling
Victoria Steele
Barbara Stewart
Janet Stewart
Carolyn Swann
Adrienne Tait
Marg Tamaki
Cayley Taylor
Diane Taylor
Marian Taylor
Gillian Telford
Ellen Tinker
Donna Tucker
Laura Wall
Margo Warrington
Grace Watson
Carolyn Whiteside
Gwyne Willmot
Sue Willoughby
Jan Wilson
Jane Wilson
Judie Wilson
Lisa Wilson
Janet Wood
Elsie Woodroffe
Elinor Young
Chricket Yule

We deeply regret that we were unable to include many recipes which were submitted due to similarity or lack of space.

A MESSAGE FROM THE PRESIDENT

As we prepare to celebrate our Diamond Jubilee, The Junior League of Toronto is pleased to present **Jubilation**—a celebration of favourite recipes compiled and produced by our Sustainers. Work began on the project in January 1984 and the result of nearly two years of labour by our dedicated Sustainers has produced this beautiful cookbook of which we are all justly proud.

Our Sustainers wished to observe our sixtieth year of volunteer service to Metropolitan Toronto by producing a major fundraiser and something which the League had not undertaken before. As with all Junior League fundraisers, the proceeds from the sales of **Jubilation** will be returned to the community through our projects.

Since 1926, The Junior League of Toronto has provided trained, committed volunteers to serve in the community. We are proud of our record of service and proud of our volunteers. Our Sustainers are certainly no exception and continue to give us their time and energies. This book is testimony to that. We salute them and we thank them.

Arlene Matheson

JUBILATION COMMITTEE

CHAIRMAN	Carol Eplett
COVER AND GRAPHIC DESIGN	Pat Benson
INTERIOR ILLUSTRATION	Lynda Bryden
PUBLISHING	Kae Matthews
PRINTING	Pat Catalano
TESTING	Nancy Barber
	Ann Collombin
	Sue Pielsticker
MARKETING	Mary Hicks
CORPORATE LIASON	Lois Mitchell
PUBLIC RELATIONS	Barbara Gyles
	Vivian Halliday
BUSINESS MANAGER	Nancy MacDonnell
TREASURER	Judie Wilson
SECRETARY	Jean Hackett
PATRON COORDINATOR	Ann Hogarth

To Barbara Donaldson we give our warm thanks for so freely giving of her time and skills to prepare the manuscript for typesetting.

The Jubilation Committee members would like to thank the following for their invaluable assistance:

Designcore
Gerry Anthony, Home Economist
Herzig Somerville
Linotext Inc.

Peter Spring News Service
Psycan Limited
Telfer's Restaurant Limited
Welch & Quest Limited

"MUDDY YORK"

The site that was to become York—or "Muddy York"—and later Toronto had been coveted by Iroquois and Mississauga Indians and by French and English fur-traders during most of the 18th century. Its Indian name, Tarantou, meant "place of meeting" or "place between the lakes" in the Huron language.

In 1787, Lord Dorchester acquired the area from the Mississauga in what is called the Toronto Purchase. A survey was done and six years later Governor John Graves Simcoe selected Toronto as the capital of the new province of Upper Canada. He called it "the arsenal of the province"—a harbour where a whole fleet could rest in safety protected from American invasion by the peninsula that is now Toronto Island. Governor Simcoe had quickly recognized what the native people had known for years—that it was on a portage route between Lake Ontario and Georgian Bay to the north, and was a link with Lake Huron on the west, the St. Lawrence route to the east and the American colonies to the south.

In July 1793, sailing vessels carrying Governor Simcoe and his Queen's Rangers landed at the capital's marsh. The entire population turned out to meet them—a few families of Mississauga Indians and a covey of water fowl. In honour of the Duke of York, son of George III, Simcoe selected the British name, York, over the Huron, Tarantou, for both the town and the fort. He laid out the town of York in ten four-acre blocks. The first street names, Palace, Princes, Duke, Duchess, Frederick, Caroline and George honoured the royal family. The northern part was allocated to officials and friends of the government. The southern part, near the marshy lakefront, was reserved for tradesmen.

Four years after establishing his government in York, Simcoe was recalled to England. He had accomplished much in that time. He had opened Yonge Street (named after Sir George Yonge, British Secretary of War in 1791), built roads along the north shore of Lake Ontario, offered free land grants and established English civil law, trial by jury, and local government. His name remains in Ontario today in a lake, a county, a town, and numerous streets and public buildings. Simcoe also left his mark by changing many place names from an Indian derivation to a British, even naming three townships for his wife's dogs, Tiny, Floss and Tay.

Simcoe's wife, Elizabeth, was a young British heiress. Her eloquent diaries enlivened by pen-and-ink sketches and maps, depict the realities of a country with which she had a natural affinity. Despite leaving 4 of her 6 children at home in England, she loved her Canadian adventure. She lived her first years in a tent purchased by her husband from Captain James Cook's estate. It was hung with deer skins for warmth—rather different from her elegant home in England. She rode through the woods on Toronto Island and painted and wrote about her new country with clarity, leaving a perceptive historical record. Sadly, she also left a baby daughter, Katharine, born shortly after her arrival, who died in 1794.

There had been little change in York by 1808. In that year a traveller recorded in his journal that the town was a "miserable apology for a metropolis". The population was just over 1,000. In 1813, the Americans attacked York. They captured Fort York, burned the government buildings as well as other public and private buildings, and stole the parliamentary mace, the symbol of government. Later British troops in return set fire to public buildings in Washington, D.C., and burned the President's mansion, which was repaired, painted and named the White House. The mace was returned to Toronto in 1934 at the request of President Roosevelt and the U.S. Congress.

In 1827, the Anglican King's College was founded in York by Bishop John Strachan. Various colleges were established later and, finally, they came together in the University of Toronto. It was here in 1921 that Doctors Fred Banting and Charles Best discovered insulin.

The name "Muddy York" which evolved in the early 1800s reflected the character of the marshy harbour town. A stroll down the street was a trek through the mud. The lack of sidewalks and paved arteries was one of the reasons that York became a city in 1834. Only by incorporation could the community borrow money to pay for civic improvements like sidewalks. At incorporation, its original Huron name, Tarantou, was restored as Toronto. The population numbered 6000 and British doctors, lawyers, and other professionals mingled with Scottish merchants and Irish store-keepers, constables, and tavern-keepers. By 1840 there were 141 licensed taverns, or one tavern for every 100 persons, as well as an unknown number of unlicensed establishments.

The first mayor of Toronto, William Lyon Mackenzie, was a fiesty Scot who led an armed rebellion in 1837 which attempted, unsuccesfully, to overthrow the provincial government. Mackenzie had many followers in Toronto and rural Ontario who resented the power of the ruling oligarchy and demanded government reform. Yonge Street was the scene of the major skirmishes. Two of Mackenzie's colleagues were captured and hanged and he fled to the United States where he remained in exile for several years. His fortunes dwindled on his return to Toronto. A group of friends bought him a house which, now restored, serves as a museum. His grandson, William Lyon Mackenzie King, was Prime Minister of Canada for twenty-two years between 1921 and 1948.

After Upper and Lower Canada were united in 1841, the location of the capital alternated among Toronto, Kingston and Montreal. Toronto went through a period of stagnation, but the railway era of the 1850s gave new impetus. At Confederation in 1867, the city became the capital of Ontario and the rapid growth of population, business, utilities and services began.

In 1883, Toronto annexed the village of Yorkville. By 1912 some twenty-five other small villages had joined the growing city. In 1953, the province established Metropolitan Toronto, ("Metro") an affiliation unique in North America combining 13 municipalities to provide vital services to its 1,300,000 residents. The next year Toronto opened Canada's first subway, which ran four and a half miles under Yonge Street and grew to the present multi-line system.

Today, the past blends with the present. High Park, the 400 acre estate of John Howard, still contains his 1836 home, Colborne Lodge. Exhibition Park houses the Canadian National Exhibition, the Royal Agricultural Winter Fair, and Scadding Cabin, the oldest dwelling in Toronto, which overlooks the modern playground, Ontario Place. Casa Loma, the castle built as a residence (1912-14) by Sir Henry Pellatt for about $3,000,000 is used for local events. Its distinguished neighbour is Spadina House (1866), recently restored and open to the public. The Grange, a beautiful neo-classical building built before 1820 stands beside the Art Gallery of Ontario and, nearby on University Avenue, is the restored home of Chief Justice Campbell. Osgoode Hall, with its courthouse and law library stands adjacent to the new City Hall, and has been beautifully restored. Two buildings from the 1850's, Dr. Henry Scadding's house and Holy Trinity Church, are nestled beside the massive and modern shopping complex, Eaton Centre. St. James Cathedral is across the street from St. Lawrence Hall, where Jenny Lind sang in July 1851. Union Station, the romanesque railway terminal of the 1920's, is a connecting link with commuter and subway lines and transcontinental travel. These and many other old buildings represent historic Toronto. They are set in the midst of a wealth of modern galleries, museums, centres of commerce, and sports and cultural facilities which serve the present population of two and a half million people.

The harbour that welcomed Governor Simcoe is now a city within a city. Condominiums and market places fill the old town of York near where Elizabeth Simcoe rode her horse in marshy and malarial York, that "miserable apology for a metropolis".

We are indebted for this factual overview of our city's heritage to sustainer Mary Byers, acclaimed co-author of "Rural Roots", "Homesteads, Toronto to Kingston" and "Governor's Road", and to June Gibson, assistant archivist at the Provincial Archives of Ontario.

Jubilation

Appetizers
Ceviche (seafood section)	132
Coquilles des Aubergines	19
Moules Marinière (seafood section)	137
Potato Latkas	20
Spinach and Smoked Salmon Salad (salad section)	70

Dips
Guacamole	21
Junior League Dill Dip	22
Layered Nacho Dip	22

Finger Food
Brie Wafers	13
Broiled Mushroom Caps	24
Capered Muffins	13
Caviar and Salmon Checkerboard	14
Cheese and Bacon Canapés	16
Cheese Puff Surprise	16
Cheese Straws	15
Cocktail Meatballs	24
Crab Puffs	21
Crispy Cheese Wafers	13
Greek Spinach and Cheese Turnovers	18
Iced Cheese Sandwiches	17
Marinated Shrimp with Snow Peas	29
Marmalade Cheese Squares	18

Mexican Nachos	29
Stuffed Mushrooms	25
Swedish Meatballs	23

Molds
Avocado Pie	12
Caviar Cheese Mold	14
Crab Mold Delight	20
Egg Watercress Mousse	28
Shrimp Spread	30

Pâté
Frosted Pâté	28
Jo Crackers Pâté Maison	11
Peppery Pâté	25
Smoked Salmon Pâté	26
Smooth and Creamy Pâté	27

Spreads
Crab Pizza	19
Homemade Herb Cheese	17
Party Cheese Ball	15

Beverages
Canadian Eggnog	31
Hot Lemon Punch	32
Innocent Juleps	33
Northern Slush	31
Rusty Pelican	33
Sparkling Spring Cooler	32
Spice-Up-Your-Coffee	34
Whispers	34
Winter Refresher	34

JO CRACKERS CHEESE
573 Eglinton Ave. W., Toronto

Jo Crackers Pâté Maison

2 Tbsp	butter	25 mL
1 lb	chicken livers	500 g
½	Spanish onion, chopped	½
1 clove	garlic, crushed	1
½	tart apple, peeled and chopped	½
2 Tbsp	Calvados	25 mL
2 Tbsp	whipping cream	25 mL
½ tsp	salt	2 mL
	ground pepper to taste	
⅛ tsp	allspice	0.5 mL
⅛ tsp	cloves	0.5 mL
⅛ tsp	nutmeg	0.5 mL
⅛ tsp	cinnamon	0.5 mL
⅛ tsp	curry	0.5 mL
¼ cup	toasted shelled pistachio nuts, coarsely chopped	50 mL

In a frying pan melt 1 Tbsp./15 mL butter, add chicken livers and cook on medium heat, turning frequently, for approximately 10 min. or until browned outside but still pink inside. Remove livers from pan and drain. Add remaining 1 Tbsp./15 mL butter to frying pan. Add onion and garlic, sauté 5 minutes. Add apples and cook 5 minutes or until apples are soft. Combine livers, onion mixture, Calvados, cream and spices in food processor. Purée until smooth. Remove to a bowl and stir in pistachio nuts. Taste for seasoning. Pour into serving dish and chill several hours before serving. Serve with bread, crackers or bagel thins.
NOTE: To toast pistachio nuts bake at 350° (180°C) 10 min.

Avocado Pie
Follow carefully for an attractive appetizer

1½ pkg	(1½ Tbsp/10 g) unflavoured gelatine	1½
¼ cup	cold water	50 mL

EGG LAYER

4	eggs, hard cooked and chopped	4
½ cup	mayonnaise	125 mL
¼ cup	minced parsley	50 mL
1	minced green onion	1
¾ tsp	each, salt and pepper	3 mL
dash	Tabasco sauce	dash

AVOCADO LAYER

1	medium avocado, mashed	1
1	medium avocado, diced	1
2	green onions, chopped	2
2 Tbsp	lemon juice	25 mL
2 Tbsp	mayonnaise	25 mL
½ tsp	each, salt and pepper	2 mL
dash	Tabasco sauce	dash

SOUR CREAM LAYER

1 cup	sour cream	250 mL
¼ cup	green onion, minced	50 mL

GARNISH (optional)

1 jar	(4 oz/125 g) black caviar (lumpfish)	1
1 tsp	fresh lemon juice	5 mL

Soften gelatine in a small dish with ¼ cup (50 mL) cold water. Place in larger dish of warm water to keep warm while working. Mix together all ingredients in egg layer and add 1½ Tbsp (25 mL) of the gelatine mixture. Oil spring form pan. Spread egg mixture on bottom of pan. Chill while making next layer. Mix together all ingredients of avocado layer. Add 1½ Tbsp (25 mL) of the gelatine mixture. Spread over egg layer. Chill. For sour cream layer, mix sour cream, onion and 1½ Tbsp (25 mL) of the gelatine mixture. Spread over avocado layer. Cover tightly and chill in refrigerator overnight. Before serving, rinse caviar under cold water in a sieve. Flavour with lemon juice. Garnish pie with caviar. Serve with small squares of pumpernickel bread.

Must make ahead   **Serves: 10 to 12**

Brie Wafers

¼ lb	butter, softened	125 g
½ lb	Brie cheese, softened	250 g
1 cup	all purpose flour	250 mL
⅛ tsp	cayenne pepper	0.5 mL
¼ tsp	seasoned salt	1 mL
½ cup	sesame seeds	125 mL

Preheat oven to 400°F (200°C). Place softened butter and cheese in medium size bowl. Add flour, cayenne and seasoned salt and beat well. Divide the mixture in half and place each portion on waxed paper. Form each half into a long round roll and wrap with waxed paper. Refrigerate for at least 12 hours. Slice the chilled rolls into thin wafers, about ¼ inch (5 mm) thick. Sprinkle with sesame seeds. Place on cookie sheet and bake at 400°F (200°C) 8 minutes. Serve immediately or store in a tightly covered container.

Must make ahead　　　　　　　　　　**Yield: 5 dozen**

Capered Muffins
Good on Triscuits too!

1 cup	mayonnaise	250 mL
1 cup	grated Cheddar cheese	250 mL
4	green onions, chopped	4
2 Tbsp	capers	25 mL
6	English muffins, split and toasted	6

Blend all ingredients except English muffins at least 24 hours in advance. Spread mixture on muffin halves and broil. Cut in small pieces for hors d'oeuvres or serve halves with a salad for lunch.

Must make ahead　　　　　　**Yield: 12 muffin halves**

Crispy Cheese Wafers

Monterey Jack or Emmenthal cheese

Preheat oven to 400°F (200°C). Cut cheese into ½ inch (1 cm) squares, approximately ¼ inch (5 mm) thick. Place on teflon pan. Bake 4 to 6 minutes. Remove from oven as soon as they stop bubbling. Wait 1 minute to remove from pan. Store in cookie tin.

Can make ahead　　　　**Can freeze**

Caviar Cheese Mold

1 pkg	(8 oz/250 g) cream cheese	1
1 can	(3 oz/85 g) ham paté	1
2 Tbsp	mayonnaise	25 mL
1	onion, chopped	1
	nutmeg to taste	
	mustard to taste	
	Worcestershire sauce to taste	
1 can	(10 oz/284 mL) consommé	1
1 Tbsp	sherry	15 mL
1 tsp	gelatine	5 mL
1 jar	(2 oz/57 g) lumpfish caviar	1

Mix cheese, paté and mayonnaise. Add onion and nutmeg, mustard and Worcestershire sauce to taste. Heat undiluted consommé, sherry and gelatine. Pour about ⅓ of this mixture into a mold. Chill until set. Sprinkle caviar over and then add cheese mixture. Avoid touching outside of mold. Pour remaining consommé over mold and chill until set. Serve with melba toast rounds or crackers.

Must make ahead   **Can freeze**   **Serves: 10**

Caviar and Salmon Checkerboard

10 slices	brown bread	10
10 slices	white bread	10
	unsalted butter, softened	
8 oz	black caviar	250 g
¼ lb	smoked salmon, thinly sliced	125 g
1	lemon, cut in half	

GARNISH   parsley and capers

Trim crusts evenly from bread and butter slices. Cut each slice into quarters. Spread caviar on brown squares. Cut forty 1¼ inch (3 cm) squares from salmon and place on white squares. Arrange squares on large platter in a checkerboard design. Garnish edges with parsley and squeeze lemon juice over all squares before serving. Small checkerboards can be formed on salad plates and served as an appetizer.

Yield: 6½ dozen

Cheese Straws

1 lb	frozen puff pastry	500 g
¾ cup	imported grated Parmesan cheese	175 mL
	salt, if desired	

Preheat oven to 350°F (180°C). Thaw pastry according to package directions. Roll out into a rectangle, 20 x 24 inches (50 x 60 cm). Spread half the cheese over the dough, pressing it in with a rolling pin. Fold dough in half cross-wise and roll it again to 20 x 24 inches (50 x 60 cm). Sprinkle on remaining cheese. Cut dough into ½ inch (1 cm) strips. Take each strip by its end and twist until it forms a corkscrew. Place twists on ungreased baking sheet so they are just touching each other. This prevents untwisting. Place on middle rack of oven and bake at 350°F (180°C) 15 to 20 minutes until puffed and lightly browned. Salt lightly, if desired. Cool 5 minutes and cut apart with a sharp knife.

Can make ahead   **Can freeze**   **Yield: 20**

Party Cheese Ball

1 pkg	(8 oz/250 g) cream cheese, softened	1
¼ lb	blue cheese, softened	125 g
½ tsp	Worcestershire sauce	2 mL
1 Tbsp	grated onion	15 mL
pinch	garlic powder (optional)	pinch
10	large pitted black olives, coarsely chopped	10
1 cup	finely chopped almonds or pecans, toasted	250 mL
¼ cup	finely chopped parsley or chives	50 mL

In medium bowl, combine cheeses, Worcestershire sauce, onion, garlic powder and olives. Blend well. Stir in ½ cup (125 mL) nuts. Shape into a ball. Wrap in waxed paper and chill. When firm, roll in remaining nuts and parsley. Wrap in waxed paper and keep chilled until ready to serve. Remove from refrigerator 30 minutes before serving. Serve with apple slices or crackers.

Can make ahead   **Serves: 8 to 10**

Cheese and Bacon Canapés

1	loaf thin sliced bread	1
½ cup	slivered almonds	125 mL
1 tsp	butter	5 mL
8	slices bacon, cooked and crumbled	8
1	small onion, grated	1
½ lb	old Cheddar cheese, grated	250 g
1 cup	mayonnaise	250 mL
2 tsp	Worcestershire sauce	10 mL

Preheat oven to 400°F (200°C). Trim crusts from bread and cut into quarters. Brown almonds in butter and mix with remaining ingredients in large bowl. Spread mixture on each piece of bread. Can be baked or frozen at this point. To freeze, place on cookie sheet in freezer until frozen and then put frozen canapés into a freezer bag. To bake, place on cookie sheet and bake at 400°F (200°C) 10 minutes. Do not overcook.

Can freeze   **Yield: 5 dozen**

Cheese Puff Surprise
Wonderful to keep on hand in the freezer

½ cup	butter	125 mL
2 cups	grated sharp Cheddar cheese	500 mL
½ tsp	salt	2 mL
1 tsp	paprika	5 mL
pinch	cayenne or red pepper	pinch
1 cup	all purpose flour, pre-sifted	250 mL
50	small stuffed green olives, drained	50

Soften butter and blend with cheese, salt, paprika and cayenne. Stir in flour, mixing well. (This may be done in a cuisinart fitted with a steel blade, using cold butter cut in small pieces). Mold 1 tsp (5 mL) of this mixture around each olive, covering it completely. Arrange on a baking sheet and chill until firm.
NOTE: It helps to rinse fingers in cold water between shaping each ball. May be frozen at this point. Bake at 400°F (200°C) 15 to 20 minutes.

Must make ahead   **Can freeze**   **Yield: 50**

Home-Made Herb Cheese
For garlic lovers

12 oz	cream cheese, softened	375 g
½ cup	butter, softened	125 mL
3	large garlic cloves, finely chopped	3
1 tsp	chopped chives	5 mL
1½ tsp	dried chervil leaves, crumbled	7 mL
1½ tsp	dried tarragon leaves, crumbled	7 mL
1 tsp	dried parsley leaves, crumbled	5 mL
½ tsp	dried thyme leaves, crumbled	2 mL
¼ tsp	white or black pepper	1 mL

Combine all ingredients in medium bowl and mix until smooth. Spoon into crock. Cover and chill. Bring to room temperature before serving. Can be kept chilled for up to three days.

Must make ahead   **Yield: 2 cups (500 mL)**

Iced Cheese Sandwiches
Keep a batch of these delicious appetizers ready for unexpected guests

1 lb	butter, softened	454 g
1 jar	(20 oz/600 g) cheese spread (Cheese Whiz)	1
1 tsp	Tabasco sauce	5 mL
1 tsp	onion powder	5 mL
1½ tsp	Worcestershire sauce	7 mL
1 tsp	Beau Monde seasoning	5 mL
1½ tsp	chopped fresh dill	7 mL
2½	loaves, thin sliced white bread	2½

In mixer or food processor, mix butter with cheese until fluffy. Add all remaining ingredients except bread. Mix well. Remove crusts from bread. Spread 3 slices with mixture and stack on top of each other. Spread sides and cut into 4 squares. Spread cut sides. Continue to do this with remaining cheese spread and bread. Place on cookie sheet covered with waxed paper and freeze. Remove and place in plastic bags to store in freezer until ready to use. Thaw and place on cookie sheet. Bake at 325°F (160°C) 15 minutes or until edges are browned.

Must freeze   **Yield: 80**

Greek Spinach and Cheese Turnovers
A party treat!

1	egg	1
½	medium onion, finely chopped	½
¼ lb	Feta cheese	125 g
1 pkg	(4 oz/125 g) cream cheese	1
1 pkg	(10 oz/284 mL) frozen, chopped spinach, thawed and drained	1
1 Tbsp	chopped parsley	15 mL
½ tsp	dried dill weed	2 mL
½ tsp	garlic powder	2 mL
4	frozen patty shells	4

Preheat oven to 450°F (230°C). In a bowl, combine egg, onion, cheeses, spinach, parsley, dill weed and garlic powder. Defrost patty shells at room temperature 15 to 20 minutes. Form each shell into a ball. Roll each ball out on floured pastry cloth, to an 11 inch (28 cm) square. Cut into 16 individual squares. Place ½ tsp (2 mL) filling on each square. Fold to form a triangle, sealing edges with milk. Place on ungreased cookie sheet and bake 12 minutes at 450°F (230°C).

Yield: 64

Marmalade Cheese Squares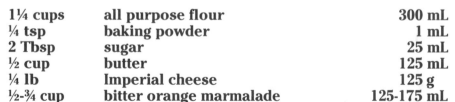

1¼ cups	all purpose flour	300 mL
¼ tsp	baking powder	1 mL
2 Tbsp	sugar	25 mL
½ cup	butter	125 mL
¼ lb	Imperial cheese	125 g
½-¾ cup	bitter orange marmalade	125-175 mL

Preheat oven to 350°F (180°C). In mixing bowl, blend flour, baking powder, sugar, butter and cheese. Mixture will be stiff. Press ⅔ of mixture lightly in a buttered 8 inch (20 cm) square pan. Spread with marmalade and crumble remaining dough on top. Bake at 350°F (180°C) 30 minutes.

Yield: 20 squares

Coquilles des Aubergines

2	medium eggplants	2
3 Tbsp	butter, divided	50 mL
1 cup	finely chopped onions	250 mL
4 Tbsp	flour	60 mL
	salt, to taste	
⅛ tsp	cayenne pepper	0.5 mL
¾ cup	milk	175 mL
3 Tbsp	Gruyère cheese, grated	50 mL
3 Tbsp	Ambrosia cheese, grated	50 mL
1 cup	sliced mushrooms	250 mL
¼ cup	dry Vermouth	50 mL
¼ cup	heavy cream	50 mL
1 tsp	dry mustard	5 mL

Peel eggplant and cut in 1 inch (2.5 cm) cubes. Cover with boiling water and simmer 10 minutes. Do not let eggplant become mushy. In saucepan, heat 2 Tbsp butter (25 mL). Add onion and sauté. Add flour, salt and cayenne pepper. Gradually add milk and cook until thickened, stirring constantly. Mix cheeses and add half to sauce. Sauté mushrooms in remaining butter, then add Vermouth, cream and mustard. Simmer 2 minutes. Combine sauces and eggplant. Place in scallop shells. Sprinkle with remaining cheese and brown under broiler.

Can make ahead   **Serves: 8**

Crab Pizza
'S wonderful!

2 pkg	(8 oz/250 g each) cream cheese	2
2 Tbsp	chopped onion	25 mL
2 Tbsp	Worcestershire sauce	25 mL
2 Tbsp	lemon juice	25 mL
2 cups	chili sauce, store bought	500 mL
2 cans	(6 oz/170 g each) crabmeat, drained	2
	chopped fresh parsley	

Cream together cream cheese, onion, Worcestershire sauce and lemon juice. Spread on an attractive plate to form a base. Mound sides up to look like a pizza. Cover with plastic wrap and refrigerate a few hours or overnight. Fill the centre with chili sauce, top with crab and sprinkle parsley over all. Serve with crackers.

Must make ahead   **Serves: 20**

Crab Mold Delight

1 pkg	(1 Tbsp/7g) unflavoured gelatine	1
3 Tbsp	cold water	50 mL
1 can	(10 oz/284 mL) cream of	1
	mushroom soup	
1 pkg	(8 oz/250 g) cream cheese, softened	1
¾ cup	mayonnaise	175 mL
1 can	(6 oz/170 g) crabmeat, drained	1
1 cup	chopped celery	250 mL
1	small onion, grated	1

GARNISH   parsley

Soften gelatine in cold water. Heat soup over low heat. Add gelatine and cream cheese and stir until well combined. Remove from heat. Add remaining ingredients and mix well. Pour into an oiled 4 cup (1 L) mold and chill until firm. Unmold and garnish with parsley. Serve with crackers.

Must make ahead   **Yield: 4 cups (1 L)**

Potato Latkas

6	medium potatoes	6
2	small onions	2
2	eggs	2
2 Tbsp	flour	25 mL
2 tsp	baking powder	10 mL
1 tsp	salt	5 mL
pinch	cinnamon (optional)	pinch
pinch	pepper (optional)	pinch
	oil for deep frying	
	sour cream or applesauce	

Preheat oil for deep frying. Grate potatoes and onions. (This may be done in food processor). Add remaining ingredients and mix well. Drop from teaspoon into hot oil and fry until well browned and crisp on both sides. Best served at once with sour cream or applesauce. To freeze: place cooked latkas on cookie sheet, freeze, then put into freezer bags. When ready to use, do not defrost. Bake at 425°F (220°C) for 20 minutes.

Can freeze   **Yield: 3 to 4 dozen**

Crab Puffs

1 can	(6 oz/170 g) king crabmeat	1
1½ cups	buttermilk Bisquick	375 mL
¼ cup	Parmesan cheese	50 mL
2 Tbsp	chopped green onion	25 mL
1	egg, beaten	1
⅓ cup	water	75 mL
½ tsp	Worcestershire sauce	3 mL
	vegetable oil	

MUSTARD DIP

½ cup	mayonnaise	125 mL
¼ cup	prepared mustard	50 mL
½ tsp	Worcestershire sauce	3 mL
4 drops	Tabasco	4

Drain crabmeat and crumble. Combine Bisquick, cheese, onion and the crabmeat. Mix egg, water and Worcestershire sauce and add to the crab mixture. Stir to barely blend. Drop by teaspoonsful into 1½ inch hot oil 375°F (190°C). Fry until golden, approximately 2 minutes, turning once. Drain on paper towels and serve immediately with mustard sauce, or make earlier in the day and reheat in moderate oven. MUSTARD DIP: Combine ingredients well.

Can make ahead   **Serves: 6 to 8**

Guacamole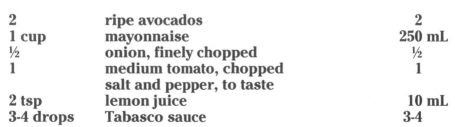

2	ripe avocados	2
1 cup	mayonnaise	250 mL
½	onion, finely chopped	½
1	medium tomato, chopped	1
	salt and pepper, to taste	
2 tsp	lemon juice	10 mL
3-4 drops	Tabasco sauce	3-4

Purée avocados. Retain one pit. Add remaining ingredients. Place avocado pit in centre of mixture and chill until ready to serve. Avocado pit keeps Guacamole from turning brown. Remove pit and serve with tortilla chips or squares of pumpernickel bread.

Yield: 2 cups (500 mL)

Junior League Dill Dip
Try it on sandwiches, with burgers— children love it!

⅔ cup	sour cream	150 mL
⅔ cup	mayonnaise	150 mL
2 Tbsp	chopped parsley or	25 mL
	1 Tbsp (15 mL) dried parsley flakes	
4	green onions chopped or 1 Tbsp	4
	(15 mL) dried onion flakes	
1 Tbsp	dill weed	15 mL
1 tsp	Beau Monde seasoning or	5 mL
	seasoned salt	

Mix all ingredients together. Allow to sit 1 hour before serving. Serve with raw vegetables.

Must make ahead   **Yield: 1½ cups (375 mL)**

Layered Nacho Dip
For a zippy change

1 can	(14 oz/398 mL) refried beans	1
1 can	(4 oz/114 mL) green chilies	1
1	medium onion, chopped	1
½ cup	chopped ripe olives	125 mL
1 Tbsp	chili powder	15 mL
1	ripe avocado, mashed	1
1 Tbsp	lemon juice	15 mL
1	garlic clove, crushed	1
	Tabasco sauce, to taste	
1 cup	sour cream	250 mL
1 cup	grated sharp Cheddar cheese	250 mL
	Tortilla chips	

Preheat oven to 350°F (180°C). Combine refried beans, chilies, onions, olives and chili powder and place in bottom of 1 qt (1 L) oven-proof casserole. Combine avocado, lemon juice, garlic and Tabasco and spread over first layer. Spread sour cream to form a third layer and sprinkle with Cheddar cheese. Bake at 350°F (180°C) for 20 minutes or until hot and bubbly. Serve with tortilla chips which should be dipped deep to scoop up all layers.

Can make ahead   **Yield: 4 cups (1 L)**

Swedish Meatballs
Oh so good, with a delicate flavour!

MEATBALLS

1 lb	ground beef	500 g
¼ lb	ground veal	125 g
¼ lb	ground pork	125 g
2 cups	bread crumbs	500 mL
½ cup	milk	125 mL
1	onion, finely chopped	1
2 Tbsp	butter	25 mL
2½ tsp	salt	12 mL
¼ tsp	pepper	1 mL
2 tsp	paprika	10 mL
2 tsp	nutmeg	10 mL
1 tsp	dry mustard	5 mL
3	eggs, beaten	3
¼ cup	butter or margarine	50 mL

SAUCE

¼ tsp	minced garlic	1 mL
5 Tbsp	butter	75 mL
2 tsp	tomato paste	10 mL
2 cups	beef bouillon or soup stock	500 mL
1 tsp	aromatic bitters (optional)	5 mL
1 cup	sour cream	250 mL

Have meat ground together twice. In large bowl, soak bread crumbs in milk, add meat and mix. In large skillet, sauté onion in 2 Tbsp (25 mL) butter. Add to meat mixture along with salt, pepper, paprika, nutmeg, mustard and eggs. Mix well. Shape into 48 small balls and brown in remaining ¼ cup (50 mL) butter. Set aside while preparing sauce. Using same skillet, add 1 Tbsp (15 mL) butter to remaining fat and sauté garlic for 1 minute. Blend in remaining ingredients, except sour cream, and stir over low heat until sauce is thickened. Pour into chafing dish, stir in sour cream, add meatballs and continue stirring to make sure all ingredients are well heated. The sauce and meatballs can be poured into a casserole dish and heated in the oven before serving, if preferred. This recipe improves if made one day ahead. Recipe would make a tasty main dish served over noodles.

Can make ahead   **Yield: 4 dozen**

Cocktail Meatballs

MEATBALLS

2 lb	medium ground beef	1 kg
1 cup	corn flake crumbs	250 mL
⅓ cup	dried parsley flakes	75 mL
2	eggs	2
2 Tbsp	soy sauce	25 mL
⅓ cup	ketchup	75 mL
2 Tbsp	dried minced onion	25 mL
¼ tsp	pepper	1 mL
½ tsp	garlic powder	2 mL

SAUCE

1 can	(14 oz/398 mL) cranberry sauce	1
1½ cups	chili sauce	375 mL
2 Tbsp	brown sugar	25 mL
1 Tbsp	lemon juice	15 mL

Preheat oven to 350°F (180°C).
MEATBALLS: Mix all meatball ingredients together and form into small balls. Place in single layer in baking dish. Bake at 350°F (180°C) for 15 minutes. Drain off fat.
SAUCE: Combine sauce ingredients together in saucepan, heat, and pour over meatballs. Bake, uncovered, at 350°F (180°C) for 30 minutes. Serve from a chafing dish. May also be served as a main course in a buffet selection.

Yield: 60 to 70

Broiled Mushroom Caps 🍒
Quick and easy

8 oz	medium size mushroom caps	250 g
¼ cup	grated Mozzarella or Emmenthal cheese	50 mL
2 Tbsp	finely chopped parsley	25 mL
½ tsp	garlic powder	3 mL
¼ cup	soft butter	50 mL

Clean mushroom caps. Make a paste of cheese, parsley, garlic powder and butter. Fill mushroom caps. Place on cookie sheet and refrigerate until serving time. Broil until cheese melts, about 1 minute.

Can make ahead   **Serves: 4 to 6**

Stuffed Mushrooms

*May be used as an attractive garnish for steak or chicken as
well as an hors d'oeuvre*

1 lb	medium mushrooms	500 g
1 or 2	celery stalks	1 or 2
1	medium onion, finely chopped	1
¼ cup	butter	50 mL
1 cup	dried bread crumbs	250 mL
	salt and pepper to taste	

Preheat oven to 350°F (180°C). Wipe or wash and dry mushrooms.
Separate stems from tops. Chop stems finely. Cut celery into thin
slivers and chop finely, making the same quantity as chopped
mushroom stems. In a frying pan, gently sauté mushroom stems,
celery and onion in butter. Cook until soft. Season with salt and
pepper. Add bread crumbs. Fill inverted mushroom caps with stuffing.
Place on greased cookie sheet. Bake 20 minutes at 350°F (180°C).

Yield: 2 dozen

Peppery Pâté

3 Tbsp	butter	50 mL
2	small onions, finely chopped	2
3	cloves garlic, chopped	3
1½ lb	chicken livers	750 g
1 tsp	salt	5 mL
½ tsp	freshly ground pepper	2 mL
2 Tbsp	green peppercorns	25 mL
1½ tsp	curry powder	7 mL
¼ cup	dry sherry	50 mL
1 cup	whipping cream	250 mL

GARNISH   lettuce leaves and parsley

Melt butter, add onions and garlic and cook 3 minutes. Add livers and
cook until pink. Add remaining seasonings and sherry and cook 5 minutes. Purée in blender or food processor. Add whipping cream. Line a
9 x 5 inch (23 x 13 cm) loaf pan with waxed paper and pour in liver
mixture. Place pan in larger pan of boiling water and bake at 350°F
(180°C) 30 minutes. Cool and refrigerate overnight. Unmold on a platter
covered with lettuce leaves and garnish with parsley. Serve with
crackers.

Must make ahead   **Serves: 10 to 12**

Smoked Salmon Pâté
Excellent for summer lunch or elegant picnic

PÂTÉ

1	small bunch watercress	1
1	small onion	1
¾ lb	fresh salmon, skinned	375 g
¼ lb	smoked salmon	125 g
2 tsp	dried dill weed	10 mL
2 tsp	fresh lemon juice	10 mL
½ tsp	white pepper, freshly ground	2 mL
1¼ cups	whipping cream, chilled	300 mL
2	eggs	2

WATERCRESS MUSTARD SAUCE

1	small bunch watercress	1
¼ cup	Dijon mustard	50 mL
½ tsp	salt, or to taste	2 mL
⅛ tsp	pepper, or to taste	0.5 mL
1 cup	vegetable oil	250 mL
2 Tbsp	sour cream	25 mL
2 tsp	fresh lemon juice	10 mL

Preheat oven to 250°F (120°C).
PÂTÉ: Butter a 1½ qt (1.5 L) loaf pan and line with buttered parchment paper. Select several perfect watercress leaves and create a design on the paper lining. Blanch remaining leaves for 15 seconds in boiling water. Drain, plunge in cold water. Drain and squeeze dry in a tea towel. In blender or food processor with steel blade, chop onion. Add fish, dill, lemon juice and pepper. Combine using 6 on/off pulses. With machine running, add cream slowly through feed tube. Add eggs and process 30 seconds. Transfer all but ¼ cup (50 mL) to a bowl. Add blanched watercress to processor and purée, stopping machine once to scrape down sides of the work bowl. Place half of pâté into prepared pan, smoothing with rubber spatula. Cut through with knife and tap pan to remove air bubbles. Spoon watercress mixture in stripes down centre. Add remaining pâté, again smoothing surface and removing air bubbles. Cover with piece of buttered parchment paper, buttered side down. Then cover top tightly with foil. Bake 250°F (120°C) 15 minutes. Reduce heat to 225°F (110°C) and continue baking 25 minutes. Pâté should feel firm but not hard to touch. Leave upright in pan 5 minutes, then invert onto serving platter. Refrigerate. Serve garnished with watercress and cherry tomatoes.

WATERCRESS MUSTARD SAUCE: In blender or food processor with steel knife, combine watercress (discard coarse stems) and mustard. Purée. Season with salt and pepper. Drizzle oil in slowly, with machine running, adding only as mixture thickens. When all oil has been added, add sour cream, combining with on/off pulses. Add lemon juice and blend 2 seconds.

Can make ahead   **Serves: 10**

Smooth and Creamy Pâté

½ lb	butter, divided	250 g
1 lb	chicken livers	500 g
½ cup	chopped onion	125 mL
2 Tbsp	chopped shallots or green onions	25 mL
¼ cup	chopped tart apple	50 mL
¼ cup	brandy	50 mL
3 Tbsp	heavy cream	50 mL
1 Tbsp	lemon juice	15 mL
1 tsp	salt	5 mL
¼ tsp	pepper	1 mL

Set aside 10 Tbsp (125 mL) butter in a bowl to soften. Wash and dry chicken livers, trim and cut in half. Sauté onion in 3 Tbsp (50 mL) butter for 5 minutes. Add shallots and apple and cook gently 5 to 10 minutes more or until apple is tender. Remove to blender. Using same pan, sauté chicken livers in remaining butter, 3 Tbsp (50 mL). Cook 5 minutes, add brandy and cook 2 minutes more. Add to blender. Add cream and blend until smooth. Cool in blender. Add softened butter and blend on high until smooth and thoroughly mixed. Add lemon juice, salt and pepper to taste. Pour into a greased mold, cover tightly and refrigerate overnight.

Must make ahead   **Serves: 20**

Frosted Pâté
No cooking!

8 oz	Braunschweiger sausage spread	250 g
½ tsp	garlic powder	2 mL
½ tsp	dried basil leaves	2 mL
2 Tbsp	grated onion	25 mL

ICING

1 pkg	(4 oz/125 g) cream cheese, softened	1
⅛ tsp	Tabasco sauce	0.5 mL
1 tsp	mayonnaise	5 mL
¼ tsp	garlic powder	1 mL

GARNISH   Chopped parsley

Mix sausage, garlic powder, basil and onion together thoroughly. Place on serving platter in smooth mound. Chill well.

ICING: Blend cheese with Tabasco, mayonnaise and garlic powder. Ice sausage mound. Cover with plastic wrap and refrigerate at least 8 hours. Garnish with chopped parsley. Serve with melba toast squares.

Must make ahead   **Serves: 10**

Egg Watercress Mousse

1 bunch	watercress, chopped	1
4	hard-boiled eggs, chopped	4
1 cup	mayonnaise	250 mL
1 pkg	(1 Tbsp/7 g) unflavoured gelatine	1
2 Tbsp	cold water	25 mL
1 Tbsp	lemon juice	15 mL
1	egg white	1
	salt and pepper to taste	

Blend watercress and egg in a bowl. Stir in mayonnaise. Soften gelatine in water. Add lemon juice. Leave for a few moments, while beating egg white. Add gelatine to egg and watercress mixture. Fold in egg white. Season with salt and pepper. Pour into 1½ qt (1.5 L) mold. Refrigerate until set. To serve, unmold onto lettuce lined plate and garnish with watercress. Serve with pumpernickel bread.

Must make ahead   **Serves: 4 to 6**

Marinated Shrimp with Snow Peas
Indulge your guests with this elegant, innovative hors d'oeuvre

MARINADE

½ cup	olive oil	125 mL
3 Tbsp	white wine vinegar	50 mL
1 Tbsp	Dijon mustard	15 mL
1	large shallot, finely chopped	1
1	clove garlic, chopped	1
1 Tbsp	fresh chopped dill	15 mL
1 tsp	grated ginger root	5 mL
	salt and pepper to taste	
1 lb	large (28 to 30), cooked shrimp, shelled and deveined	500 g
28 to 30	snow peas toothpicks	28-30

Combine marinade ingredients and mix well. Pour over shrimp. Cover and refrigerate for at least four hours, tossing once or twice. Remove top and string from peas. Blanch in boiling water for about 30 seconds or until bright green and pliable. Drain. Cool in ice water and drain again. Wrap a pea pod around each shrimp and fasten with a toothpick. Keep refrigerated until serving time.

Can make ahead **Yield: 30**

Mexican Nachos

Tortilla chips
Mozzarella cheese, sliced
hot banana peppers, cut up and
drained

Preheat oven 350°F (180°C). Lay chips on cookie sheet. Top each with cheese and a piece of hot pepper. Place in oven or under broiler until cheese melts.

Shrimp Spread or Mold

½ cup	water	125 mL
2 pkg	(2 Tbsp/14 g) unflavoured gelatine	2
1 can	(10 oz/284 mL) cream of tomato soup	1
1 pkg	(8 oz/250 g) cream cheese	1
½ cup	finely chopped onion	125 mL
½ cup	finely chopped celery	125 mL
1 cup	finely chopped green pepper	250 mL
1 cup	mayonnaise	250 mL
2 cups	cooked, peeled, deveined and chopped shrimps	500 mL
1 Tbsp	horseradish	15 mL
¼ cup	ketchup	50 mL

Place water in small saucepan and sprinkle gelatine over it. Let stand 1 minute to soften, and then stir in soup. Place pan over moderate heat and stir constantly until gelatine is dissolved. Pour soup mixture into blender or food processor. Add cream cheese and process until smooth. Place onion, celery, green pepper, mayonnaise, shrimps, horseradish and ketchup in a large bowl and toss well to mix. Fold in soup mixture and mix well. Pour into 6 cup (1.5 L) mold or soufflé dish. Chill several hours or overnight until set. Unmold or leave in soufflé dish. Serve with crackers.

Must make ahead   **Serves: 20**

Canadian Eggnog
Start early to make this party pleaser

40 oz	rye whiskey	1.14 L
40 oz	white rum	1.14 L
5 cups	pure maple syrup	1.25 L
12	eggs	12
2 cups	whipping cream	500 mL
	nutmeg	

Mix rye, rum and maple syrup, and allow to blend for 4 days in a cool place. The day before serving, separate eggs. Beat yolks until a pale yellow colour. Beat whites until stiff. Blend yolks into rye mixture. Add whites and stir gently. Refrigerate for 24 hours. Before serving, whip cream and stir into eggnog. Top each glass with dash of nutmeg. Enjoy!

Must make ahead   **Serves: a crowd**

Northern Slush

1 can	(48 oz/1.36 L) pineapple juice	1
1 can	(12½ oz/355 mL) frozen orange juice, thawed	1
1 can	(6¼ oz/178 mL) frozen lemonade, thawed	1
1 bottle	(26 oz/750 mL) gin	1
1 cup	cold, strong tea	250 mL
	7-Up, to taste	

GARNISH   orange or lemon slices

Mix together juices, gin and tea and freeze for at least 48 hours in a large container. Scoop slush into serving glass and top up with 7-Up, to taste. Stir with straws as swizzle sticks.

Must make ahead   **Serves: 20 to 25**

Sparkling Spring Cooler

2 cans	(12½ oz/355 mL each) frozen orange juice	2
2 cans	(12½ oz/355 mL each) frozen lemonade	2
2 bottles	(26 oz/750 mL each) gingerale, chilled	2
2 bottles	(26 oz/750 mL each) dry white wine, chilled	2
⅔ cup	Triple Sec	150 mL
	ice cubes or fruited ice mold*	
	fruit slices	

Mix undiluted orange juice and lemonade, gingerale, wine and Triple Sec in a large punch bowl. Add ice cubes or fruited ice mold and decorate with thin slices of fruit.

*TO MAKE FRUITED ICE MOLD

3 cups	frozen lemonade	750 mL
2	limes, thinly sliced	2
2	lemons, thinly sliced	2

Arrange fruit slices in bottom of ring mold in a decorative pattern. Pour 1 cup (250 mL) lemonade into mold and freeze. Remove from freezer and add remaining lemonade. Refreeze for 24 hours. To unmold, dip bottom of mold in warm water for 5 to 10 seconds, and invert. Place in punch immediately or keep in freezer until ready to use.

Serves: 25

Hot Lemon Punch 🍒

5 cups	water	1.25 L
1 cup	sugar	250 mL
1 cup	lemon juice	250 mL
1 cup	gin	250 mL
	lemon slices	

Heat first three ingredients together until sugar dissolves and punch just begins to boil. Add gin and lemon slices.

Yield: 15-4 oz (125 mL) servings

Innocent Juleps

1⅓ cups	sugar	325 mL
1 cup	hot water	250 mL
1 cup	pineapple juice	250 mL
1 cup	lemon or lime juice	250 mL
1 cup	orange juice	250 mL
	gingerale	

| GARNISH | mint leaves, fruit slices or maraschino cherries | |

Mix sugar and hot water. Stir to dissolve sugar. Add fruit juices. Cool. Pour into ice cube trays and freeze. For punch, pour chilled gingerale over fruit cubes. For individual drinks, drop 2 or 3 fruit cubes into a tall glass and fill with chilled gingerale. Stir until mix is slushy. Garnish with mint, fruit slices or maraschino cherries.

Yield: 5⅓ cups (1.325 L) fruit juice base

Rusty Pelican

End a hot summer day with this refreshing drink

	juice of 1½ limes	
	juice of 1 lemon	
2 Tbsp	grenadine	25 mL
¼-½ tsp	Angostura bitters	1-2 mL
1 cup	pink or white grapefruit juice	250 mL
½ cup	vodka	125 mL
½ cup	cognac or Grand Marnier	125 mL
2 cups	amber rum	500 mL
4 cups	orange juice	1 L

Mix all ingredients, adding orange juice last to dilute to desired strength. Serve with lots of ice. Makes approximately 8 cups (2 L) of punch.

Serves: 4 to 6

Spice-Up-Your-Coffee 🍒

2 Tbsp	gound cinnamon	25 mL
1 Tbsp	ground nutmeg	15 mL
1 lb	coffee, regular or decaffeinated	500 g

Empty coffee into a large bowl. Add spices and mix well. Return to coffee tin or sealed jar. Keep in freezer and use as needed.

Winter Refresher 🍒
Hot and delicious

6 tsp	loose tea	25 mL
2 cups	boiling water	500 mL
1 can	(6¼ oz/178 mL) frozen lemonade	1
1 can	(6¼ oz/178 mL) frozen orange juice	1
1½ cups	sugar	375 mL
10 cups	water	2.5 L
2	cinnamon sticks	2

Pour boiling water over tea and let cool. Strain and add remaining ingredients. Simmer mixture for 20 minutes. If too strong add more water. Add extra sugar to taste.

Yield: 15 cups (3.75 L)

Whispers 🍒

1 part	brandy (or rye)	1
1 part	coffee liqueur	1
5 parts	vanilla ice cream	5

Mix in blender and serve.

Serves: 1

Jubilation

🍒 ...designates "Company in a Minute"

ALL THE BEST BREADS,
1099 Yonge St., Toronto

Apricot Tea Loaf
A delicious fruity variation of the traditional pound cake
Keeps and travels well

¾ cup	chopped dried apricots	175 mL
½ cup	golden raisins	125 mL
1 tsp	grated lemon rind	5 mL
1 tsp	vanilla extract	5 mL
2 Tbsp	cognac (optional)	25 mL
1 cup	soft, unsalted butter	250 mL
¾ cup	fine sugar	175 mL
4	large eggs, (at room temperature)	4
2 cups	cake and pastry flour	500 mL
1 tsp	baking powder	5 mL
pinch	salt	pinch
½ cup	sliced almonds	125 mL

LEMON SYRUP

2 Tbsp	water	25 mL
2 Tbsp	lemon juice	25 mL
¼ cup	sugar	50 mL

Preheat oven to 325°F (160°C). Mix together apricots, raisins, lemon rind, vanilla and cognac and set aside for half and hour. (If you don't use cognac, allow apricots to soften in hot water for 30 minutes. Drain off excess liquid before mixing with other fruits). Cream butter with sugar until light. Add eggs, beating well. Sift flour, baking powder and salt. Fold into creamed mixture and add fruits. Butter and flour a 9 x 5 inch (23 x 13 cm) loaf pan and fill with batter. Smooth top and sprinkle with almonds. Bake at 325°F (160°C) until done, about 1 hour. Let rest in pan for 5 minutes, turn out and spoon lemon syrup over hot cake. Cool before slicing.
LEMON SYRUP: Swirl water, lemon juice and sugar over moderate heat. Raise heat and simmer for 2 minutes.

Can freeze   **Yield: 1 loaf**

Cinnamon Ring
Remember this for Christmas morning

2	loaves frozen white bread dough	2
2 Tbsp	butter	25 mL
¼ cup	brown sugar	50 mL
2 Tbsp	raisins	25 mL
2 Tbsp	slivered almonds	25 mL
2 Tbsp	chopped maraschino cherries	25 mL
¼ cup	butter	50 mL
1 cup	sugar	250 mL
4 tsp	cinnamon	20 mL

Remove bread dough from freezer. Place in refrigerator to soften overnight. Next day, melt 2 Tbsp (25 mL) butter and stir in brown sugar until smooth. Pour into bundt or tube pan. Sprinkle with raisins, almonds and cherries. Melt ¼ cup (50 mL) butter. Mix sugar and cinnamon until blended. Cut each loaf into 12 slices. Dip bread slices, first into melted butter, then into sugar-cinnamon mixture until well coated. Stand pieces on their edges around pan. Sprinkle remaining cinnamon mixture over top. Let rise 2 hours in warm place. Bake at 350°F (180°C) 30 minutes. Let stand 10 minutes before inverting on a platter.

Yield: 1 ring

Maraschino Cherry Loaf

1¾ cups	unsifted all purpose flour	425 mL
4 tsp	baking powder	20 mL
½ tsp	salt	2 mL
¾ cup	sugar	175 mL
1 bottle	(12 oz/375 mL) red maraschino cherries	1
2 tsp	grated lemon or orange rind	10 mL
2	eggs, beaten	2
1 cup	milk	250 mL
3 Tbsp	vegetable oil	50 mL

Preheat oven to 375°F (190°C). Sift all dry ingredients together into large bowl. Drain and dry cherries. Cut into small pieces. Toss with dry ingredients. Combine remaining ingredients and stir into dry mixture. Pour into greased 9 x 5 inch (23 x 13 cm) loaf pan. Bake at 375°F (190°C) for 50 minutes, until crust is browned.

Can freeze   **Yield: 1 loaf**

Frypan Blueberry Cornbread 🍒
An oven or frypan success

1 cup	cornmeal	250 mL
1½ cups	all purpose flour	375 mL
⅓ cup	sugar	75 mL
2 tsp	baking powder	10 mL
¼ tsp	salt	1 mL
2	eggs, beaten	2
1½ cups	milk	375 mL
¼ cup	butter, melted	50 mL
1 cup	blueberries	250 mL
	maple syrup for serving	

Sift dry ingredients. Mix eggs, milk and butter and add to dry ingredients. Stir to blend. Add blueberries. Mix lightly.

METHOD ONE: Grease electric frypan. Pour in batter. Cover and cook, with vent open, at 250°F (120°C) 25 to 30 minutes.

METHOD TWO: Grease ovenproof frypan. Pour in batter. Cover lightly with foil and bake at 375°F (190°C) 25 minutes.

Cut into wedges and serve hot with butter and maple syrup.

Serves: 8

Savoury Cheddar Bread
A great brunch bread

2 cups	all purpose flour	500 mL
4 tsp	baking powder	20 mL
1 Tbsp	sugar	15 mL
1 tsp	onion salt	5 mL
½ tsp	ground oregano	2 mL
¼ tsp	dry mustard	1 mL
1¼ cups	grated Cheddar cheese	300 mL
1	egg, well beaten	1
1 cup	milk	250 mL
1 Tbsp	butter, melted	15 mL

Preheat oven to 350°F (180°C). Sift together flour, baking powder, sugar, onion salt, oregano and dry mustard. Add cheese. Combine egg, milk and butter. Add all at once to dry ingredients, stirring just until moistened. Spread batter in greased 9 x 5 inch (23 x 13 cm) loaf pan. Bake at 350°F (180°C) 45 minutes.

Can freeze　　　　　**Yield: 1 loaf**

Granny's Coffee Cake
Just like you remember

½ cup	butter	125 mL
1 cup	brown sugar	250 mL
2	eggs	2
1 cup	sour cream	250 mL
2 cups	flour	500 mL
1 tsp	baking soda	5 mL
1 tsp	baking powder	5 mL
½ tsp	salt	2 mL
1 cup	golden raisins	250 mL

TOPPING AND FILLING

¼ cup	brown sugar	50 mL
1 tsp	cinnamon	5 mL
1 cup	broken nuts	250 mL
¼ cup	golden raisins	50 mL

Preheat oven to 350°F (180°C). Cream butter and sugar. Beat in eggs and sour cream. Sift dry ingredients and add to creamed mixture. Fold in raisins. Mix together topping ingredients. Spread half of batter into greased and floured spring form or tube pan. Cover with half the topping mixture. Spoon on the remaining batter and lightly press in remaining topping. Bake at 350°F (180°C) 40 to 50 minutes or until toothpick comes out clean. Let sit for 10 minutes before removing from pan.

Can freeze   **Serves: 16 to 18**

Good Melba Toast
Excellent with soups and appetizers

1	French stick loaf (long thin type)	1
	butter, melted	
	onion salt (or any seasoning salt)	
	celery seed	

Preheat oven to 200°F (100°C). Slice French stick in thin slices. Butter and sprinkle generously with onion salt and celery seed, or any other desired seasonings. Bake at 200°F (100°C) until crisp (approximately 2 hours).
NOTE: Bread slices more easily if frozen.

Must make ahead

Old Fashioned Plum Cake
Absolutely sinful!

½ cup	brown sugar	125 mL
1 tsp	ground cinnamon	5 mL
½ cup	butter, softened	125 mL
1 cup	sugar	250 mL
2	eggs, separated	2
1½ cups	all purpose flour, sifted	375 mL
1 tsp	baking powder	5 mL
½ cup	milk	125 mL
1 tsp	vanilla	5 mL
12-15	fresh or canned blue or red plums pitted and quartered	12-15

GLAZE

¾ cup	icing sugar	175 mL
1 Tbsp	milk	15 mL
½ tsp	vanilla or almond extract	2 mL

Preheat oven to 350°F (180°C). Combine brown sugar, cinnamon and ¼ cup (50 mL) butter and set aside. Cream remaining butter with sugar and egg yolks until light and fluffy. Sift flour with baking powder and add to creamed mixture alternately with milk and vanilla. Beat egg whites until stiff, and fold into above mixture. Pour into greased 9 inch (23 cm) square pan or 9 inch (23 cm) spring form pan. Arrange plums neatly on top, in rows. Spread brown sugar, cinnamon and butter mixture over top. Bake at 350°F (180°C) 45 minutes or until cake tester comes out clean.

GLAZE: Mix icing sugar, milk and vanilla and drizzle on top of cake, while still hot. Glaze will be shiny when cool.

NOTE: Cake may be served with flavoured whipped cream instead of glaze, if desired.

Can make ahead   **Serves: 8**

Cranberry Holiday Bread
Ideal for Christmas entertaining

1 cup	fresh cranberries	250 mL
1 cup	nuts	250 mL
2 cups	all purpose flour	500 mL
1 cup	sugar	250 mL
1½ tsp	baking powder	7 mL
1 tsp	salt	5 mL
½ tsp	baking soda	2 mL
1 tsp	grated orange peel	5 mL
¼ cup	butter, frozen, cut into small pieces	50 mL
1	egg	1
¾ cup	orange juice	175 mL

Preheat oven to 350°F (180°C). Place cranberries and nuts in food processor. Use steel blade to chop. Do not purée. Remove and place in large bowl. Put flour, sugar, baking powder, salt, soda and orange peel into food processor bowl and pulse on/off only to mix. Then add butter and process until mixture has a granular appearance. Hand beat egg and add enough orange juice to make 1 cup (250 mL). With food processor motor running, add juice until mixed. Combine batter mixture with cranberry and nuts and stir to mix. Place in a greased and floured 9 x 5 inch (23 x 13 cm) loaf pan. Bake at 350°F (180°C) 1 hour or until bread tests done. Cool on rack and remove from pan when bread releases easily.

Can freeze　　　　　　　　**Yield: 1 loaf**

Quick Cheese Bread
A picture to behold

2	loaves frozen white bread dough	2
¼-⅓ lb	butter, melted	125-150 g
½ lb	old Cheddar cheese, grated	250 g

Thaw dough in refrigerator overnight. Cut each loaf into 12 slices. Roll each slice in melted butter, then in grated cheese. Place slices side by side in bundt or tube pan. Place in warm place until dough rises to top of pan, 2 to 4 hours. Bake at 350°F (180°C) 30 minutes. Remove from pan to serve.

Can make ahead　　　　　　　**Serves: 10 to 12**

Cherry Pecan Tea Bread
An old Kentucky recipe for Christmas gift giving

1 lb	butter	454 g
3 cups	sugar, divided	750 mL
½ tsp	mace	2 mL
8	eggs separated, room temperature	8
3 cups	all purpose flour, sifted and divided	750 mL
⅓ cup	rye or bourbon	75 mL
1 lb	chopped red glacé cherries	500 g
4 cups	finely chopped pecans	1 L

Preheat oven to 350°F (180°C). Cream butter, 2 cups (500 mL) sugar and mace until fluffy. Gradually add egg yolks, one at a time, beating well after each addition. Stir in 2¾ cups (675 mL) flour. Add rye or bourbon. Toss remaining flour with cherries. Fold cherries and nuts into batter. Beat egg whites to soft peaks, then add remaining 1 cup (250 mL) sugar and continue beating until stiff. Fold into batter. Spoon mixture into 3 well greased or parchment lined loaf pans. Bake at 350°F (180°C) 1½ hours until well done. For last 30 minutes cover with foil. Test with toothpick to see if fully baked.

Can freeze　　　**Yield: 3 loaves**

Zucchini Bread

2 cups	loosely packed shredded zucchini	500 mL
3	eggs	3
2 cups	sugar	500 mL
1 cup	vegetable oil	250 mL
1 Tbsp	vanilla	15 mL
2 cups	all purpose flour	500 mL
1 Tbsp	cinnamon	15 mL
2 tsp	baking soda	10 mL
1 tsp	salt	5 mL
¼ tsp	baking powder	1 mL

Preheat oven to 350°F (180°C). Prepare zucchini and set aside. Beat eggs until foamy. Add sugar, oil and vanilla. Beat until thick. Sift flour, cinnamon, baking soda, salt and baking powder and add to egg mixture. Beat to combine well. Fold in the zucchini with spatula. Mix well. Pour into 2 greased 9 x 5 inch (23 x 13 cm) loaf pans. Bake at 350°F (180°C) 50 to 60 minutes until tester comes out clean.

Can freeze　　　**Yield: 2 loaves**

Pumpkin Tea Bread
Moist and delicious

1½ cups	brown sugar	375 mL
1½ cups	granulated sugar	375 mL
1 cup	vegetable oil	250 mL
4	eggs	4
¼ cup	orange juice concentrate	50 mL
1 tsp	grated orange rind	5 mL
2½ cups	pumpkin purée	625 mL
3½ cups	flour	875 mL
1½ tsp	salt	7 mL
2 tsp	baking soda	10 mL
1 tsp	nutmeg	5 mL
1 tsp	cinnamon	5 mL
1 tsp	pumpkin pie spice	5 mL
1 tsp	ground cloves	5 mL
1½ cups	chopped walnuts (optional)	375 mL

Preheat oven to 350°F (180°C). Beat together sugars and oil. Beat in eggs one at a time. Add orange juice, rind and pumpkin. Combine dry ingredients and add to pumpkin mixture. Blend thoroughly but do not overmix. Pour batter into 2 well greased 9 x 5 inch (23 x 13 cm) loaf pans. Bake at 350°F (180°C) 1 hour and 10 minutes or until toothpick inserted in centre comes out clean. Cool on rack for 10 minutes, then remove from pan.

Can freeze   **Yield: 2 loaves**

No Knead Bread 🍒
A delicious bread even children can make

2½ cups	whole wheat flour	625 mL
1½ cups	all purpose flour	375 mL
3 Tbsp	sugar	50 mL
1½ tsp	baking soda	7 mL
1 tsp	salt (optional)	5 mL
2 cups	yogurt	500 mL
2	eggs	2

Preheat oven to 350°F (180°C). Sift dry ingredients together. Mix yogurt and eggs together. Add dry ingredients to yogurt mixture. It will be very sticky. Put in well greased and floured 9 x 5 inch (23 x 13 cm) loaf pan. Bake at 350°F (180°C) for 55 minutes, or until done.

Can freeze   **Yield: 1 loaf**

Processor Egg Bread
For a beginner—you can't go wrong!

1 pkg	dry yeast	1
1 tsp	sugar	5 mL
½ cup	warm water	125 mL
½ cup	butter, melted	125 mL
3	eggs	3
¾ tsp	salt	3 mL
3 cups	all purpose flour, divided	750 mL
2 tsp	sugar	10 mL
1	egg yolk	1
1 Tbsp	water	15 mL
	sesame seeds or poppy seeds (optional)	

In a bowl combine yeast, 1 tsp (5 mL) sugar and ½ cup (125 mL) warm water. Let stand 10 minutes. In food processor, using steel blade, whirl together melted butter, yeast mixture, eggs and salt in 4 on-off turns. Add 2½ cups (625 mL) flour, 2 tsp (10 mL) sugar and process for 20 seconds. Add 2 Tbsp (25 mL) flour, whirl 5 seconds. Then add an additional 2 Tbsp (25 mL) flour, whirl 3 seconds. Finally add remaining ¼ cup (50 mL) flour and process 2 seconds. Leave in food processor bowl and cover with towel. Let rise 1 hour. Process a final 5 seconds. Remove dough from bowl and divide in thirds making strips. Braid together and fold ends under. Place on greased cookie sheet. Beat egg yolk and 1 Tbsp (15 mL) water together to make a wash. Paint top of bread with wash using pastry brush and sprinkle with seeds. Let stand in warm place, to rise, covered with tea towel for 30 minutes. Bake at 375°F (190°C) 10 minutes then reduce heat to 350°F (180°C) for 35 minutes.

Can freeze   **Yield: 1 loaf**

Swiss Cheese Loaf 🍒

½ lb	butter, softened	250 g
½ cup	chopped green onions	125 mL
3 Tbsp	poppy seeds	50 mL
1 Tbsp	dry mustard	15 mL
1	large loaf French or Italian bread	1
16	slices Swiss cheese	16
8	slices cooked ham, diagonally cut (optional)	8

Preheat oven to 400°F (200°C). Mix butter, onions, poppy seeds and mustard. Cut top and side crusts off loaf and cut 16 slices to bottom crust, but not through. Spread mixture on both sides of slices reserving enough to frost the top and sides completely. Place cheese and ham between each slice. Frost top and sides with reserved spread. Wrap loaf in foil, leaving top open. Bake at 400°F (200°C) 15 minutes or until cheese melts and top is golden.

Can freeze   **Yield: 16 slices**

Pumpernickel Bread

3 cups	Red River cereal	750 mL
1 cup	whole wheat flour	250 mL
2 tsp	baking soda	10 mL
1 tsp	salt	5 mL
3 cups	hot water	750 mL
½ cup	dark molasses	125 mL

Combine all dry ingredients. Mix molasses and hot water and stir into dry ingredients. Mix well. Let stand for 2 hours or overnight. Turn into a greased 9 x 5 inch (23 x 13 cm) loaf pan. Cover with foil and bake at 275°F (140°C) for 3 hours or until firm. Cool, wrap and chill in refrigerator before slicing. Store in refrigerator.

Can freeze   **Yield: 1 loaf**

Poppy Seed Coffee Cake
May be served for dessert with puréed raspberries

1 pkg	(18 oz/510 g) "super moist" lemon cake mix	1
1 pkg	(4 oz/106 g) instant lemon pudding	1
1 cup	warm water	250 mL
½ cup	vegetable oil	125 mL
4	eggs	4
½ cup	poppy seeds	125 mL

GLAZE

¼ cup	butter	50 mL
⅔ cup	sugar	150 mL
⅓ cup	lemon juice	75 mL
	grated rind of 1 lemon	

Preheat oven to 350°F (180°C)

CAKE: Grease and flour angel cake pan. Pour all ingredients into large bowl. Mix well then beat at medium speed for 3 minutes. Pour into pan and bake at 350°F (180°C) 1 hour and 15 minutes or until done. Remove from pan while warm and glaze.

GLAZE: Melt butter and combine with remaining ingredients. Boil 1 to 2 minutes. While glaze is hot spoon over cake.

Can freeze   **Serves: 8 to 10**

Aloha Muffins

1	orange, peeled	1
½ cup	orange juice	125 mL
3 oz	crystallized ginger, chopped or	90 g
	5 stems of preserved ginger, chopped	
1	egg	1
½ cup	oil or melted butter	125 mL
1½ cups	all purpose flour	375 mL
1 tsp	baking soda	5 mL
1 tsp	baking powder	5 mL
¾ cup	sugar	175 mL
pinch	salt	pinch

Preheat oven to 400°F (200°C). Cut orange into small pieces and chop. (Food processor works well). In a small bowl, mix chopped orange, orange juice, chopped ginger, egg and oil. Stir well. Put dry ingredients in large bowl and make a well in centre. Add orange liquid and stir gently until just moistened. Spoon into greased or paper lined muffin tins three-quarters full. Bake at 400°F (200°C) 15 minutes.

Can freeze   **Yield: 12**

Chocolate Chip Almond Muffins

1½ cups	all purpose flour	375 mL
1½ tsp	baking powder	7 mL
½ tsp	salt	2 mL
1 cup	semi-sweet chocolate chips	250 mL
½ cup	soft butter or margarine	125 mL
1 cup	sugar	250 mL
2	eggs	2
1 cup	sour cream or plain yogurt	250 mL
1 tsp	baking soda	5 mL
½ cup	slivered almonds	125 mL

Preheat oven to 350°F (180°C). Combine flour, baking powder, salt and chocolate chips in small bowl. In large bowl, cream together butter and sugar. Add eggs to butter mixture and beat until mixture is light and fluffy. Combine sour cream or yogurt and soda in a bowl. Blend into creamed mixture. And dry ingredients. Mix until just blended. Fold in almonds. Spoon into 18 greased or paper lined muffin tins, filling three-quarters full. Bake at 350°F (180°C) 30 minutes or until golden brown.

Can freeze   **Yield: 18**

Yogurt Bran Muffins

2 cups	plain yogurt	500 mL
2 tsp	baking soda	10 mL
1½ cups	brown sugar	375 mL
2	eggs	2
1 cup	vegetable oil	250 mL
2 cups	bran	500 mL
2 tsp	vanilla	10 mL
2 cups	all purpose flour	500 mL
4 tsp	baking powder	20 mL
½ tsp	salt	2 mL
1 cup	blueberries, fresh or frozen	250 mL
	or	
½ cup	chopped nuts and	125 mL
½ cup	raisins	125 mL

Preheat oven to 350°F (180°C). Combine yogurt and baking soda in a large bowl. Set aside. Beat sugar, eggs and oil together. Add bran and vanilla. Mix remaining dry ingredients and add to bran mixture, alternating with yogurt. Fold in blueberries or nuts and raisins. Fill 24 greased or paper lined muffin tins. Bake at 350°F (180°C) for 20 to 25 minutes.

Can freeze **Yield: 24**

Oatmeal Banana Muffins

½ cup	sugar	125 mL
½ cup	butter or margarine	125 mL
¾ cup	honey	175 mL
2	eggs	2
3	medium bananas, well mashed	3
1½ cups	all purpose flour	375 mL
1 Tbsp	baking powder	15 mL
1 tsp	baking soda	5 mL
¾ tsp	salt	3 mL
1 cup	quick-cooking rolled oats	250 mL

Preheat oven to 375°F (190°C). In medium sized bowl, cream sugar and butter. Stir in honey, eggs and mashed bananas. Combine flour, baking powder, baking soda and salt and stir into creamed mixture until blended. Gently stir in rolled oats. Fill greased or paper lined muffin tins three-quarters full. Bake at 375°F (190°C) 18 to 20 minutes.

Can freeze **Yield: 24**

Orange and Date Blender Muffins

1	orange	1
½ cup	orange juice, fresh or frozen	125 mL
1	egg	1
½ cup	chopped dates	125 mL
½ cup	butter	125 mL
1½ cups	all purpose flour	375 mL
1 tsp	baking soda	5 mL
1 tsp	baking powder	5 mL
¾ cup	sugar	175 mL
1 tsp	salt	5 mL

Preheat oven to 400°F (200°C). Cut orange into pieces. Remove seeds. Process in blender or food processor until rind is finely ground. Add juice, egg, dates and butter and process briefly. Sift dry ingredients into a mixing bowl. Pour in orange mixture. Blend lightly. Fill 18 greased or paper lined muffin tins with batter. Bake at 400°F (200°C) 15 minutes or until lightly browned.

Can freeze   **Yield: 18**

Poppy Seed Muffins

¾ cup	sugar	175 mL
¼ cup	butter, softened	50 mL
½ tsp	grated orange rind	2 mL
2	eggs	2
2 cups	all purpose flour	500 mL
2½ tsp	baking powder	12 mL
½ tsp	salt	2 mL
¼ tsp	nutmeg	1 mL
1 cup	milk	250 mL
½ cup	golden raisins	125 mL
½ cup	pecans, chopped	125 mL
¼ cup	poppy seeds	50 mL

Preheat oven to 400°F (200°C). In large bowl cream together sugar, butter and orange rind. Add eggs, one at a time, beating well after each addition. Stir together flour, baking powder, salt and nutmeg. Add flour mixture to creamed mixture alternating with milk. Beat well after each addition. Fold in raisins, pecans and poppy seeds. Fill greased or paper lined muffin tins three-quarters full. Bake at 400°F (200°C) 20 minutes or until done.

Can freeze   **Yield: 16**

Marmalade Muffins

2 cups	all purpose flour	500 mL
½ cup	sugar	125 mL
1 Tbsp	baking powder	15 mL
½ tsp	salt	2 mL
⅔ cup	raisins	150 mL
⅓ cup	sunflower seeds or nuts	75 mL
½ cup	undiluted frozen orange juice, thawed	125 mL
1	egg	1
⅓ cup	soft butter or margarine	75 mL
¾ cup	marmalade	175 mL

Preheat oven to 400°F (200°C). Sift dry ingredients into a large bowl. Stir in raisins and seeds. In small bowl combine juice, egg, butter or margarine and marmalade. Add liquid to dry ingredients and stir only until moistened. Spoon into greased or paper lined muffin tins. Bake at 400°F (200°C) for 15 to 20 minutes. These may brown quickly.

Can freeze   **Yield: 12**

Mandarin Muffins

1½ cups	all purpose flour	375 mL
1¾ tsp	baking powder	8 mL
½ tsp	salt	2 mL
½ cup	sugar	125 mL
¼ tsp	allspice (optional)	1 mL
½ tsp	nutmeg (optional)	2 mL
⅓ cup	shortening	75 mL
¼ cup	milk	50 mL
1	egg, slightly beaten	1
1 can	(10 oz/284 mL) mandarin orange sections, drained and halved	1

TOPPING
2 Tbsp	melted butter	25 mL
¼ cup	sugar, scant	50 mL
½ tsp	cinnamon	2 mL

Preheat oven to 350°F (180°C). Sift flour with other dry ingredients into bowl. Cut in shortening. Combine milk and egg. Mix all together until just moistened. Fold in oranges. Spoon into greased or paper lined muffin tins. Bake at 350°F (180°C) 20 to 25 minutes. While muffins are hot, dip tops in melted butter, then in sugar cinnamon mixture.

Can freeze   **Yield: 12**

Rhubarb Muffins
Spicy, light— a nice change

2	eggs	2
1 cup	sugar	250 mL
½ cup	vegetable oil or melted shortening	125 mL
2 cups	all purpose flour	500 mL
1 tsp	baking soda	5 mL
1 tsp	cinnamon	5 mL
¼ tsp	cloves	1 mL
¼ tsp	allspice	1 mL
dash	salt	dash
⅓ cup	milk	75 mL
3 cups	finely chopped red rhubarb, fresh or frozen	750 mL

TOPPING

⅓ cup	brown sugar	75 mL
1 tsp	cinnamon	5 mL
¼ cup	finely chopped pecans (optional)	50 mL

Preheat oven to 400°F (200°C). In large bowl beat together eggs, sugar and oil or shortening. Sift flour together with other dry ingredients and add to sugar mixture alternately with milk. Fold in rhubarb. Batter will be stiff. Fill greased or paper lined muffin tins three-quarters full. Combine topping ingredients and sprinkle over batter. Bake at 400°F (200°C) 20 minutes.

Can freeze   **Yield: 16**

Jubilation

...designates "Company in a Minute"

JONATHAN'S OF OAKVILLE,
120 Thomas St., Oakville

Jonathan's Broccoli Soup

2 Tbsp	oil	25 mL
2	heads of broccoli, chopped	2
1	medium onion, diced	1
¼ tsp	rubbed sage	1 mL
1	clove garlic, minced	1
1	large baking potato, diced	1
4 cups	chicken stock	1 L
1	bay leaf	1
	salt and pepper, to taste	
½ cup	35% cream	125 mL
	Stilton cheese	
1 pkg	frozen puff pastry	1

In a large saucepan sauté in oil, over medium heat, broccoli, onion, sage and garlic. Add potato, chicken stock, bay leaf, salt and pepper. Bring to a boil, reduce heat and simmer for approximately 20 minutes or until potato is fully cooked. Purée in a food processor and return to heat. Adjust seasoning and add cream. Simmer gently. Do not boil.

Preheat oven to 425°F (220°C). Place hot soup in individual serving bowls and add a bit of Stilton. Cover with puff pastry which has been rolled out, making sure it does not touch the soup. Brush the top of the pastry with an egg wash (egg and water mixed). Bake at 425°F (220°C) 10 minutes. Watch carefully so that it doesn't burn.

Serves: 6

Cream of Almond Soup

4 oz	almonds, ground	125 g
2 cans	(10 oz/284 mL each) chicken broth	2
	bouquet garni*	
2 Tbsp	butter	25 mL
2 Tbsp	all purpose flour	25 mL
2 cups	10% cream, heated	500 mL
	salt to taste	

GARNISH   slivered almonds, toasted

In a large saucepan, combine almonds, broth and bouquet garni. Bring to boil, reduce heat and simmer 30 minutes. Discard the bouquet. In a small saucepan, melt butter and stir in flour, stirring constantly 2 to 3 minutes. Add hot cream and beat vigorously until smooth. Stir this into the almond broth mixture. Bring to boil, add salt and serve immediately. Garnish with toasted almonds.
*NOTE: Bouquet garni—wrap in cheesecloth and tie: 2 sprigs parsley, thyme, ½ onion, sliced, and 1 stalk celery.

Serves: 6

Avocado Soup

1 can	(10 oz/284 mL) cream of	1
	celery soup	
½ cup	chopped avocado	125 mL
¼ cup	chopped cucumber	50 mL
¼ cup	chopped tomato	50 mL
1 Tbsp	chopped green pepper	15 mL
1 Tbsp	chopped green onion	15 mL
2 Tbsp	vegetable oil or olive oil	25 mL
1 Tbsp	vinegar	15 mL
1¼ cups	cold water	300 mL

GARNISH

¼ cup	peeled, seeded and chopped tomato	50 mL
¼ cup	peeled and chopped avocado	50 mL

Blend all ingredients, except garnish, in blender. Refrigerate until serving time. Serve cold, garnished with chopped tomato and avocado.

Can make ahead   **Serves: 4**

Chilled Strawberry Soup
Perfect for a ladies' luncheon

2 qts	strawberries	2 L
1 cup	orange juice	250 mL
4 tsp	corn starch	20 mL
pinch	allspice	pinch
pinch	cinnamon	pinch
1 cup	buttermilk	250 mL
½ cup	sugar (less, if desired)	125 mL
2 Tbsp	lemon juice	25 mL
1 tsp	grated lemon peel	5 mL

GARNISH   fresh mint leaves

Wash and hull strawberries. Slice 8 berries and set aside. Purée remaining berries with orange juice. Strain into large saucepan. Mix cornstarch with a little of the purée, and add to saucepan. Stir in allspice and cinnamon. Heat gently until boiling. Cook until thickened, stirring constantly. Remove from heat and pour into a large bowl. Stir in buttermilk, sugar, lemon juice and peel. Cover and chill 8 hours or overnight. Garnish with sliced strawberries and mint leaves.

Must make ahead   **Serves: 8**

Cherry Soup

2 cans	(14 oz/398 mL each) waterpacked pitted sour cherries	2
⅓ cup	sugar	75 mL
4 tsp	cornstarch	20 mL
½ tsp	salt	2 mL
½tsp	cinnamon	2 mL
	grated rind of 1 orange	
1 cup	orange juice	250 mL
1 cup	dry red wine	250 mL

GARNISH: sour cream

Combine cherries, sugar, cornstarch, salt, cinnamon, orange rind and orange juice in a blender or food processor. Blend until smooth. Pour soup into saucepan, add wine and cook, stirring, until slightly thickened. Serve hot or cold with a dollop of sour cream.

Serves: 6 to 8

Creamy Zucchini Soup 🍒
A wonderful way to use garden zucchini

3 Tbsp	butter	50 mL
½ cup	chopped green onions	125 mL
6 cups	chicken stock	1.5 L
5 cups	unpeeled, sliced zucchini	125 L
1½ tsp	red wine vinegar	7 mL
¾ tsp	dried dill weed or tarragon	3 mL
⅓ cup	cream of wheat	75 mL
½ cup	sour cream (optional)	125 mL
	seasonings to taste	

Melt butter in a large, heavy saucepan or Dutch oven. Cook onions in butter, slowly. Do not brown. Add chicken stock, zucchini, vinegar and dill weed. Bring to boil. Slowly add cream of wheat, stirring constantly. Reduce heat and simmer, partially covered, 20 to 30 minutes or until zucchini is tender. Purée soup in blender or food processor until smooth. Return to saucepan and season to taste. Reheat to simmer and beat in sour cream. Serve hot or cold.
NOTE: Cream of wheat makes a good thickener and is also good for people with possible allergies to cream.

Can freeze **Serves: 6**

Cider Soup 🍒
What could be easier!

1 can	(10 oz/284 mL) consommé	1
2 cups	apple juice	500 mL
	curry powder to taste	

Combine consommé and apple juice in a saucepan. Heat over medium heat. Stir in curry powder.

Can make ahead **Serves: 4**

Simply Chowder Soup

A crowd pleaser

1	large onion, chopped	1
1 lb	frozen sole fillets	500 g
¼ cup	butter	50 mL
7 cans	(10 oz/284 mL each) cream of potato soup	7
7	soup cans (10 oz/284 mL each) milk	7
4 cans	(5 oz/142 g each) baby clams, drain off ½ of juice	4
3 cans	(4 oz/113 g each) tiny shrimp, drained	3

Sauté onion and fish fillets in butter until onion is soft and fish is flaky. Add soup, milk, clams with juice and shrimp. Serve hot.

Can freeze　　　　　　　　　　　**Serves: 20**

Clam Chowder

Good for a cross-country skiing excursion

2 Tbsp	butter	25 mL
1	medium onion, finely chopped	1
½ cup	finely chopped celery	125 mL
½ cup	finely diced carrots	125 mL
2 cups	finely diced potatoes	500 mL
1 tsp	salt	5 mL
½ tsp	pepper	2 mL
2 cups	boiling water	500 mL
1 can	(5 oz/142 g) baby clams	1
1 cup	milk	250 mL
½ cup	dry sherry (optional)	125 mL

Melt butter in a large saucepan. Add onion, celery and carrots and sauté until softened, 5 to 10 minutes. Add potatoes, salt, pepper and water. Cover and simmer 10 to 15 minutes. Add clams and cook an additional 10 minutes. Add milk and sherry. Reheat but do not boil.

Can make ahead　　　　　　　　　　　**Serves: 6**

Spinach and Lentil Soup
A meal in a bowl or an excellent vegetarian dish

1½ cups	red or green lentils	375 mL
¼ cup	vegetable oil	50 mL
2	large onions, chopped	2
2	cloves garlic, chopped	2
3	celery stalks, chopped	3
½ lb	fresh spinach, chopped	250 g
3	large tomatoes, chopped	3
2½ cups	beef stock	675 mL
pinch	salt and pepper	pinch
pinch	dried basil and oregano leaves	pinch

Cover lentils with water and soak for a minimum of 2 hours. Heat oil in heavy saucepan and sauté onions, garlic, celery, spinach and tomatoes until softened. Add beef stock and drained lentils. If a thinner soup is desired, add some of the water used to soak the lentils. Add seasonings to taste. Simmer for 2 hours before serving. Serve with rye bread.

Can freeze   **Serves: 6 to 8**

Plaza III Steak Soup
From the Plaza III Restaurant in Kansas City

½ cup	butter or margarine	125 mL
½ cup	all purpose flour	125 mL
8 cups	hot water	2 L
2 lb	lean ground beef	1 kg
2 Tbsp	powdered beef bouillon base	25 mL
1 cup	chopped onion	250 mL
1 cup	diced carrots	250 mL
1 cup	sliced celery	250 mL
2 cups	frozen mixed vegetables	500 mL
1 can	(19 oz/540 mL) tomatoes	1
1 tsp	pepper	5 mL
1 Tbsp	Accent (optional)	15 mL

Melt butter or margarine in a large saucepan. Blend in flour to make a smooth paste. Add hot water a little at a time. Simmer until smooth. Sauté beef in a large skillet and drain off fat. Add meat, bouillon base, all vegetables and seasonings to saucepan. Bring to boil. Reduce heat and simmer until vegetables are cooked. Do not add salt.

Can freeze   **Serves: 8 to 10**

Minted Pea Soup
Serve hot or cold

1 tsp	butter or margarine	5 mL
¼ cup	chopped onion	50 mL
1½ cups	chicken stock	375 mL
2 cups	frozen peas	500 mL
2	leaves iceberg or romaine lettuce, chopped	2
¼ cup	chopped fresh parsley	50 mL
2	sprigs fresh mint or 1½ tsp (7 mL) dried mint	2
1 cup	skim milk	250 mL
GARNISH	chopped mint or chives or grated orange rind	

Melt butter in saucepan. Add onions and ½ cup (125 mL) chicken stock. Cook over medium heat until onions are soft. Add peas, lettuce, parsley and mint. Cover and cook 20 minutes. Add remaining stock and bring to boil. Cool. Purée in blender or food processor. Stir in milk. If serving cold, chill well and garnish. If serving hot, reheat and garnish.

Can make ahead   **Serves: 4**

Consommé Surprise
So easy it's embarrassing!

1 can	(10 oz/284 mL) consommé	1
1 pkg	(8 oz/250 g) plain cream cheese	1
	curry powder to taste	

Pour ½ can of consommé into 6 demi-tasse cups. Chill until set. Thoroughly mix remaining consommé with softened cream cheese. Add curry powder to taste and pour over jellied consommé. Chill until set. Garnish with slice of green olive or sprig of watercress or parsley.

Must make ahead   **Serves: 6**

Chinese Consommé 🍒

2 cups	chicken stock	500 mL
2 cups	tomato juice	500 mL
1 Tbsp	vegetable oil	15 mL
½ cup	dry white wine or 1½ Tbsp (25 mL) lemon juice	125 mL
1 cup	combination of thinly sliced, crisp vegetables such as celery, radishes, carrots, cucumber and green onion.	250 mL

Mix together chicken stock and tomato juice and bring to a boil. In a tureen, place the oil, white wine or lemon juice and vegetables. Pour the boiling stock into the tureen and serve.
NOTE: If the vegetables have been sliced paper thin, they will float, and their different shapes and colours will make a very attractive dish.

Serves: 4 to 6

Dutch Pea Soup
A family favourite

1	pork hock	1
7 cups	cold water	1.75 L
1 Tbsp	salt	15 mL
⅛ tsp	pepper	0.5 mL
1 pkg	(12 oz/350 g) dried split peas	1
1¼ cups	chopped celery	300 mL
1 Tbsp	chopped parsley	15 mL
⅓ cup	chopped carrots	75 mL
¾ cup	chopped onion	175 mL
1	medium potato, cubed	1
1	smoked sausage, sliced	1
2	bouillon cubes	2

In a large saucepan, place pork hock, water, salt and pepper. Simmer for 1½ hours. Add peas and simmer for another hour. Stir occasionally. Add celery, parsley, carrots, onion and potato. Continue simmering until vegetables are tender. Remove pork hock from soup and cut meat into bite size pieces, return to pot. Add sausage slices and bouillon cubes. Serve with crusty rolls.

Can make ahead   **Serves: 8**

Carrot Soup

2 Tbsp	butter	25 mL
¾ cup	finely chopped onion	175 mL
3 cups	finely chopped carrots	750 mL
4 cups	chicken stock	1 L
2 tsp	tomato paste	10 mL
2 Tbsp	long grain white rice	25 mL
	salt and pepper to taste	
½ cup	whipping cream	125 mL

Melt butter over medium heat in large heavy saucepan. Add onions and cook until soft but not browned. Add carrots, chicken stock, tomato paste and rice. Simmer gently for 30 minutes. Pour soup into blender or food processor and blend until smooth. Return to saucepan and stir in seasonings and cream. May be served hot or cold. If serving hot, heat over medium heat, stirring constantly. Do not boil. Garnish with parsley sprigs or carrot curls.

Can make ahead   **Serves: 4 to 6**

Cool Cucumber Soup
...with a shrimp surprise!

1	large English cucumber, peeled and grated	1
1 cup	cold chicken stock	250 mL
2 cups	plain yogurt	500 mL
½ cup	tomato juice	125 mL
1	small garlic clove, chopped	1
½ cup	18% cream	125 mL
2 Tbsp	white vinegar	25 mL
¾ cup	small shrimp, rinsed and drained well	175 mL

Squeeze water from grated cucumber. Add cucumber to remaining ingredients. Serve well chilled, garnished with a cucumber slice. Keeps well up to one week.

Can make ahead   **Serves: 6 to 8**

Oyster Bisque Florentine 🍒
Easily doubled or tripled

2 cups	oysters, with liquor	500 mL
½ lb	frozen spinach	250 g
¾ cup	18% cream	175 mL
¼ cup	butter	50 mL
2 Tbsp	all purpose flour	25 mL
2 cups	chicken stock	500 mL
2 tsp	lemon juice	10 mL
pinch	salt	pinch
pinch	cayenne pepper	pinch
½ cup	sour cream	125 mL

Cut oysters in half, saving liquor. Cook spinach in boiling water just until it falls apart. Drain and blend in blender with ½ cup (125 mL) cream. Melt butter in heavy saucepan. Blend in flour. Add oyster liquor, spinach and chicken stock. Cook slowly, stirring constantly, until soup thickens slightly. Add oysters and lemon juice. Beat remaining ¼ cup (50 mL) cream with sour cream. Add to soup. Season. Reheat but do not boil. Serve with crackers.

Serves: 4

Oktoberfest Soup
A meal in itself!

1 lb	Oktoberfest sausage	500 g
1	small onion, chopped	1
1 can	(28 oz/796 mL) tomatoes, chopped	1
1 can	(19 oz/540 mL) kidney beans	1
3	medium zucchini, sliced	3
3	stalks celery, sliced thickly	3
½	head cauliflower, broken into flowerets	½
GARNISH	Parmesan cheese	

Parboil sausage in a saucepan for 15 minutes. Drain and cool slightly. Remove casing from sausage and cut into chunks. Place in Dutch oven with chopped onion and sauté until onion is golden. Add tomatoes, kidney beans (including liquid), zucchini, celery and cauliflower and simmer 45 minutes to 1 hour. Serve piping hot. Sprinkle with Parmesan cheese and serve with hot crusty bread.

NOTE: Other vegetables of your choice may be added (potatoes, broccoli etc.).

Can freeze   Serves: 6 to 8

Acorn Squash Soup

2	acorn squash, halved and seeded	2
	salt and pepper	
2 Tbsp	unsalted butter	25 mL
⅓ cup	diced carrots	75 mL
⅓ cup	diced celery	75 mL
⅓ cup	chopped onion	75 mL
½	bay leaf	½
½ tsp	dried thyme leaves	2 mL
2½ cups	chicken stock	625 mL
½ cup	half and half cream	125 mL

Preheat oven to 350°F (180°C). Sprinkle the squash with salt and pepper and bake, cut side down, on a buttered baking pan at 350°F (180°C) 45 minutes to 1 hour. When cool, scoop out the flesh. In a saucepan, melt butter and sauté carrots, celery and onion with bay leaf and thyme for 10 minutes. Add chicken stock, bring to boil and simmer 20 minutes. Discard bay leaf and purée soup in blender or food processor until smooth. Transfer to saucepan, add cream and heat, but do not boil. Thin with extra chicken stock, if desired, and season with salt and pepper. May be served hot or cold. This recipe can be multiplied to suit any number.

Can make ahead   **Serves: 6 to 8**

Quick Spinach Soup 🍒

2 pkgs	(10 oz/284 g each) spinach	2
	cooked and puréed	
2 cans	(10 oz/284 g each) cream of	2
	mushroom or cream of celery soup	
dash	onion salt	dash
1 cup	chicken stock	250 mL
1 cup	sour cream	250 mL
1 cup	cream, evaporated milk or milk	250 mL
	salt and pepper to taste	
	sherry to taste (optional)	

GARNISH   croutons

Combine spinach, soup, onion salt, chicken stock, sour cream, cream and seasonings. Heat but do not boil. Serve garnished with croutons.

Serves: 8

61

Garden Tomato Soup

1	small onion, finely chopped	1
3	scallions, finely chopped	3
3 Tbsp	olive oil	50 mL
8-10	tomatoes, peeled, seeded and quartered, reserving juice	8-10
1	clove garlic	1
4 cups	tomato juice	1 L
1 Tbsp	dried parsley or 3 fresh sprigs, chopped	15 mL
1 Tbsp	basil, fresh if possible, chopped	15 mL
	salt and pepper to taste	
pinch	sugar	pinch
3 drops	Tabasco sauce	3

GARNISH chopped green pepper

Sauté onion and scallions in olive oil about 5 minutes. Add drained tomatoes and garlic. Cook over high heat for 2 to 3 minutes. Add reserved tomato juice and enough canned juice to make 4 cups (1 L) liquid. Add parsley and basil. Simmer, partially covered, 20 minutes. Add seasonings to taste. Refrigerate covered 24 hours to develop flavour. Heat, garnish with chopped green pepper and serve with cheese straws.

Must make ahead **Serves: 6**

Cold Pea Soup
Zippy and refreshing! An unusual taste for summer!

1 can	(10 oz/284 mL) pea soup	1
1 can	(10 oz/284 mL) beef bouillon or consommé	1
2 tsp	curry powder	10 mL
1½ cups	half and half cream	375 mL
	salt and pepper to taste	

GARNISH paprika or parsley

Combine pea soup, beef bouillon and curry powder in a saucepan. Bring to a boil, stirring occasionally. Cool. Add cream and seasonings. Chill and serve garnished with paprika or parsley.

Must make ahead **Serves: 4 to 6**

Pumpkin Soup
Once you taste this you'll know why chic restaurants serve it!

2 Tbsp	butter	25 mL
¼ cup	chopped green pepper	50 mL
2 Tbsp	chopped onion	25 mL
1	large sprig parsley, chopped	1
⅛ tsp	dried thyme leaves	0.5 mL
1	bay leaf	1
1 cup	canned tomatoes	250 mL
1 can	(14 oz/398 mL) pumpkin	1
2 cups	chicken stock	500 mL
1 Tbsp	flour	15 mL
1 cup	milk or half and half cream	250 mL
1 tsp	salt	5 mL
⅛ tsp	pepper	0.5 mL

Melt butter and add green pepper, onion, parsley, thyme and bay leaf. Cook 5 minutes. Add tomatoes, pumpkin and chicken stock. Cover and simmer 30 minutes, stirring occasionally. Purée in blender or food processor. Blend together flour and milk and stir into soup. Add salt and pepper and cook, stirring frequently, until mixture boils and thickens. Store in refrigerator until serving time. Serve hot or cold.

Can make ahead   **Serves: 6**

Leek Soup

6	leeks	6
2	onions, chopped	2
4	garlic cloves, chopped	4
2 Tbsp	butter	25 mL
7	potatoes, sliced	7
9 cups	chicken stock	2.25 L
4	carrots, grated	4
2 cups	cream	500 mL
3 Tbsp	butter	50 mL
½ cup	chopped parsley	125 mL
¼ cup	chopped chives	50 mL
¼ cup	chopped savory	50 mL

Wash leeks and chop (use white part and ⅓ of green). Sauté leeks, onions and garlic, in butter until softened. Add sliced potatoes and chicken stock. Simmer, covered, 1 hour. Blend, in small portions, in blender or food processor. Return to saucepan. Add carrots, cream and butter. Just before serving stir in parsley, chives and savory.

Can make ahead   **Serves: 8 to 10**

Vichyssoise
An elegant soup for a summer dinner

3 cups	sliced potatoes	750 mL
3 cups	sliced leeks, white part only	750 mL
6 cups	chicken stock	1.5 L
	salt and white pepper to taste	
½-1 cup	whipping cream	125-250 mL
GARNISH	chopped chives or green onion tops	

Simmer potatoes and leeks in chicken stock until tender. Cool. Purée in blender or food processor. Stir in cream. Season to taste. Over salt slightly as salt loses flavour when cold. Chill. Serve in chilled soup cups and garnish.

Must make ahead   **Serves: 8**

Main Dish Salads

Babsi's Warm Salad of Romaine and Slivers of Beef Tenderloin	65
Chicken and Pasta Primavera	81
Chicken Salad Elizabeth	67
Chinese Chicken Salad	77
Royal Curried Chicken Salad	73
Shrimp Salad	75
South Sea Salad	72
Spinach and Smoked Salmon Salad	70

Molded Salads

Broccoli Mold	69
Cherry Sherry Mold	74
Divine Horseradish Mold	72
Quick Tomato Aspic	80
Summertime Egg Salad	68
Tomato Aspic in Cheese Crust	75

Rice and Pasta Salads

Artichoke and Wild Rice Salad	79
Chicken and Pasta Primavera	81
Garden Rice Salad	71
Greek Pasta Salad	79
Rice Stuffed Tomato Salad	78
Sunshine Salad	76

Vegetable Salads

Celeri Remoulade	73
Greek Salad	68
Hot German Potato Salad	69
Marinated Cherry Tomatoes	76
Pretty Potato Salad	66
Scandinavian Stuffed Tomatoes	80
Shaker Salad	66
Tabouleh	71
Watercress and Apple Salad	74

Dressings

Basil Salad Dressing	85
Brick Cheese Salad Dressing	84
Buttermilk Dressing	81
Creamy Salad Dressing	86
Green Goddess Salad Dressing	86
Mayonnaise	85
Orange Salad Dressing	82
Processor Salad Dressing	83
Red Wine Vinegar Dressing	65
Tangy French Dressing	84
Tarragon Dressing	82
Thousand Island Dressing	83
Walnut Oil Dressing	65

... designates "Company in a Minute"

BABSI'S RESTAURANT
1731 Lakeshore Road West, Mississauga

Warm Salad of Romaine and Slivers of Beef Tenderloin

1 head	romaine lettuce	1
1	red pepper, cut in julienne strips	1
¾ cup	red wine vinegar dressing or walnut oil dressing (see below)	175 mL
2 Tbsp	olive oil	25 mL
10 oz	beef tenderloin slivers	300 g
	salt and coarse pepper, to taste	
¼ cup	red wine	50 mL

Cut, wash and dry the romaine lettuce. Add the red pepper and dressing and toss. In a sauté pan, heat olive oil until it smokes. Add the tenderloin, salt and pepper. Sauté rare and then deglaze the pan with red wine. Pour over the salad.

Serves: 4

Red Wine Vinegar Dressing

¾ cup	olive oil	175 mL
¼ cup	red wine vinegar	50 mL
	salt and pepper to taste	
	dry mustard to taste	

Combine all ingredients. Mix well.

Yield: 1 cup (250 mL)

Walnut Oil Dressing

¼ cup	walnut oil	50 mL
½ cup	corn oil	125 mL
¼ cup	white wine vinegar	50 mL
	salt and pepper to taste	
	sugar to taste	

Combine all the ingredients. Mix well.

Yield: 1 cup (250 mL)

Pretty Potato Salad

1 lb	red boiling potatoes	500 g
1 lb	white boiling potatoes (new if possible)	500 g
3 Tbsp	fresh lemon juice, divided	40 mL
	salt to taste	
½ lb	snow peas	250 g
¼ cup	coarsely chopped onion	50 mL
1 Tbsp	mustard seed	15 mL
⅓ cup	olive oil	75 mL
	dillweed, to taste	

Cut potatoes, unpeeled, into bite size pieces and cook until just tender. Toss while hot with 1 Tbsp (15 mL) lemon juice and salt to taste. Cool. Discard strings from snow peas, cut in half diagonally and blanch in boiling water for 5 seconds. Drain and refresh under cold water. Add to potatoes along with chopped onion. In small bowl, whisk together 2 Tbsp (25 mL) lemon juice, mustard seed and olive oil. Add to salad, toss gently and sprinkle with dillweed. Serve at room temperature or slightly chilled. Wonderful with cold meats.

Can make ahead   **Serves: 6 to 8**

Shaker Salad
Wonderful accompaniment to fish, seafood or poultry

½ lb	green beans, washed and trimmed	250 g
⅓ cup	olive or vegetable oil	75 mL
3 Tbsp	tarragon vinegar	50 mL
1 Tbsp	finely chopped onion	15 mL
½ tsp	dried thyme leaves, crumbled	2 mL
½ tsp	dry mustard	2 mL
¼ tsp	ground savoury	1 mL
	salt and pepper to taste	
2	firm heads Boston or Bibb lettuce	2
2	green onions, chopped, including 1 inch (2 cm) green tops	2

Cook beans in salted water until crisp tender. Immerse in cold water to cool. Pat dry and refrigerate. Whisk together oil and vinegar. Add onion, thyme, mustard, savoury, salt and pepper. Break lettuce into bite size pieces. Combine with green onions and beans. Toss with dressing in a glass bowl and serve immediately.

Serves: 4 to 6

Chicken Salad Elizabeth
Created for the Coronation in 1953

CHICKEN

1	(3 lb/1.5 kg) roasting chicken	1
4 cups	chicken stock	1 L
2	sprigs parsley	2
1	slice lemon	1
1 Tbsp	thyme	15 mL

SAUCE

1	small onion, chopped	1
1½ Tbsp	vegetable oil	25 mL
1 Tbsp	curry powder	15 mL
1 tsp	tomato paste	5 mL
¼ cup	water	50 mL
1	bay leaf	1
½ cup	red wine	125 mL
1	slice lemon	1
1 tsp	lemon juice	5 mL
½ tsp	salt	2 mL
⅛ tsp	pepper	0.5 mL
2 Tbsp	apricot jam	25 mL
1 cup	mayonnaise	250 mL
2 Tbsp	whipping cream, lightly whipped (optional)	25 mL

CHICKEN: Place chicken in pot of simmering stock. Add parsley, lemon and thyme. Cover and cook gently for 1¼ to 1½ hours, until tender. Remove immediately from stock and set aside to cool. Cover with foil to prevent drying out. When cool, remove meat from the bones and cut into bite size pieces.

SAUCE: In skillet, sauté onion in oil for 4 minutes. Add curry powder and cook 1 minute more. Add tomato paste, water, bay leaf, wine, lemon slice and juice, salt, pepper and jam. Simmer for 8 minutes. Strain mixture through sieve. Flavour mayonnaise with sauce to desired consistency. Add whipped cream. A few hours before serving, mix chicken with sauce. Reserve a little sauce to coat top. Chill in refrigerator. Serve garnished with watercress or parsley.

Must make ahead   **Serves: 4 to 6**

Greek Salad

1	English cucumber, thinly sliced, or 2 regular cucumbers	1
2	large tomatoes, thinly sliced	2
1	zucchini (8 inches/20 cm), sliced	1
2	stocks celery, thinly sliced	2
2	red onions, very thinly sliced	2
8 oz	feta cheese, cubed	250 g
1 Tbsp	dried oregano leaves	15 mL
½ cup	Greek olives	125 g
2	cloves garlic chopped	2

DRESSING

3 Tbsp	lemon juice	50 mL
½ cup	Greek olive oil	125 mL
1	clove garlic, chopped salt and pepper, to taste	1

Mix all ingredients for salad together and chill.
DRESSING: Add oil slowly to lemon juice, garlic, salt and pepper. Add dressing to vegetables and toss.

Must make ahead   **Serves: 8 to 10**

Summertime Egg Salad

1 pkg	(1 Tbsp/7 g) unflavoured gelatine	1
¼ cup	cold water	50 mL
1 cup	mayonnaise	250 mL
4	hard-boiled eggs, chopped	4
½ cup	chopped celery	125 mL
2 Tbsp	pickle relish	25 mL
1 Tbsp	chopped pimento	15 mL
1 Tbsp	fresh lemon juice	15 mL
1 tsp	salt	5 mL

Soften gelatine in cold water and dissolve over hot water. Combine next 7 ingredients, add gelatine and combine thoroughly. Pour into 4 cup (1 L) mold which has been rinsed in cold water. Refrigerate 6 hours or overnight. Unmold, garnish with leaf lettuce and radishes. Variations: Add chopped black or green olives, chopped parsley, chopped green onion. Can be doubled to serve 8 to 10.

Must make ahead   **Serves: 4 to 6**

Broccoli Mold

1 pkg	(1 Tbsp/7 g) unflavoured gelatine	1
¼ cup	cold beef stock	50 mL
¾ cup	hot beef stock	175 mL
¾ cup	mayonnaise	175 mL
¼ cup	plain yogurt or sour cream	50 mL
½ tsp	Worcestershire sauce	2 mL
	salt to taste	
2 pkg	(10 oz/250 g each) frozen, chopped broccoli, cooked and drained	2
6	hard-boiled eggs, chopped	6

Dissolve gelatine in cold broth. Add to hot broth. Add mayonnaise, yogurt, Worcestershire sauce and salt. Mix well. Stir in broccoli and eggs. Turn into a 5 cup (1.25 L) mold. Chill until firm. Unmold. For a luncheon dish, use a ring mold and fill centre with chicken salad.

Must make ahead   **Serves: 8**

Hot German Potato Salad
Superb!

4 cups	cooked potatoes cut in ½ inch (1 cm) cubes	1 L
16	slices bacon, cooked and crumbled	16
1 cup	chopped green onions, including tops	250 mL
½ tsp	seasoned salt	2 mL
pinch	pepper	pinch
pinch	paprika	pinch
pinch	fresh dill	pinch
1½ cups	mayonnaise	375 mL
¼ cup	prepared mustard	50 mL
¼ cup	horseradish	50 mL
1 cup	diced celery	250 mL
¼ cup	finely chopped carrots	50 mL

In large bowl, gently mix potatoes, bacon, onions, salt, pepper, paprika and dill. In saucepan, combine mayonnaise, mustard and horseradish. Heat, stirring constantly. When hot, not boiling, add celery and carrots. Reheat until very hot. Pour over potato mixture. Toss lightly. Sprinkle with additional paprika and dill. Serve immediately. Potato mixture may be prepared ahead but bring to room temperature before adding dressing.

Can make ahead   **Serves: 8**

Spinach and Smoked Salmon Salad
Party pretty and delicious as an appetizer

2	bunches fresh spinach	2
6	green onions, chopped	6
3	hard-boiled eggs, chopped	3
½ lb	smoked salmon	250 g
GARNISH	capers	

YOGURT AND HERB DRESSING

¼ cup	lemon juice	50 mL
¼ cup	white wine vinegar	50 mL
2 tsp	chopped fresh dill	10 mL
½ tsp	dry mustard	2 mL
½ tsp	dried marjoram leaves	2 mL
½ tsp	dried tarragon leaves	2 mL
1 tsp	sugar	5 mL
1	garlic clove, chopped	1
1 cup	plain yogurt	250 mL
1 cup	vegetable oil	250 mL
	salt and pepper, to taste	

Wash, dry and tear spinach into bite size pieces. Arrange spinach on individual salad plates. Sprinkle each salad with chopped onions and hard-boiled eggs. Cut smoked salmon into strips and arrange on top. Garnish with capers and dress with Yogurt and Herb dressing.

YOGURT AND HERB DRESSING: Whisk together all ingredients except oil and yogurt. When well blended, add oil, yogurt, salt and pepper. Whisk again and chill. Yield: 2 cups (500 mL).

Must make ahead   **Serves: 6 to 8**

Tabouleh
Light and refreshing!

1 cup	uncooked bulgur wheat	250 mL
2	bunches parsley, snipped	2
2	medium tomatoes, chopped	2
1	medium English cucumber, diced	1
1	medium Spanish onion, chopped	1
1	green pepper, chopped	1
2	green onions, chopped	2
¼ cup	chopped fresh mint	50 mL
	juice of 1 lemon	
¾ cup	olive oil	175 mL
1	clove garlic, chopped	1
	salt	
	dried basil leaves, to taste	
	romaine lettuce	

Cover bulgar wheat with boiling water and soak until softened. Drain. Add all remaining ingredients except lettuce. Toss well. Chill for 2 hours. Serve on a bed of romaine lettuce. May fill pocket of pita bread as a tasty sandwich. Keeps well in refrigerator for 3 to 4 days.

Must make ahead   **Serves: 6**

Garden Rice Salad

1 pkg	(6 oz/170 g) long grain and wild rice	1
½ cup	mayonnaise	125 mL
¼ cup	plain yogurt	50 mL
1 cup	finely diced celery	250 mL
1 cup	chopped tomatoes	250 mL
½ cup	diced cucumbers	125 mL
2 Tbsp	chopped parsley	25 mL
⅛ tsp	salt	0.5 mL
⅛ tsp	pepper	0.5 mL

GARNISH

¼ cup	finely chopped peanuts	50 mL

Cook rice according to package directions but omit butter. Cool. Toss lightly with mayonnaise, yogurt, celery, tomatoes, cucumbers, parsley, salt and pepper. Cover and chill. Garnish with nuts, if desired.

Must make ahead   **Serves: 4**

South Sea Salad

8 cups	mixed salad greens	2 L
2 cups	fresh strawberries, hulled and halved	500 mL
2 cups	fresh pineapple chunks	500 mL
2-3	kiwi fruit, peeled and sliced	2-3
½ cup	chopped green onions	125 mL

POPPY SEED DRESSING

¾ cup	vegetable oil	175 mL
¼ cup	cider vinegar	50 mL
2 Tbsp	lemon juice	25 mL
2 Tbsp	granulated sugar	25 mL
2 Tbsp	honey	25 mL
2 Tbsp	sesame seeds	25 mL
2 Tbsp	poppy seeds	25 mL
2 Tbsp	chopped green onions	25 mL
½ tsp	salt	2 mL

Combine salad greens, strawberries, pineapple, kiwi fruit and onions in a large bowl. Chill.

POPPY SEED DRESSING: Combine remaining ingredients in a blender. Blend until thick. Cover and chill until serving time. Add enough dressing to coat greens and fruit. Toss gently.

Must make ahead   **Serves: 10**

Divine Horseradish Mold

1 pkg	(3 oz/85 g) lime flavoured jelly powder	1
½ cup	cold water	125 mL
1 cup	hot water	250 mL
1 cup	cottage cheese	250 mL
½ cup	mayonnaise	125 mL
½ cup	sour cream	125 mL
3 Tbsp	grated horseradish	50 mL
½ tsp	salt	2 mL
	juice of 1 lemon	

Soak jelly powder in cold water. Dissolve in hot water. Chill. When slightly set, fold in all remaining ingredients. Pour into 1 qt (1 L) mold or individual molds.

Must make ahead   **Serves: 6**

Céleri Remoulade
Very different, interesting and light first course

1	celery root (celeriac) approximately 2 cups/500 mL when sliced	1
1	egg yolk, hard-boiled	1
1	egg yolk, raw	1
1½ tsp	Dijon mustard	7 mL
	salt and pepper, to taste	
2 Tbsp	tarragon vinegar or lemon juice	25 mL
½ cup	chilled olive oil or vegetable oil	125 mL
	fresh parsley or chives, chopped	

Pare off all tough outer peel from celery root. Shred or cut into julienne strips. Mash hard boiled yolk with raw yolk. Add mustard, salt, pepper and vinegar or lemon juice. Blend to a smooth paste. While beating with wire whisk, add oil little by little until dressing resembles mayonnaise. Combine celery root with dressing and chill. Serve on a bed of lettuce and sprinkle with parsley or chives.

Must make ahead   **Serves: 6 to 8**

Royal Curried Chicken Salad

2 cups	cooked, diced chicken	500 mL
¼ cup	sliced water chestnuts	50 mL
½ lb	halved seedless green grapes	250 g
1 can	(8 oz/227 mL) pineapple chunks, drained	1
½ cup	chopped celery	125 mL
½ cup	slivered, toasted almonds	125 mL

DRESSING

¾ cup	mayonnaise	175 mL
1 tsp	curry powder	5 mL
2 tsp	lemon juice	10 mL
2 tsp	soy sauce	10 mL

Combine all ingredients for the salad together in a serving bowl. Beat together all ingredients for dressing and pour over salad. Chill several hours before serving.

Must make ahead   **Serves: 6**

Watercress and Apple Salad 🍒

2 Tbsp	wine vinegar	25 mL
½ tsp	salt	2 mL
	pepper to taste	
⅓-½ cup	olive oil	75-125 mL
½ tsp	Dijon mustard	2 mL
2	bunches watercress	2
2	large tart apples	2
1	red onion, thinly sliced	1

Mix together wine vinegar, salt and pepper. Slowly add oil while continuing to mix. Stir in mustard. Wash and dry leaves and young stems of watercress. Core apples and slice thinly. Separate onion slices into rings. Arrange apple and onion slices over the watercress in a salad bowl or on individual salad plates. Drizzle with dressing. Serve immediately.

Serves: 4

Cherry Sherry Mold
An elegant touch with cold ham, green salad and croissants

1 can	(14 oz/398 g) Bing cherries	1
1 pkg	(3 oz/85 g) cherry flavoured jelly powder	1
¾ cup	hot water	175 mL
½ cup	dry sherry	125 mL
¾ cup	reserved cherry syrup	175 mL
½ cup	sour cream	125 mL
¼ cup	sliced almonds	50 mL

Drain cherries, reserving syrup. Pit cherries if necessary. Dissolve jelly powder in hot water. Stir in sherry and cherry syrup. Chill mixture until consistency of unbeaten egg whites. Add cherries, sour cream and almonds. Pour into mold and set in refrigerator.

Must make ahead   **Serves: 6**

Shrimp Salad 🍒
Interesting way to stretch the shrimp!

2 cups	cooked shrimp	500 mL
6	slices thick bread, crusts removed buttered and cubed (crouton size)	6
4	hard-boiled eggs, chopped	4
1	small onion, chopped	1
1 cup	mayonnaise salt and pepper to taste	250 mL
4	tomatoes, peeled and chopped	4

Mix together all ingredients except tomatoes. Let stand several hours or overnight. Just before serving add tomatoes. Serve on lettuce.

Must make ahead   **Serves: 4**

Tomato Aspic in Cheese Crust
Party pretty

CHEESE CRUST

1 cup	finely crushed cheese crackers (Ritz)	250 mL
¼ cup	melted butter	50 mL

ASPIC

1 pkg	(3 oz/85 g) lemon flavoured jelly powder	1
1¼ cups	boiling water	300 mL
1 can	(7½ oz/213 mL) tomato sauce	1
2 Tbsp	vinegar	25 mL
½ tsp	salt	2 mL
dash	pepper	dash
1 drop	Tabasco sauce	1
½ cup	chopped stuffed olives	125 mL
¼ cup	sliced green onions	50 mL
¼ cup	chopped celery	50 mL

Preheat oven to 375°F (190°C).
CHEESE CRUST: Blend finely crushed cheese crackers with melted butter and pat into 8 inch (20 cm) pie plate. Bake at 375°F (190°C) 6 to 7 minutes. Cool.
ASPIC: Dissolve jelly powder in boiling water. Add tomato sauce, vinegar, salt, pepper and Tabasco sauce. Mix well. Chill until partially set. Stir in olives, onions and celery. Pour into cheese crust and chill until firm.

Must make ahead   **Serves: 6 to 8**

Sunshine Salad
Crunchy and pretty as a luncheon dish

1 cup	long grain rice	250 mL
1 cup	celery slices	250 mL
2 cups	ham, cubed	500 mL
1 can	(10 oz/284 mL) mandarin orange segments, drained	1
¾ cup	green pepper strips	175 mL
½ cup	carrot slices	125 mL
¾ cup	mayonnaise	175 mL
½ tsp	salt	2 mL
¼ tsp	pepper	1 mL

Cook rice according to package directions. Cool slightly. Combine rice, celery, ham, oranges, green peppers, carrots, mayonnaise, salt and pepper. Chill.

Must make ahead   **Serves: 4**

Marinated Cherry Tomatoes
Easy and tasty

2 cups	cherry tomatoes, halved	500 mL
6 Tbsp	olive oil	100 mL
1 Tbsp	finely chopped fresh dill or 1½ tsp (7 mL) dried dill weed	15 mL
2	green onions, chopped	2
2 Tbsp	chopped fresh parsley	25 mL
	salt	
	freshly ground black pepper	

Place tomatoes in serving bowl. Add remaining ingredients and toss gently. Cover and chill at least 6 hours. Can be prepared up to 3 days ahead.

Must make ahead   **Serves: 4**

Chinese Chicken Salad
A hot summer's day dinner

2	whole chicken breasts, split	2
1	(2 inch/5 cm) piece of ginger root, coarsely chopped	1
	water	
1	head lettuce torn into bite size pieces	1
4	green onions, cut in diagonal	4
4 oz	toasted, slivered almonds	125 g
8 oz.	Chinese rice sticks	227 g

DRESSING

¼ cup	sugar (or less, to taste)	50 mL
½ tsp	salt	2 mL
½ tsp	pepper	2 mL
¼ cup	vinegar	50 mL
½ cup	vegetable oil	125 mL

Place ginger and chicken in saucepan and add water to cover well. Bring water to boil and simmer 20 minutes or until chicken is tender. Remove chicken and cool. Shred chicken with fingers into bowl. Add lettuce and green onion. Chill.

RICE STICKS: These are available in Chinatown and may be cooked ahead but not mixed with other ingredients until the end. In a deep pot place at least 2 inches (6 cm) of oil. Heat to 375°F to 400°F (190°C to 200°C) and fry rice sticks briefly until they puff. Remove with slotted spoon and drain on paper towels. Chinese noodles may be substituted if time is short.

DRESSING: Combine all ingredients and heat until sugar dissolves, then cool to room temperature. Just before serving, toss as much dressing as needed with salad. Add almonds and rice sticks and toss again.

Must make ahead   **Serves: 4 to 6**

Rice Stuffed Tomato Salad
A basic recipe to vary as you wish

4	firm ripe tomatoes	4
	salt and pepper to taste	
2 cups	cooked rice (warm if possible)	500 mL
¼ cup	French dressing (oil and vinegar)	50 mL
¼ cup	mayonnaise	50 mL
½ cup	chopped celery	125 mL
¼ cup	chopped green onion	50 mL
¼ cup	chopped green pepper (optional)	50 mL
½ cup	chopped unpeeled seedless cucumber	125 mL
1 cup	cooked small shrimp or cubed chicken or salmon	250 mL
¼ tsp	dried rosemary or basil or 1 tsp (5 mL) fresh	1 mL
GARNISH	lettuce, whole shrimp, cucumber twists or fresh parsley	

To prepare tomatoes for stuffing, cut a small slice from tops; scoop out seeds and pulp, using a grapefruit knife or spoon. Sprinkle insides lightly with salt. Invert on paper towels to drain about 15 minutes. For rice stuffing, toss warm rice with French dressing, then add enough mayonnaise to moisten. Add remaining ingredients. Toss to mix, and season to taste. Spoon into tomatoes. Chill. Serve on lettuce, with desired garnish on top.

Variations: Add a little curry powder to the shrimp variation for added colour and flavour. Substitute chopped green and red peppers for the celery. Add sliced mushrooms, cooked green peas or grated carrot.

Can make ahead   **Serves: 4**

Artichoke and Wild Rice Salad

1 pkg	(170 g) long grain and wild rice	1
1 jar	(6 oz/170 mL) marinated artichoke hearts	1
½ cup	chopped green pepper	125 mL
⅓ cup	finely chopped red onion	75 mL
1½ tsp	vinegar	7 mL
10	cherry tomatoes, halved	10

Cook rice according to package directions but omit butter. Put into a bowl, cover and chill. Drain and coarsely chop artichoke hearts, reserving marinade. Add chopped artichoke hearts, green pepper, and onion to the chilled rice, mixing lightly. Stir vinegar into reserved marinade and toss well with rice mixture. Chill. Toss in tomatoes at serving time. Serve in a large glass bowl. Good with roast chicken.

Must make ahead   **Serves: 6**

Greek Pasta Salad
A spectacular buffet dish

½ lb	green noodles (fresh if possible)	250 g
⅓ cup	olive oil	75 mL
3 Tbsp	lemon juice	50 mL
1	clove garlic, finely chopped	1
½ tsp	Tabasco sauce	2 mL
¼ tsp	salt	1 mL
½ tsp	anise seed (optional)	2 mL
½ lb	Feta cheese, crumbled	250 g
2	tomatoes, coarsely chopped	2
½ cup	sliced pitted Greek olives	125 mL
¼ cup	chopped fresh parsley	50 mL
¼ cup	pine nuts (optional)	50 mL

Cook noodles and drain. Rinse with cold water and drain again. Mix olive oil, lemon juice, garlic, Tabasco sauce, salt and anise seed in a bowl. Add pasta and mix. Add cheese, tomatoes, Greek olives, parsley and pine nuts. Toss well. Chill for at least 24 hours. Excellent with baked ham or roast beef.

Must make ahead   **Serves: 8 to 10**

Scandinavian Stuffed Tomatoes

6	medium tomatoes	6
	salt	
2	large cucumbers	2
1½ tsp	salt	7 mL
2	hard-boiled eggs	2
2 tsp	sugar	10 mL
2 Tbsp	chopped fresh dill	25 mL
¼ cup	mayonnaise	50 mL
¼-⅓ cup	sour cream	50-75 mL
	lettuce or watercress	

Cut tops from tomatoes and scoop out pulp. Sprinkle lightly with salt and invert on paper towel to drain well. Chill. Peel cucumbers, seed and chop very finely. Add salt and let stand at least 30 minutes, stirring often. Put in sieve to drain, pressing gently with back of spoon to drain off all excess moisture. Cut hard-boiled eggs in half. Lift out yolks and put them through a coarse sieve. Set aside to use later. Chop whites finely and add to cucumber with sugar, dill, mayonnaise and enough sour cream to make a moist, but not wet mixture. Chill. At serving time, spoon cucumber mixture into tomatoes. Sprinkle egg yolks on top as a garnish. Serve each tomato on a bed of lettuce or watercress.

Must make ahead   **Serves: 6**

Quick Tomato Aspic
A tangy treat! Recipe can be increased to serve a cast of thousands!

1 pkg	(3 oz/85 g) lemon flavoured jelly powder	1
1 cup	boiling water	250 mL
1 cup	ketchup	250 mL
4 drops	onion juice	4
¼ tsp	celery powder	1 mL

Stir boiling water into jelly powder until dissolved. Add remaining ingredients. Pour into oiled mold. Chill until set. Turn out onto platter garnished with lettuce leaves. Chopped celery and/or chopped green pepper may also be added for a difference.

Must make ahead   **Serves: 4 to 6**

Chicken and Pasta Primavera

½ lb	spaghettini	250 g
1	clove garlic, chopped	1
2 tsp	salt	10 mL
½ tsp	pepper	2 mL
½ tsp	sugar	2 mL
1 tsp	Dijon mustard	5 mL
½ cup	vegetable oil	125 mL
3 Tbsp	red wine vinegar	50 mL
10	mushrooms, sliced	10
1 cup	broccoli flowerets, blanched 3 minutes	250 mL
1 cup	snow peas, blanched 1 minute	250 mL
14	cherry tomatoes	14
2 cups	cooked chicken	500 mL
⅓ cup	pine nuts	75 mL
⅓ cup	chopped fresh basil	75 mL
⅓ cup	chopped fresh parsley	75 mL

Cook pasta according to package directions. Make a vinaigrette by combining garlic, salt, pepper, sugar, mustard, oil and vinegar. Combine pasta with ⅓ cup (75 mL) of vinaigrette. Toss and chill for 3 hours. In another bowl combine vegetables with the remaining vinaigrette. Just before serving, toss chicken with pasta. Add vegetables, nuts, basil and parsley. Mix well and serve.

Must make ahead   **Serves: 6**

Buttermilk Dressing

1⅓ cups	mayonnaise	325 mL
1 cup	buttermilk	250 mL
1 tsp	garlic powder	5 mL
1 tsp	monosodium glutamate (Accent)	5 mL
½ tsp	salt	2 mL
1 tsp	pepper	5 mL
2 Tbsp	chopped fresh parsley	25 mL

Place all ingredients in a jar with tight fitting lid. Shake well. Dressing keeps well in the refrigerator up to 2 weeks. Goes well on tomatoes, greens or tuna fish salad.

Yield: 2 cups (500 mL)

Tarragon Dressing

¼ cup	fresh lemon juice, divided	50 mL
2 Tbsp	Dijon mustard	25 mL
4 tsp	red wine vinegar	20 mL
1	egg yolk	1
2 tsp	fresh tarragon leaves or 1 tsp (5 mL) dried tarragon	10 mL
2 tsp	fresh thyme leaves or 1 tsp (5 mL) dried thyme	10 mL
1½ tsp	freshly ground pepper salt to taste	7 mL
2 cups	vegetable oil	500 mL

In medium bowl combine 2 Tbsp (25 mL) lemon juice with mustard, vinegar, egg yolk and seasonings. Beat at medium speed of electric mixer until thick, 2 to 3 minutes. Gradually add oil beating constantly until mixture is smooth and creamy, about 3 minutes. Blend in remaining 2 Tbsp (25 mL) lemon juice. Store in tightly covered jar in refrigerator.

Can make ahead   **Yield: 3 cups (750 mL)**

Orange Salad Dressing
Refreshing, and improves with age!

½ tsp	grated orange peel	2 mL
¼ cup	orange juice	50 mL
½ cup	vegetable oil	125 mL
2 Tbsp	wine vinegar	25 mL
1 Tbsp	lemon juice	15 mL
¼ tsp	salt	1 mL
2 Tbsp	sugar	25 mL

Combine all ingredients in jar and shake until well blended. Refrigerate until ready to serve. Especially good served with a salad of mixed greens, mandarin oranges and any combination of: sliced cucumber, red onion rings, tomatoes, sliced, raw mushrooms and croutons.

Can make ahead   **Yield: 1 cup (250 mL)**

Processor Salad Dressing
A good basic recipe

¾ cup	vegetable oil	175 mL
¼ cup	white vinegar	50 mL
1 tsp	salt	5 mL
1 tsp	sugar	5 mL
1 tsp	dry mustard	5 mL
1 tsp	fresh lemon juice	5 mL
1 tsp	Worcestershire sauce	5 mL
1 tsp	Beau Monde seasoning	5 mL
	ground pepper to taste	
1	clove garlic	1

Add all ingredients, except garlic clove, one at a time to food processor or blender. Process until well blended. Pour into jar, add garlic clove, cover tightly and store in refrigerator. Garlic is for flavour and should be removed before serving.

Must make ahead   **Yield: 1¼ cups (300 mL)**

1000 Island Dressing

2 cups	mayonnaise	500 mL
¼ cup	chili sauce	50 mL
2 Tbsp	ketchup	25 mL
1 tsp	paprika	5 mL
2 Tbsp	sweet relish	25 mL
½ cup	chopped green onion	125 mL
½ cup	chopped dill pickles	125 mL
1	hard-boiled egg, chopped	1
⅓ cup	chopped olives, green or black	75 mL
¼ cup	chopped pimento	50 mL
¼ cup	chopped green pepper	50 mL

Blend mayonnaise, chili sauce, ketchup, paprika and sweet relish. Add chopped ingredients and stir well. Bottle and store in refrigerator. Let sit for a few hours to allow flavours to blend.

Must make ahead   **Yield: 4 cups (1 L)**

Tangy French Dressing
An easy and delicious recipe

¼ tsp	garlic powder	1 mL
¾ cup	sugar	175 mL
1 Tbsp	salt	15 mL
1 tsp	black pepper	5 mL
1 tsp	dry mustard	5 mL
1 Tbsp	Worcestershire sauce	15 mL
1 can	(10 oz/284 mL) cream of tomato soup	1
1 cup	vegetable oil	250 mL
1 cup	malt vinegar	250 mL
1	onion, halved	1

Place all ingredients except onion in blender or food processor and mix well. Pour into large jar. Add onion halves. Seal jar well and store in refrigerator several hours before using, to allow flavours to combine. Discard onion. Keeps several weeks. Stir or shake well before using.

Must make ahead　　　　　　　　　　**Yield: 4 cups (1 L)**

Brick Cheese Salad Dressing

½ cup	white vinegar	125 mL
1½ cups	vegetable oil	375 mL
¼ cup	Parmesan cheese	50 mL
2	garlic cloves	2
2 tsp	dried oregano leaves	10 mL
½ tsp	salt	2 mL
2 tsp	sugar	10 mL
¼ tsp	pepper	1 mL
8 oz	Brick cheese, cubed	250 g

Put all ingredients, except cheese, in blender. Whirl for 2 seconds. Drop cheese cubes and purée for 15 to 20 seconds. Wonderful tossed with romaine lettuce.

Can make ahead　　　　　　　　　　**Yield: 4 cups (1 L)**

Basil Salad Dressing
Wonderful!

2 Tbsp	rice wine vinegar	50 mL
1 Tbsp	Dijon mustard	25 mL
6 Tbsp	safflower oil	100 mL
¼ cup	finely chopped fresh basil leaves	50 mL
	salt and freshly ground pepper to taste	
2 Tbsp	yogurt (optional)	25 mL

Dissolve mustard in rice wine vinegar. Add oil, a little at a time, whisking well until smooth and thoroughly blended. Whisk in basil leaves, salt and freshly ground pepper. If you wish, 2 Tbsp (25 mL) of yogurt can be added to make a creamy texture. Do not vary any of the ingredients. Safflower oil gives a pleasant nutty flavour to dressing, the rice wine vinegar gives a sweet pungent flavour, and fresh basil is incomparable to the dried. An ideal recipe for the food processor.

Can make ahead   **Yield: about ½ cup (125 mL)**

Mayonnaise

1	egg yolk	1
½ tsp	salt	2 mL
1 scant tsp	dry mustard	5 mL
1 scant tsp	curry powder	5 mL
5 drops	Tabasco or shake of cayenne	5 drops
½ tsp	sugar	2 mL
1 Tbsp	vinegar	15 mL
1 cup	olive or corn oil, divided	250 mL
1 Tbsp	lemon juice	15 mL

Beat egg yolk, seasonings and sugar together. Add vinegar. Beating continuously, add drop by drop, 2 Tbsp (25 mL) oil, then ½ tsp (2 mL) oil at a time until all oil has been added and dressing is thick. Add lemon juice. Store in sealed jar.

Can make ahead   **Yield: 1¼ cups (300 mL)**

Green Goddess Salad Dressing

1 cup	mayonnaise	250 mL
1	garlic clove	1
2 Tbsp	anchovy paste	25 mL
¼ cup	chopped fresh parsley	50 mL
3 Tbsp	chopped chives or scallions	50 mL
½	lemon	½
3 Tbsp	tarragon vinegar	50 mL
	salt and pepper to taste	
½ cup	18% cream	125 mL

In blender or food processor, mix all ingredients and blend 20 seconds. Bottle and chill. Will keep refrigerated for several weeks. Excellent with mixed greens.

Can make ahead   **Yield: 2 cups (500 mL)**

Creamy Salad Dressing
Fantastic flavour

1 Tbsp	salt	15 mL
1 Tbsp	sugar	15 mL
2 tsp	black pepper	10 mL
2 Tbsp	chopped parsley	25 mL
2 Tbsp	Dijon mustard	25 mL
1 cup	olive oil	250 mL
⅔ cup	18% cream	150 mL
½ cup	red wine vinegar	125 mL
2	large garlic cloves	2

Combine all ingredients in blender or food processor. Blend thoroughly. Pour into jar with tightly-fitting lid. Store in refrigerator.

Can make ahead   **Yield: 2¼ cups (550 mL)**

...designates "Company in a Minute"

Jubilation

Eggs and Cheese

Breakfast Casserole	89
Cheddar and Onion Pie	88
Cheddar Quiche	91
Christmas Breakfast Quiche	91
Crustless Crab Quiche	93
Devilled Eggs with Salted Almonds	92
Green Onion Tart	90
Scrambled Egg Bake	89
Spinach Quiche	90
Tasty Brunch	92

Pasta

Christopher's Secret Spaghetti Sauce	100
Fettuccine	98
Fettuccine with Smoked Salmon	98
Herbed Summer Lasagna	94
Linguini Vongole	95
Noodles Florentine	99
Pork Lasagna	96
Ravioli with Snow Peas and Mushrooms	95
Tagliolini alla Francescana 4 Formaggi, Pronto's	87
Tomato Fettuccine with Basil Cream and Fresh Vegetables	97

● ...designates "Company in a Minute"

PRONTO RISTORANTE
692 Mt. Pleasant Rd., Toronto

Tagliolini Alla Francescana 4 Formaggi

6 Tbsp	butter	100 mL
1	small onion, finely chopped	1
¼ lb	Fontina cheese, cubed	125 g
¼ lb	Gorgonzola cheese, cubed	125 g
¼ lb	Bel Paese cheese, cubed	125 g
1 oz	Scotch whiskey	25 mL
1½ cups	35% cream	375 mL
1½ lb	fresh Tagliolini	750 g
⅙ lb	freshly grated Parmigiano	85 g
	salt and freshly ground pepper	
	pistachio nuts	
	curry powder	
GARNISH	fresh mint	

In a large casserole, heat the butter, add chopped onion and over low heat add the Fontina, Gorgonzola and Bel Paese until the cheeses melt. Allow cheeses to cook for a minute. Add the whiskey and the cream, reduce to one-third. Keep the sauce warm over low heat. Cook the noodles in plenty of boiling, salted water, stirring often. Do not overcook. Drain the noodles and put them into the casserole with the sauce. Add the Parmigiano, salt and pepper to taste. Sprinkle with curry and pistachio nuts. Toss and serve very hot. Garnish the centre with fresh mint. Buon Appetito!

Serves: 4 to 6

Cheddar and Onion Pie
A tasty winter dish

CRUST

1⅓ cups	all purpose flour	325 mL
2 Tbsp	lard	25 mL
⅓ cup	butter	75 mL
½ tsp	salt	2 mL
3 Tbsp	ice water (approximately)	50 mL

FILLING

2	large eggs	2
1 cup	milk	250 mL
1 Tbsp	all purpose flour	15 mL
½ tsp	salt	2 mL
pinch	freshly ground black pepper	pinch
pinch	cayenne	pinch
2 Tbsp	butter	25 mL
2	medium onions, finely chopped	2
10	bacon slices, cooked and crumbled	10
¾ lb	sharp Cheddar cheese, grated	350 g

Preheat oven to 450°F (230°C).

CRUST: Blend flour, lard and butter with pastry blender. Add salt and water and continue blending until crumbly. Form ball and chill 2 to 3 hours. Roll out and line a 9 inch (23 cm) pie plate, crimping the edges. Set a slightly smaller pie plate on top to hold down crust or line with a piece of aluminum foil filled with dried beans. Bake in bottom third of preheated 450°F (230°C) oven for 8 minutes. Then remove extra plate or filled foil, prick bottom all over and bake another 2 or 3 minutes or until crust begins to colour. Crust may be made ahead and frozen.

FILLING: Preheat oven to 375°F (190°C). Beat eggs lightly. Add milk, flour, salt, pepper and cayenne. Beat until well blended. Melt butter in frying pan and sauté onions slowly until translucent (do not brown). Combine crumbled bacon, egg mixture, sautéed onions and grated cheese and pour into partially baked shell. Bake at 375°F (190°C) 30 minutes. Remove from oven and allow to sit for 5 to 10 minutes before cutting. Can be frozen after cooking.

Can freeze   **Serves: 4 to 6**

Scrambled Egg Bake
A family favourite

3 Tbsp	chopped green onions	50 mL
2 Tbsp	butter	25 mL
5	eggs	5
1 tsp	salt	5 mL
pinch	pepper	pinch
1 cup	whipping cream	250 mL
6	strips bacon, cooked	6
½ cup	grated Cheddar cheese	125 mL

Preheat oven to 350°F (180°C). Sauté onions in butter. Beat eggs, salt and pepper until frothy. Add cream and onions. Combine well and pour into 9 inch (23 cm) pie plate. Bake at 350°F (180°C) 25 to 30 minutes. Arrange bacon, pinwheel fashion, on top of baked egg dish. Top with grated cheese. Broil just until cheese is melted.

Serves: 6

Breakfast Casserole
An excellent make ahead breakfast for a "non-morning person"

6	eggs, beaten	6
2 cups	milk	500 mL
1 tsp	salt	5 mL
1 tsp	dry mustard	5 mL
3	slices bread, cubed	3
1 lb	bulk sausage	500 g
1 cup	grated sharp cheese	250 mL

Preheat oven to 350°F (180°C). In a bowl, mix eggs, milk, salt and mustard. Grease a 9 x 13 inch (23 x 33 cm) baking dish. Place cubed bread over bottom. In a frying pan, brown sausage, breaking it up into small pieces. Drain well. Spread sausage over bread layer. Sprinkle grated cheese over sausage. Pour egg mixture over all. There are 3 cooking options for this recipe:
1. Refrigerate overnight and then bake at 350°F (180°C) 45 minutes.
2. Bake immediately at 350°F (180°C) 30 minutes and then reheat at serving time for 15 minutes.
3. Bake at 350°F (180°C) 45 minutes and then freeze. Reheat frozen casserole at serving time.

Can make ahead   **Can freeze**   **Serves: 6 to 8**

Spinach Quiche

1	unbaked 9 or 10 inch (23 or 25 cm) deep dish pie shell	1
1	egg yolk	1
2 Tbsp	water	25 mL
14	slices bacon	14
2	medium onions, chopped	2
8 oz	Swiss cheese	250 g
1 pkg	(10 oz/284 g) fresh spinach, cooked drained and chopped	1
2 cups	10% cream	500 mL
4	eggs	4
pinch	salt, pepper, garlic powder and nutmeg	pinch

Preheat oven to 375°F (190°). Mix egg yolk and water and brush over pie shell. In skillet, fry bacon until crisp. Crumble and sprinkle in pie shell. Sauté onions in bacon fat until translucent. Spread onions over bacon. Cut cheese into small chunks, and sprinkle over onions. Cover with spinach. Mix cream and eggs and beat well. Add seasonings, and pour custard into pie shell. Bake at 375°F (190°C) 10 minutes to set pastry. Reduce heat to 300°F (150°C). Cook approximately 35 minutes or until custard is set.

Serves: 6 to 8

Green Onion Tart
Just add a salad to accompany this Maritime favourite

1 cup	packaged biscuit mix	250 mL
⅓ cup	milk	75 mL
2 cups	chopped green onions	500 mL
1 Tbsp	butter	15 mL
1 pkg	(8 oz/250 g) cream cheese	1
1	egg	1
½ cup	milk	125 mL
	salt, Tabasco sauce, to taste	

Preheat oven to 350°F (180°C). Mix biscuit mix and ⅓ cup (75 mL) milk. In a well greased 8 inch (20 cm) pie plate, pat mixture on bottom and sides. Sauté onions in butter until wilted but still bright green. Beat cream cheese, egg and ½ cup (125 mL) milk until smooth. Place onions on top of biscuit shell. Pour cheese mixture over all. Bake at 350°F (180°C) 35 minutes, or until knife inserted in the centre comes out clean.

Serves: 6 to 8

Christmas Breakfast Quiche
This make-ahead breakfast makes Christmas morning a breeze

1	unbaked 9 inch (23 cm) pie shell	1
1½ cups	grated Natural Swiss cheese	375 mL
4 tsp	all purpose flour	20 mL
½ cup	diced ham or cooked bacon bits	125 mL
3	eggs	3
1 cup	evaporated milk	250 mL
¼ tsp	salt	1 mL
¼ tsp	dry mustard	1 mL

Toss grated cheese with flour. Place in pie crust. Sprinkle ham or bacon bits on top. In bowl combine eggs, evaporated milk, salt and mustard. Beat until smooth. Pour over cheese and flour mixture. Place in freezer. When frozen, cover with foil.
CHRISTMAS MORNING: Preheat oven to 400°F (200°C). Bake 1 hour, cool slightly and serve. Serve with fruit cocktail and raisin bread.

Can freeze   **Serves: 4 to 6**

Cheddar Quiche

CRUST

¾ cup	all purpose flour	175 mL
1 cup	grated Cheddar cheese	250 mL
¼ tsp	dry mustard	1 mL
¼ cup	butter, melted	50 mL
	salt and pepper to taste	

FILLING

3	large onions, chopped	3
1 cup	egg noodles, cooked	250 mL
2	eggs, beaten	2
½ cup	hot milk	125 mL
1 cup	Cheddar cheese, grated	250 mL
	salt and pepper to taste	

GARNISH   grated cheese and bacon bits

Preheat oven to 325°F (160°C). Mix crust ingredients together. Roll out and line an 8 inch (20 cm) pie plate. In fry pan sauté onions. Mix with cooked noodles. Add beaten eggs, hot milk, cheese, salt and pepper. Pour mixture into unbaked pie shell. Sprinkle additional cheese and bacon bits on top. Bake at 325°F (160°C) 30 to 40 minutes.

Can make ahead   **Serves: 6 to 8**

Tasty Brunch
Guests always seem to want seconds

12	slices white bread	12
¾ lb	sharp Cheddar cheese, grated	375 g
1 pkg	(10 oz/284 g) frozen broccoli, cooked and drained	1
2 cups	diced ham	500 mL
6	eggs, beaten	6
3½ cups	milk	875 mL
2 Tbsp	chopped onion	25 mL
½ tsp	salt	2 mL
¼ tsp	prepared mustard	1 mL
¼ cup	grated Cheddar cheese	50 mL

With round cookie cutter, cut a circle out of each slice of bread. Set aside. Break up remaining bread and sprinkle over the bottom of a 9 x 13 inch (23 x 33 cm) buttered baking dish. On top, layer ¾ lb (375 g) grated cheese, broccoli, ham, and bread circles. Combine remaining ingredients (except ¼ cup/50 mL grated cheese) and pour over. Cover and refrigerate overnight or at least 6 hours. Uncover and bake at 325°F (160°C) 45 minutes. Sprinkle ¼ cup (50 mL) grated cheese over top and bake another 10 minutes. Remove from oven and allow to sit for 10 minutes before cutting into squares.

Can make ahead   **Serves: 12**

Devilled Eggs with Salted Almonds

12	hard cooked eggs	12
¼ cup	mayonnaise	50 mL
¼ cup	sour cream	50 mL
1 tsp	salt	5 mL
1 Tbsp	Dijon mustard	15 mL
⅓ cup	chopped salted almonds	75 mL

Cut eggs in half and scoop out yolks. Mash yolks with mayonnaise and sour cream. Add salt and mustard, blending well. Taste for seasonings, adding more if desired. Refill eggs and sprinkle with chopped almonds.

Serves: 12

Crustless Crab Quiche
A crisp green salad and warm French bread make this a meal

½ lb	mushrooms, sliced	250 g
4	green onions, chopped	4
2 Tbsp	butter	25 mL
4	eggs	4
1 cup	sour cream	250 mL
1 cup	small curd cottage cheese	250 mL
½ cup	grated Parmesan cheese	125 mL
¼ cup	all purpose flour	50 mL
¼ tsp	salt	1 mL
4 drops	Tabasco sauce	4
½ lb	Monterey Jack or Brick cheese, grated	250 g
1 can	(6 oz/170 g) crabmeat	1

Preheat oven to 350°F (180°C). Sauté mushrooms and onions in butter and drain off excess liquid. In food processor or blender blend eggs, sour cream, cottage cheese, Parmesan cheese, flour, salt and Tabasco sauce. Pour into large bowl. Stir in mushrooms and onions, Monterey Jack cheese and crabmeat. Pour into lightly buttered 10 inch (25 cm) pie plate or shallow casserole. Bake at 350°F (180°C) 45 minutes or until puffed and golden brown. Let stand 5 to 10 minutes before serving.
NOTE: Do not use low fat cottage cheese!

Serves: 4 to 6

Herbed Summer Lasagna
Well worth the effort!

1 pkg	(10 oz/284 g) spinach, washed, trimmed and blanched	1
⅓ cup	18% cream	75 mL
2 tsp	fresh chopped chives	10 mL
1 tsp	dried thyme leaves	5 mL
1 tsp	dried marjoram leaves	5 mL
	salt, pepper, nutmeg to taste	
	squeeze of lemon juice	
1 lb	lasagna noodles	500 g
4 Tbsp	butter	50 mL
4 Tbsp	all purpose flour	50 mL
1½ cups	milk	375 mL
½ cup	white wine or chicken stock	125 mL
1 cup	sliced mushrooms	250 mL
2 Tbsp	butter	25 mL
½ tsp	fresh chopped chives	2 mL
¼ tsp	dried thyme leaves	1 mL
¼ tsp	dried marjoram leaves	1 mL
	salt, pepper, nutmeg to taste	
2 cups	grated Mozzarella or medium white Cheddar cheese	500 mL
⅓ cup	grated Parmesan cheese	75 mL
2 Tbsp	butter	25 mL

Preheat oven to 350°F (180°C). Purée spinach in food processor with cream until smooth. Add herbs, seasonings and lemon juice. Set aside. Cook lasagna noodles until al dente and drain well. Set aside. Melt 4 Tbsp (50 mL) butter in heavy saucepan, stir in flour and cook, stirring 2 to 3 minutes. Whisk in milk and white wine. Cook over medium heat until thickened and smooth. If required, add more wine to make medium consistency. Sauté mushrooms in 2 Tbsp (25 mL) butter and add to the sauce. Add herbs and season to taste.

TO ASSEMBLE: Grease 12 x 8 inch (30 x 20 cm) baking dish. Cover bottom of dish with a thin layer of sauce. Layer with half the noodles, spinach purée and sauce. Sprinkle with half of Mozzarella cheese. Repeat with remaining noodles, spinach purée, sauce and Mozzarella cheese. Dot with butter. Bake at 350°F (180°C) for 30 minutes. Sprinkle with Parmesan cheese and bake 10 minutes more or until bubbly and golden brown. Let sit for 10 minutes before serving. Cut into squares.

Can make ahead   **Can freeze**   **Serves: 6**

Linguine Vongole
Clam lovers will applaud this dish!

3	cloves garlic, thinly sliced	3
½	small onion, chopped	½
¼ cup	olive oil	50 mL
2 cans	(5 oz/142 g each) baby clams	2
1	bunch parsley, chopped	1
1	large tomato, chopped	1
	salt to taste	
½ tsp	pepper	2 mL
1 cup	water	250 mL
½ can	(5½ oz/156 mL) tomato paste	½
¾ lb	linguine noodles	375 g
¼ cup	butter	50 mL

In large fry pan sauté garlic and onion in olive oil until onion is soft. Drain clams and reserve juice. To garlic-onion mixture, add clams, half the chopped parsley, tomato, salt and pepper. Cook gently for 15 minutes. Slowly add reserved clam juice making sure the sediment is not added to mixture. Stir in water and tomato paste and simmer 1 hour. Cook linguine noodles according to package directions. Drain. Stir butter and remaining parsley into clam sauce. Mix well until butter melts. Pour sauce over noodles and serve immediately.

Serves: 4

Ravioli with Snow Peas and Mushrooms
Delicious appetizer or accompaniment to main meal

¼ lb	snow peas	125 g
1 lb	meat ravioli, fresh or frozen	500 g
⅓ cup	unsalted butter	75 mL
1	clove garlic, halved	1
¼ lb	small mushrooms	125 g
¼ cup	grated Parmesan cheese	50 mL
	salt and pepper to taste	

Steam snow peas over boiling water for 2 minutes. Immediately cool peas in cold water to set colour. Drain well. Cook ravioli in large pot of boiling water until tender. Drain and set aside. In large fry pan, melt butter over medium high heat. Sauté garlic and mushrooms lightly, about 5 minutes. Remove garlic and discard. Add ravioli and peas to mushrooms in fry pan. Add cheese and mix well. Season to taste. Serve at once.

Serves: 6

Pork Lasagna

MEAT AND TOMATO SAUCE

4	garlic cloves, peeled	4
¼ cup	olive oil	50 mL
¼ cup	butter	50 mL
6 Tbsp	chopped onion	100 mL
1 can	(5½ oz/156 mL) tomato paste	1
2 tsp	fresh chopped oregano (or 1 tsp/5 mL dried)	10 mL
2 tsp	fresh chopped sweet basil (or 1 tsp/5 mL dried)	10 mL
2 cans	(28 oz/796 mL each) tomatoes	2
2 lbs	ground lean pork	1 kg

WHITE SAUCE

2 cups	milk	500 mL
	peppercorns, bay leaf, celery leaves, onion slices	
½ cup	butter	125 mL
½ cup	all purpose flour	125 mL
1-2 cups	chicken stock	250-500 mL
	salt, pepper, nutmeg, to taste	

NOODLES, SPINACH AND CHEESE

3 pkg	(10 oz/284 mL each) frozen spinach cooked, drained and squeezed	3
1½ lb	lasagna noodles, preferably fresh, rolled very thin	750 g
2 lb	Ricotta cheese	1 kg
2 pkg	(12 oz/340 g each) Mozzarella cheese slices	2
½ lb	Gruyère cheese, grated	250 g
½ lb	Parmesan cheese, grated	250 g

MEAT AND TOMATO SAUCE: Sauté garlic in olive oil and butter until golden. Remove garlic and discard. Sauté onion until soft and translucent. Add tomato paste and herbs, cook 2 minutes. Add tomatoes and bring to boil. Reduce heat and simmer about 1 hour or until thick. Partially cover and simmer longer, if necessary, to reach desired thickness. Brown pork in fry pan. Drain off fat and add pork to tomato sauce. Simmer while preparing remaining ingredients.

WHITE SAUCE: Prepare sauce by heating milk with a few peppercorns, bay leaf, celery leaves and onion slices to the boiling point. Cool and strain. In a medium saucepan melt butter, add flour and blend well. Slowly add strained milk and cook, stirring until mixture comes to a boil. Add chicken stock, a little at a time to get the desired thickness. Add salt, pepper and nutmeg to taste.

NOODLES, SPINACH AND CHEESE: Cook and drain spinach. Prepare noodles. Fresh noodles don't require cooking but dry noodles will require boiling in salted water until barely tender.

TO ASSEMBLE: In 2–9 x 13 inch (23 x 33 cm) pans, layer in the following order using ¼ of each of the ingredients: noodles, meat sauce, Ricotta cheese, Mozzarella cheese, spinach, sauce. Repeat. Top with grated Gruyère and a sprinkling of Parmesan. Bake at 350°F (180°C) 45 to 55 minutes until hot and bubbly. Let stand 10 to 15 minutes before cutting. Pass additional grated Parmesan cheese.

Can make ahead   **Can freeze**   **Serves: 16 to 20**

Tomato Fettuccine with Basil Cream and Fresh Vegetables ●
A wonderfully flavourful dish

¾ lb	tomato fettuccine	375 g
2 cups	whipping cream	500 mL
¼ cup	fresh chopped basil	50 mL
	(1 Tbsp/15 mL dried basil and	
	1 Tbsp/15 mL dried parsley may be	
	substituted)	
2 Tbsp	olive oil	25 mL
	salt and freshly ground pepper	
	to taste	
1	medium carrot, peeled and thinly sliced	1
1 cup	mushrooms, halved	250 mL
¼ lb	snow peas	125 g
2	scallions, sliced	2
½ cup	freshly grated Parmesan cheese	125 mL

Cook pasta according to package directions. While pasta cooks, combine cream, basil, olive oil, salt and pepper in a fry pan. Simmer until slightly reduced. Add carrots and mushrooms to basil cream and simmer 3 to 4 minutes until barely cooked. Add snow peas and scallions and simmer an additional 2 minutes. Pour sauce over drained pasta and add cheese. Serve immediately.

NOTE: Tomato fettuccine simply provides colour; spinach or plain pasta are equally as good.   **Serves: 4 to 6**

Fettuccine with Smoked Salmon 🍒

May be served in small quantities as an appetizer or larger portions as a main dish.

8 cups	water	2 L
2 Tbsp	salt	25 mL
1 Tbsp	olive oil	15 mL
1 lb	fresh fettuccine noodles	500 g
6 Tbsp	unsalted butter	100 mL
3 oz	smoked salmon, cut in julienne strips	100 g
¾ cup	whipping cream	175 mL
½ cup	freshly grated Parmesan cheese	125 mL
	nutmeg, freshly grated	
	pepper	

Bring water to a boil in a large pot. Add salt, olive oil and noodles and cook 1 to 2 minutes, until the fettuccine is "al dente". Drain, transfer to a shallow bowl and toss with 2 Tbsp (25 mL) softened butter. Keep warm. While the fettuccine is cooking, melt remaining butter over moderate heat. Add smoked salmon and cream and bring to a boil, stirring. Remove the pan from the heat, add Parmesan cheese, nutmeg and pepper to taste and stir until the cheese is melted. Pour sauce over the fettuccine, toss and serve on heated plates.

Serves: 2 to 4 as an appetizer

Fettuccine 🍒

Fresh pasta will make this irresistible

½ cup	butter, softened	125 mL
1 cup	whipping cream	250 mL
1¼ cups	freshly grated Parmesan cheese	300 mL
1 lb	fettuccine noodles, green or white	500 g
	salt and pepper (white if possible) to taste	

GARNISH   grated Parmesan cheese

Using electric mixer or food processor, cream butter until light and fluffy. Alternately add cream and cheese, mixing after each addition. Cook fettuccine according to package directions. Do not overcook. Drain noodles. Toss with cream mixture in heated casserole over low heat until every strand is well coated. Season with salt and pepper. Sprinkle additional cheese over top. Serve immediately.

**Serves: 2 as a main course or
4 as an appetizer**

Noodles Florentine

6 oz	noodles (¼ inch/5 mm wide) about 4 cups/1 L packed	170 g
1 pkg	(10 oz/284 g) fresh spinach	1
½ cup	sliced mushrooms	125 mL
2 cups	cottage cheese	500 mL
½ cup	grated Parmesan cheese	125 mL
½ cup	sour cream or yogurt	125 mL
½ tsp	salt	2 mL
¼ tsp	Tabasco or Worcestershire sauce	1 mL
¼ tsp	dried basil leaves	1 mL
¼ tsp	dried thyme leaves	1 mL
¾ cup	fine bread crumbs	175 mL
1 Tbsp	melted butter	15 mL

SAUCE

1 cup	chicken stock	250 mL
1 Tbsp	all purpose flour	15 mL
1 Tbsp	melted butter	15 mL

Cook noodles in salted water and drain. Wash spinach. Cook, just with water clinging to leaves, turning once, until almost tender. Drain well and chop. Turn into a large bowl. Add mushrooms, cheeses, sour cream, salt, Tabasco sauce, basil and thyme. Gently stir in noodles. Turn into 1½ qt (1.5 L) casserole. To make sauce, blend flour with melted butter. Stir in chicken stock and continue to cook, stirring constantly until thick. Pour over casserole. Mix bread crumbs and 1 Tbsp (15 mL) melted butter. Sprinkle over sauce. Bake at 350°F (180°C) 40 to 50 minutes. Serve with sliced tomatoes and crusty bread.

Can freeze   **Serves: 6**

Christopher's Secret Spaghetti Sauce

3 Tbsp	olive oil	50 mL
1 lb	lean ground beef	500 g
2	cloves garlic, finely chopped	2
1	large onion, finely chopped	1
½	green pepper, finely chopped	½
1 can	(28 oz/796 mL) tomato sauce	1
1 can	(5½ oz/156 mL) tomato paste	1
1 can	(10 oz/284 mL) button mushrooms	1
⅓ can	(10 oz/284 mL) Chinese sweet and sour sauce	1
2	bay leaves	2
2 tsp	oregano	10 mL
1 tsp	salt	5 mL
1 tsp	pepper	5 mL

Heat olive oil in a large fry pan. Add meat, garlic, onion and green pepper. Cook until meat is browned and onions translucent. Drain excess fat. Transfer mixture to large pot. Add all other ingredients. Lower heat, cover pot and simmer for one hour. Remove cover, or keep partially covered and simmer for an additional 30 minutes, until sauce reaches desired consistency. Should it become too thick, add some dry red wine or water. Remove bay leaf and pour sauce onto cooked spaghetti.

NOTE: This is an excellent sauce to use in making Lasagna. Simply increase sweet and sour sauce to ½ can.

Can freeze   **Serves: 6 to 8**

● ...designates "Company in a Minute"

GEOFFREY'S RESTAURANT
30 Wellington St. E., Toronto

Geoffrey's Braised Zucchini and Tomato

1	medium size onion	1
2 Tbsp	butter	25 mL
	salt and pepper, to taste	
12	cherry tomatoes	12
6	small whole zucchini	6
	seasoning, to taste	
	chicken stock, heated	

Preheat oven to 350°F (180°C). Slice onion very thinly. Sauté the onion without colouring for 2 to 3 minutes in butter, salt and pepper. Spread this mixture evenly over the bottom of 4 individual vegetable dishes. Slice the tomatoes and the zucchini evenly and arrange on top of the onions in alternating layers down the vegetable dish. Season. Add enough chicken stock to cover the bottom of the dish and bake at 350°F (180°C) 6 to 10 minutes. Serve at once.

Serves: 4

Green Beans Gourmet ❧
Party pretty

¼ cup	butter	50 mL
1 pkg	(10 oz/300 g) frozen green beans thawed and drained	1
¾ tsp	Italian herb seasonings or ¼ tsp (1 mL) each dried oregano leaves, marjoram leaves, basil leaves	3 mL
¼ tsp	garlic salt	1 mL
⅛ tsp	rubbed sage leaves	0.5 mL
1 jar	(2 oz/57 mL) pimento, undrained	1
1 can	(14 oz/398 mL) artichoke hearts, drained and quartered	1
½ cup	chopped pecans	125 mL

In a 2 qt (2 L) saucepan, melt butter over medium heat. Stir in all ingredients except artichokes and pecans. Cover and cook 5 to 7 minutes stirring occasionally, until green beans are tender-crisp. Stir in artichokes and pecans. Cover and continue cooking until artichokes are heated through (2 to 3 minutes).

Serves: 4

Baked Apples and Onions
This hot fruit and vegetable combination is unique and mouthwatering

6	apples, peeled and sliced	6
4	onions, peeled, sliced and separated into rings	4
½ cup	brown sugar or to taste	125 mL
1 tsp	salt	5 mL
¼ cup	butter	50 mL
½ cup	bread or cracker crumbs	125 mL

Preheat oven to 300°F (150°C). Butter an 8 inch (20 cm) casserole. Place a layer of apple slices in casserole and then a layer of onion rings. Sprinkle generously with brown sugar and sparingly with salt. Repeat layers until casserole is heaping. Top with crumbs and generous dabs of butter. Cover and bake slowly at 300°F (150°C) 3 hours. The longer it is baked, the better it is! (Onions cooked this long are completely digestible). Uncover for the last half hour so breadcrumbs will brown and some of the juice will evaporate.

Serves: 4 to 6

Bean Casserole

2 cans	(14 oz/398 mL each) lima beans, drained	2
1 can	(19 oz/540 mL) kidney beans, drained	1
2 cans	(19 oz/540 mL each) baked beans	2
1 can	(19 oz/540 mL) pineapple chunks, drained	1
½ lb	bacon	250 g
3	medium onions, chopped	3
¾ cup	brown sugar	175 mL
¼ cup	vinegar	50 mL
¼ cup	molasses	50 mL
½ cup	ketchup	125 mL
2 Tbsp	prepared mustard	25 mL
½ tsp	garlic salt	2 mL
1	green pepper, chopped	1

Preheat oven to 350°F (180°C). In Dutch oven, mix together all beans and pineapple. In skillet, cook bacon, drain and crumble. Reserve 2 Tbsp (25 mL) bacon fat. In reserved fat, brown onions and drain. Add bacon and onions to beans. In small bowl, mix together remaining ingredients. Add to bean mixture and mix well. Bake at 350°F (180°C) 1 hour. If consistency is too thin, bake an additional 15 minutes.
MICROWAVE INSTRUCTIONS: Cook 25 minutes at medium power, stirring twice.
Excellent served with fried chicken or ham.

Can freeze   **Serves: 18 to 20**

Rice, Broccoli and Tomatoes
Good with chicken and pork dishes

5 cups	chicken stock	1.25 L
2 cups	long grain white rice	500 mL
1½ tsp	salt	7 mL
2 Tbsp	butter	25 mL
2	small onions, chopped	2
1 lb	broccoli, coarsely chopped	500 g
4	tomatoes, chopped	4
¼ tsp	pepper	1 mL

Bring chicken stock to a boil in saucepan. Stir in rice, salt, butter, onion and broccoli. Reduce heat to medium and cook, covered, until stock is absorbed, about 20 minutes. Stir in tomatoes and pepper. Return to heat just to warm tomatoes. Serve immediately.

Serves: 10

Broccoli Casserole
Your guests will ask for this recipe

1	clove garlic, chopped	1
1	large onion, chopped	1
¼ cup	butter	50 mL
4 cups	broccoli pieces	1 L
1 can	(10 oz/284 mL) sliced mushrooms, drained	1
¼ cup	chopped almonds	50 mL
1 can	(10 oz/284 mL) cream of mushroom soup	1
1 jar	(7½ oz/213 mL) Cheese Whiz	1
½ cup	buttered bread crumbs	125 mL
¼ cup	slivered almonds	50 mL

Preheat oven to 350°F (180°C). In skillet, sauté garlic and onion in butter 5 minutes, until softened. Spoon into greased 1½ qt (1.5 L) casserole. Cook, (steam, boil or microwave) broccoli until crunchy. Add to casserole. Spread mushrooms and almonds over broccoli. In separate bowl, blend soup and cheese. Pour over vegetables. Sprinkle slivered almonds and buttered bread crumbs over top. Bake at 350°F (180°C) for 35 minutes.

Can make ahead   **Serves: 4 to 6**

Broccoli Pie

½ cup	sliced mushrooms	125 mL
1	onion, chopped	1
¼ cup	butter	50 mL
½ tsp	dried oregano leaves	2 mL
⅛ tsp	pepper	0.5 mL
¾ tsp	salt	3 mL
1 cup	cooked, chopped broccoli	125 mL
1	slice bread, finely crumbled	1
1 pkg	(4 oz/125 g) Philadelphia cream cheese	1
1 cup	18% cream	250 mL
½ cup	Parmesan cheese	125 mL
2	eggs, slightly beaten	2

Preheat oven to 425°F (220°C). Sauté mushrooms and onions in butter until onions are soft. Stir in oregano, pepper and salt. Remove from heat. Add broccoli and bread crumbs. Set aside. In small bowl, blend cream cheese, cream, Parmesan cheese and eggs. Add to broccoli mixture and turn into a greased 10 inch (25 cm) pie plate. Bake at 425°F (220°C) 25 minutes or until knife inserted in centre of pie comes out clean. Do not undercook. The vegetable and cheese mixtures can each be prepared ahead and mixed together just prior to baking.

Can make ahead   **Serves: 6 to 8**

Cauliflower Casserole 🍒

1	cauliflower	1
1 tsp	curry powder	5 mL
1 can	(10 oz/284 mL) cream of mushroom soup or cream of chicken soup	1
1 cup	grated Cheddar cheese	250 mL
⅓ cup	mayonnaise	75 mL
¼ cup	bread crumbs	50 mL

Preheat oven to 300°F (150°C). Break cauliflower into flowerets and boil for 5 minutes. Drain and place in casserole. Blend curry, soup, cheese and mayonnaise. Pour sauce over top. Sprinkle with bread crumbs and bake at 300°F (150°C) 30 minutes.

Serves: 4 to 6

Cheese Stuffed Cauliflower

1	large cauliflower, trimmed and washed	1
	juice of ½ lemon	
¼ lb	Swiss cheese, cut in strips	125 g
	salt and pepper to taste	
¼ cup	butter or margarine, melted	50 mL
1 cup	herb flavoured stuffing mix, finely crushed	250 mL

Preheat oven to 350°F (180°C). Soak cauliflower, head down, in cold salted water for 15 minutes. Cook, covered in about 1 inch (2.5 cm) boiling, salted water with lemon juice until cauliflower is tender but still firm, approximately 10 minutes. Drain well. Place whole head in shallow baking pan. Press strips of cheese into head. Sprinkle with salt and pepper. Mix butter and stuffing mix together and stuff between the flowerets. Bake at 350°F (180°C) 20 minutes or until crumbs are lightly browned.

Serves: 6

Carrot Cauliflower Casserole

4 cups	sliced carrots (8 carrots)	1 L
1	large cauliflower	1
2 Tbsp	butter	25 mL
2 Tbsp	all purpose flour	25 mL
¼ cup	Dijon mustard	50 mL
1 cup	chicken stock	250 mL
½ cup	whipping cream	125 mL
1¼ cup	grated Swiss cheese (Emmenthal)	300 mL

GARNISH green onions, chopped

Peel carrots. Cut into ¼ inch (5 mm) diagonal slices. Separate cauliflower into flowerets. Cook vegetables in boiling salted water 5 minutes. Plunge into cold water. Drain. In large pan, melt butter over medium heat. Stir in flour and mustard, until mixture is bubbly. Remove from heat, and add chicken stock and cream. Return to heat and cook, stirring, until thickened. Add 1 cup (250 mL) cheese. Stir until melted. Combine vegetables and sauce in 2 qt (2 L) casserole. Sprinkle with remaining cheese. Refrigerate until serving time. Bake at 350°F (180°C) uncovered, 35 minutes if chilled, 20 minutes if at room temperature. Garnish with chopped green onions.

Can make ahead　　　　　　　　　　　　　　　　　**Serves: 6**

Cauliflower Cheese Puff Soufflé

1	medium cauliflower	1
1 tsp	lemon juice	5 mL
¼ cup	butter	50 mL
2 Tbsp	flour	25 mL
1 cup	milk	250 mL
3	eggs, separated	3
1 cup	grated Cheddar cheese	250 mL
	salt and pepper to taste	
¼ cup	bread crumbs	50 mL

Preheat oven to 400°F (200°C). Cook cauliflower in salted water with lemon juice until tender. Set aside until cool. Break cauliflower into flowerets and place in a greased 9 x 13 inch (23 x 33 cm) baking dish. Melt butter in saucepan. Add flour and cook 2 to 3 minutes. Gradually stir in milk. Stir in egg yolks, grated cheese, salt and pepper. Continue cooking over low heat until mixture is smooth. Beat egg whites until stiff and fold into cheese mixture. Pour over cauliflower. Sprinkle with bread crumbs. Bake at 400°F (200°C) for 30 minutes until puffy and brown.

Serves: 8

Glazed Carrots and Parsnips
A colourful vegetable for a dinner party

10	medium carrots	10
5	medium parsnips	5
2 cups	water	500 mL
2 cups	apple juice	500 mL
⅓ cup	butter	75 mL
⅓ cup	honey	75 mL
2 Tbsp	lemon juice	25 mL
1 tsp	dried mint leaves or 1 Tbsp (15 mL) fresh mint leaves	5 mL
pinch	nutmeg	pinch
pinch	pepper	pinch

Peel and cut vegetables into 3 inch (7 cm) julienne strips. Cook in mixture of water and apple juice until tender. Drain. Add remaining ingredients and cook uncovered 3 minutes over medium heat, stirring to glaze.

Serves: 6 to 8

Mashed Celery Root 🍒

Try something new
Celery root is a round, knarled white vegetable!

2	celery roots	2
2 Tbsp	butter	25 mL
	salt, pepper and nutmeg to taste	

Peel and dice celery root. Boil as you would potato. Drain. Mash with butter, salt, pepper and a little nutmeg. For finer texture purée in blender or food processor. Excellent with beef and fowl.

Serves: 6 to 8

Sweet and Sour Carrots

Great to take to a pot luck supper

2 lb	carrots, sliced in rounds	1 kg
1	onion, chopped or sliced	1
1	green pepper, chopped	1

SAUCE		
1 cup	sugar	250 mL
½ cup	vegetable oil	125 mL
½ cup	white vinegar	125 mL
1 tsp	dry mustard	5 mL
1 can	(10 oz/284 mL) cream of tomato soup	1
1 tsp	salt	5 mL
1 tsp	pepper	5 mL

Cook carrots until tender. Drain and cool. Arrange carrots in serving dish. Scatter onion and green pepper over top. In saucepan combine sauce ingredients. Bring to a boil, while stirring. Pour over carrots. Let stand 24 hours. Can be served hot or cold. Carrots will keep in refrigerator for several days.

Must make ahead   **Serves: 6 to 8**

Celery Oriental 🍒
An inexpensive, pretty and delicious dish

1	bunch celery	1
1 can	(10 oz/284 mL) cream of chicken soup	1
1 jar	(2 oz/57 mL) pimento, finely chopped and drained	1
1 can	(10 oz/284 mL) water chestnuts, drained	1
GARNISH	croutons and slivered almonds, toasted	

Preheat oven to 350°F (180°C). Cut celery into bite sized pieces. Mix all ingredients in an 8 inch (20 cm) square pan. Sprinkle croutons and slivered almonds on top. Bake at 350°F (180°C) 35 to 40 minutes.

Serves: 4

Eggplant Casserole
Deliciously Italian

1	medium onion, chopped	1
2	cloves garlic, finely chopped	2
2 Tbsp	vegetable oil	25 mL
1 can	(14 oz/398 mL) tomato sauce	1
½ cup	water	125 mL
2	chicken bouillon cubes	2
1	medium eggplant	1
2	eggs, beaten	2
42	Ritz crackers, finely crushed	42
½ cup	vegetable oil	125 mL
1 lb	Mozzarella cheese	500 g
	Parmesan cheese for topping	
	Italian seasoning (optional)	

Preheat oven to 350°F (180°C). Sauté onion and garlic in 2 Tbsp (25 mL) oil until tender. Add tomato sauce, water and bouillon cubes. Simmer while preparing eggplant. Wash and cut eggplant into 12 slices. Dip into beaten eggs and coat with cracker crumbs. Fry, until brown, in ½ cup (125 mL) vegetable oil. Place half the eggplant slices in 9 x 13 inch (23 x 33 cm) casserole. Top with half the Mozzarella cheese. Repeat layers. Pour on sauce. Sprinkle with Parmesan cheese. Bake at 350°F (180°C) 20 minutes or until bubbly.

Serves: 8 to 10

Creole Okra

½ cup	chopped onion	125 mL
½ cup	chopped green pepper	125 mL
3 Tbsp	bacon drippings	50 mL
3 cups	sliced okra, fresh or frozen	750 mL
3 cups	sliced tomatoes	750 mL
¼ cup	chopped parsley	50 mL
4 tsp	sugar	20 mL
1½ tsp	salt	7 mL
¾ tsp	pepper	3 mL
⅛ tsp	lemon juice	0.5 mL
	tomato juice or water as required	

Sauté onion and green pepper in bacon drippings until tender. Add okra, and cook over medium heat 5 minutes, stirring constantly. Stir in sliced tomatoes, parsley, sugar, salt, pepper and lemon juice. Simmer uncovered 1 hour. Add a small amount of tomato juice or water if necessary.

Serves: 6 to 8

Sweet and Sour Limas
An unusual vegetable recipe receives rave notices

1	medium onion, chopped	1
1 cup	chopped celery	250 mL
1	green pepper, chopped	1
1 Tbsp	butter	15 mL
2 cans	(14 oz/398 mL each) lima beans, drained	2
1 cup	ketchup	250 mL
½ cup	brown sugar	125 mL
¼ cup	vinegar	50 mL
1 Tbsp	prepared mustard	15 mL
	juice of 1 lemon	
	salt and pepper to taste	

Preheat oven to 350°F (180°C). Sauté onion, celery and green pepper in butter in large skillet about 5 minutes. Add remaining ingredients and combine thoroughly. Pour into oven proof dish and bake at 350°F (180°C) 30 minutes.
NOTE: Beans may be cooked on top of stove by cooking over medium-low heat 20 minutes.

Can make ahead **Serves: 6**

Eggplant Tomato Casserole

1	medium eggplant	1
1	medium onion, chopped	1
2 Tbsp	butter, melted	25 mL
2	medium tomatoes, cut in eighths	2
1 tsp	salt	5 mL
⅛ tsp	pepper	0.5 mL
½ tsp	oregano	2 mL
½ cup	dry bread crumbs	125 mL
¼ cup	grated Parmesan cheese	50 mL
2 Tbsp	butter, melted	25 mL

Preheat oven to 375°F (190°C). Peel eggplant and cut in 1 inch (2.5 cm) cubes. Sauté onion in 2 Tbsp (25 mL) butter until transparent. Combine eggplant, tomatoes, onion and seasonings. Toss crumbs and cheese in 2 Tbsp (25 mL) melted butter. Put half the vegetable mixture in greased baking dish and sprinkle with half the crumb mixture. Add remaining vegetables and sprinkle remaining crumbs on top. Bake uncovered, at 375°F (190°C) until tender and lightly browned, 55 to 60 minutes.

Serves: 6 to 8

Zucchini and Tomato Kebabs
A colourful combination for the barbecue season

2	medium zucchini	2
1	egg, lightly beaten	1
⅓ cup	bread crumbs	75 mL
⅓ cup	freshly grated Parmesan cheese	75 mL
¼ tsp	dried thyme leaves	1 mL
	salt and pepper to taste	
16	cherry tomatoes	16
	olive oil	

Scrub the zucchini and cut into 1 inch (2.5 cm) pieces. Cook in boiling, salted water to cover for 5 to 7 minutes until almost tender. Drain zucchini, refresh under cold running water and pat dry with paper towel. Dip pieces into egg and coat with mixture of the bread crumbs, cheese, thyme, salt and pepper. Thread zucchini on four 8 inch (20 cm) metal skewers, alternately with cherry tomatoes. Baste kebabs with olive oil and grill over hot coals or under the broiler for 4 to 5 minutes until crumbs are golden.

Can make ahead   **Serves: 4**

Sweet Potato Casserole
A fabulous companion to Easter ham

2 cups	mashed sweet potatoes	500 mL
1 cup	milk	250 mL
2	eggs, slightly beaten	2
¾ cup	sugar	175 mL
½ tsp	ground nutmeg	2 mL
½ tsp	ground cinnamon	2 mL
⅓ cup	butter, softened	75 mL
¾ cup	slightly crushed cornflakes	175 mL
½ cup	brown sugar	125 mL
½ cup	chopped pecans	125 mL
¼ cup	butter, softened	50 mL

Preheat oven to 400°F (200°C). In a bowl, mix sweet potatoes, milk, eggs, sugar, nutmeg, cinnamon and ⅓ cup (75 mL) butter. Transfer to 1½ qt (1.5 L) casserole dish and bake uncovered at 400°F (200°C) 20 minutes. Mix cornflakes, brown sugar, nuts and ¼ cup (50 mL) butter to a crumbly mixture. Remove casserole from oven, sprinkle nut mixture on top and return for 10 minutes at same temperature, uncovered.

Serves: 4 to 6

Cheesed Green Peas
Just a little different

2 lb	green peas, shelled or 10 oz (300 g) frozen peas	1 kg
½ cup	diced celery	125 mL
4	scallions, sliced	4
6 Tbsp	butter	100 mL
1 Tbsp	grated Gruyère cheese	15 mL
1 Tbsp	grated Parmesan cheese	15 mL
1 Tbsp	whipping cream	15 mL

Cook green peas in boiling salted water to cover for 15 minutes or until barely tender. Drain. In a fry pan, cook celery and scallions in butter, covered, over low heat for 2 to 3 minutes or until barely tender. Add peas, stir together, and sprinkle the mixture with grated cheeses. Stir in cream. Cook, covered, over low heat 1 minute, or just until cheese is melted.

Serves: 4

Olive Creamed Potatoes
A popular buffet item

6	medium potatoes, peeled and cooked	6
2 cups	sour cream	500 mL
3 Tbsp	finely chopped onion	50 mL
2 Tbsp	finely chopped green olives	25 mL
1 tsp	salt	5 mL
½ tsp	pepper	2 mL
½ tsp	paprika	2 mL
1 Tbsp	chopped parsley	15 mL

Dice potatoes. Pour sour cream into skillet. Add potatoes and heat slowly until bubbly. Add onion, olives, salt and pepper. Place into serving bowl and sprinkle with paprika and parsley.

Serves: 6 to 8

Sweet Potatoes 🍒

6	sweet potatoes, boiled or baked and then peeled	6
	or	
2 cans	(19 oz/540 mL each) sweet potatoes	2

SAUCE		
1 cup	fresh orange juice	250 mL
1 Tbsp	grated orange rind	15 mL
1 Tbsp	cornstarch	15 mL
⅓ cup	butter	75 mL
⅓ cup	brown sugar, firmly packed	75 mL
⅓ cup	sugar	75 mL

Preheat oven to 350°F (180°C). Arrange sweet potatoes in casserole dish. Mix sauce ingredients and cook until thick. Pour sauce over potatoes. Bake covered in 350°F (180°C) oven 20 minutes and then 15 minutes uncovered.

Can make ahead   **Serves: 6 to 8**

Pecan Rice Casserole
Gives the effect of wild rice without the expense

1 cup	butter	250 mL
1	clove garlic, chopped	1
3	green onions, chopped	3
1 lb	mushrooms, sliced	500 g
3 cups	long grain white rice	750 mL
¼ tsp	turmeric	1 mL
½ tsp	thyme	2 mL
1 tsp	salt	5 mL
¼ tsp	pepper	1 mL
1½ cups	chopped pecans	375 mL
6 cups	beef stock	1.5 L

GARNISH   sliced green onion tops and pecans

Preheat oven to 400°F (200°C). Melt butter in Dutch oven and sauté garlic, onions and mushrooms about 5 minutes, or until onions are golden. Add rice and stir 2 minutes until rice is hot. Stir in turmeric, thyme, salt and pepper. Add pecans and stock and bring to a boil. Bake covered at 400°F (200°C) 1 hour and 20 minutes. Garnish with green onion tops and pecans. Can be prepared in advance and refrigerated until baking time.

Can make ahead   **Serves: 10 to 12**

Cheesy Rice and Broccoli
Add sliced water chestnuts for crunch

2 Tbsp	butter	25 mL
1	small onion, chopped	1
1 pkg	(10 oz/300 g) frozen chopped broccoli	1
1 can	(10 oz/284 mL) cream of chicken or cream of celery soup	1
1 jar	(8.8 oz/250 g) Cheese Whiz	1
½ cup	milk	125 mL
2 cups	cooked rice	500 mL

Preheat oven to 350°F (180°C). Melt butter in frying pan, add onion, and sauté until soft. Add broccoli and cook until thawed, stirring occasionally. Add soup, Cheese Whiz and milk. Combine well, and cook 5 minutes, stirring occasionally. Pour mixture over cooked rice and bake at 350°F (180°C) for 30 minutes until hot.

Can make ahead   **Serves: 6**

Curried Rice with Vegetables

3 Tbsp	butter	50 mL
1	onion, chopped	1
1	large tomato, peeled, seeded and chopped	1
¼ tsp	cumin	1 mL
½ tsp	curry powder	2 mL
1 cup	long grain white rice	250 mL
2 cups	chicken stock	500 mL
1 Tbsp	raisins	15 mL
6-7	dried apricots, chopped	6-7

Melt butter in saucepan, add onion and sauté. Add tomato and cook 2 minutes. Add cumin, curry, rice and stock. Bring to boil, reduce heat and simmer covered 20 minutes. Remove from heat. Add raisins and apricots. Cover and simmer 10 minutes or until rice is tender and stock is absorbed.

MICROWAVE METHOD: Place butter and onion in glass dish with cover. Cook 1 minute at high power. Add tomato and cook 1 minute at high power. Add cumin, curry, rice and stock and stir. Cook 4 to 5 minutes at medium-high power. Remove and add raisins and apricots. Finish cooking at medium high power 5 to 6 minutes or until all stock is absorbed.

Serves: 4 to 6

Fried Rice Casserole

1 bunch	green onions, chopped	1
1 cup	diced celery	250 mL
2 Tbsp	salad oil	25 mL
2 cups	cooked rice	500 mL
2 Tbsp	soy sauce	25 mL

GARNISH toasted almonds

Preheat oven to 350°F (180°C). Sauté onions and celery in oil, but do not brown. Add rice and soy sauce. Mix and place in casserole. Bake at 350°F (180°C) 30 minutes or until well heated. Sprinkle almonds on top just before serving. This casserole can be made as a main dish by adding cooked chicken, ham or turkey.

Can freeze **Serves: 4**

Saffron Rice with Raisins

2 Tbsp	butter	25 mL
1 cup	uncooked long grain rice	250 mL
2 cups	boiling water	500 mL
1 stick	cinammon (2 inches/5 cm) long	1
½ tsp	ground turmeric	2 mL
pinch	crumbled saffron	pinch
1 tsp	salt	5 mL
½ cup	seedless raisins	125 mL
1 tsp	sugar	5 mL

Melt butter in a large saucepan. Add rice and stir to coat. Add water, cinnamon, turmeric, saffron and salt. Stir constantly and bring to boil. Reduce heat, cover and simmer 20 minutes. Remove from heat, discard cinnamon stick, add raisins, fluff with fork and stir in sugar. Cut circle of foil and place inside pan on top of rice. Cover with lid, and let stand at room temperature for 20 minutes. Fluff with fork and serve. Doubles well. Good with meats or for stuffing tomatoes.

Serves: 4 to 6

Oven Baked Rice

3 Tbsp	butter	50 mL
⅓ cup	minced onion	75 mL
1½ cups	uncooked rice	375 mL
2¼ cups	water	550 mL
2	sprigs parsley	2
	salt and freshly ground pepper	
½ tsp	dried thyme (2 sprigs fresh)	2 mL
½	bay leaf	½
	Tabasco to taste	

Preheat oven to 400°F (200°C). Melt half the butter in large fry pan or Dutch oven. Add onion. Cook, stirring, until soft. Add rice and stir to blend. Add water and stir. Add remaining ingredients. Cover with tight fitting lid and place in oven. Bake exactly 17 minutes. Remove cover and discard parsley, bay leaf and thyme sprigs (if used). Fluff rice with remaining butter.

Serves: 4 to 6

Julienne of Curried Sweet Peppers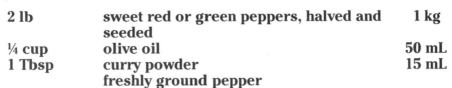

2 lb	sweet red or green peppers, halved and seeded	1 kg
¼ cup	olive oil	50 mL
1 Tbsp	curry powder	15 mL
	freshly ground pepper	

Slice peppers into thin strips. Heat oil in large skillet or wok until hot but not smoking. Add curry powder and stir. Add pepper strips and stir fry 4 to 6 minutes until tender-crisp. Season with pepper.

Serves: 4

Onions Stuffed with Broccoli

4	large Spanish onions	4
1 pkg	(10 oz/300 g) frozen chopped broccoli, defrosted	1
½ cup	grated Parmesan cheese	125 mL
⅓ cup	mayonnaise	75 mL
2 tsp	lemon juice	10 mL
2 Tbsp	butter or margarine	25 mL
2 Tbsp	all purpose flour	25 mL
1 cup	milk	250 mL
¼ tsp	salt	1 mL
⅛ tsp	paprika	0.5 mL
1 pkg	(4 oz/125 g) cream cheese, cubed	1

Preheat oven to 375°F (190°C). Peel and halve onions. Parboil in salted water 10 to 12 minutes. Remove centres of onions leaving ¾ inch (2 cm) shell. Chop enough of the centre portion of onions to equal 1 cup (250 mL). Reserve remainder for other uses. Combine chopped onion, broccoli, Parmesan cheese, mayonnaise and lemon juice. Spoon mixture into centre of onion halves. Can be prepared to this point in advance. In small sauce pan, melt butter and blend in flour. Gradually add milk, salt and paprika and cook until thick, stirring constantly. Remove from heat and blend in cream cheese until smooth. Place onions in greased flat baking dish. Spoon sauce over them. Sprinkle with more paprika, if desired. Bake uncovered at 375°F (190°C) 20 minutes.

Can make ahead   **Serves: 8**

Ratatouille

1	medium eggplant, peeled and cubed	1
	flour for dredging	
½ cup	olive oil	125 mL
2	garlic cloves, chopped	2
1 cup	chopped onion	250 mL
2	zucchini, unpeeled and cut in ½ inch (2 cm) slices	2
2	green peppers, cut in strips	2
4	whole tomatoes, peeled and chopped or 1 can (19 oz/540 mL) drained	4
1½ tsp	salt	7 mL
¼ tsp	black pepper	1 mL
½ tsp	Italian seasonings	2 mL
	Mozzarella cheese slices	
½ cup	grated Parmesan cheese	125 mL

Preheat oven to 350°F (180°C). Dredge eggplant in flour. Heat 3 Tbsp (50 mL) oil in fry pan and sauté eggplant, adding additional oil if necessary. Remove from pan and place in greased 9 x 13 inch (23 x 30 cm) baking pan. Add more oil to fry pan and sauté garlic and onion until golden (about 3 minutes). Add zucchini and green peppers to pan and sauté 5 minutes, stirring occasionally. Add tomatoes and seasoning. Simmer 10 minutes. Cover eggplant with vegetables. Top with Mozzarella cheese slices and sprinkle with Parmesan cheese. Bake at 350°F (180°C) 45 minutes. Bake 1½ hours if frozen.

Can make ahead   **Can freeze**   **Serves: 6 to 8**

Stir Fry Vegetables

1 lb	snow peas	500 g
2	bunches broccoli, broken into flowerets	2
1 cup	water chestnuts, drained and sliced	250 mL
1 cup	chopped green onions	250 mL
2 Tbsp	minced ginger root	25 mL
1 lb	fresh mushrooms, sliced	500 g
¼ cup	peanut oil	50 mL
¼ cup	soy sauce	50 mL
6 Tbsp	dry sherry	100 mL

Prepare snowpeas, broccoli, water chestnuts, green onions, ginger and mushrooms early in the day. Cover and refrigerate until ready to use. To cook, heat oil in fry pan or wok. First, sauté ginger for 2 minutes to flavour the oil. Add broccoli and water chestnuts. Stir in soy sauce and sherry, cooking 2 to 3 minutes stirring occasionally. Add peas, mushrooms and onions. Stir until vegetables are heated through.

Serves: 12

Pear Filled Squash
Two Fall favourites make a winning combination

3	small acorn squash	3
¼ cup	butter	50 mL
2	onions, chopped	2
2	pears, peeled and diced	2
2 Tbsp	brown sugar	25 mL
2 Tbsp	sherry	25 mL
½ tsp	salt	2 mL
¼ tsp	ground ginger	1 mL
¼ tsp	ground cinnamon	1 mL
¼ cup	sliced almonds, toasted	50 mL

Preheat oven to 350°F (180°C). Halve squash lengthwise and remove seeds. Arrange squash, cut side down, in greased baking dish. Bake at 350°F (180°C) 45 minutes or until fork tender. In saucepan, melt butter and cook onions until soft. Stir in pears, brown sugar, sherry, salt, ginger and cinnamon. Cook, stirring constantly until pears are tender, about 4 minutes. Turn squash over, mound pear mixture into centre. Bake 10 minutes longer. Before serving, garnish with toasted almonds.

Serves: 6

Zucchini Au Gratin
Delicious for a party served with chicken or lamb

4 or 5	zucchini, cut in ¼ inch (5 mm) slices	4 or 5
2 Tbsp	butter	25 mL
2 cups	sour cream	500 mL
½ cup	butter	125 mL
¼ cup	grated Parmesan cheese	50 mL
	salt and pepper, to taste	
4	egg yolks, well beaten	4
4 Tbsp	chopped green onions	50 mL
1 cup	dry bread crumbs	250 mL
¼ cup	melted butter	50 mL
⅔ cup	grated Parmesan cheese	150 mL

Sauté zucchini in 2 Tbsp (25 mL) butter until barely tender. (Add more butter, if needed.) Place in shallow 2 qt (2 L) casserole. In saucepan, blend sour cream ½ cup (125 mL) butter, ¼ cup (50 mL) cheese, salt and pepper. Cook gently until cheese is melted. Remove from heat and beat in egg yolks and green onions. Pour this mixture over zucchini. Blend bread crumbs with ¼ cup (50 mL) melted butter. Spread over zucchini. Sprinkle with ⅔ cup (150 mL) Parmesan cheese. Refrigerate overnight. Bake at 350°F (180°C) 30 minutes.

Must make ahead　　　　　　　　　　　**Serves: 10 to 12**

Sautéed Cherry Tomatoes and Snow Peas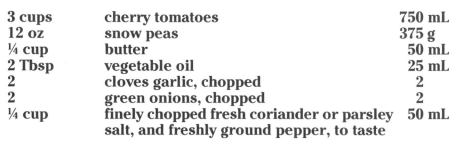
A pretty dish

3 cups	cherry tomatoes	750 mL
12 oz	snow peas	375 g
¼ cup	butter	50 mL
2 Tbsp	vegetable oil	25 mL
2	cloves garlic, chopped	2
2	green onions, chopped	2
¼ cup	finely chopped fresh coriander or parsley	50 mL
	salt, and freshly ground pepper, to taste	

Wash and stem tomatoes. Trim snow peas. In large skillet heat butter with oil. Add snow peas, garlic and onions. Stir fry over medium high heat about 2 minutes. Add tomatoes and cook 2 minutes longer, stirring gently until tomatoes are just heated through, (do not overcook). Add coriander, salt and pepper. Cook and stir gently 30 seconds.

Serves: 6 to 8

Spinach Artichoke Casserole

1 can	(10 oz/284 mL) mushroom pieces, drained	1
6 Tbsp	butter	100 mL
1 Tbsp	flour	15 mL
½ cup	milk	125 mL
½ tsp	salt	2 mL
pinch	pepper	pinch
1 can	(14 oz/398 mL) artichoke hearts, drained	1
2 pkg	(10 oz/300 g each) frozen chopped spinach, cooked	2
½ cup	sour cream	125 mL
2 Tbsp	lemon juice	25 mL
½ cup	mayonnaise	125 mL
1 can	(10 oz/284 mL) whole mushrooms, drained	1
1 Tbsp	butter	15 mL

Preheat oven to 350°F (180°C). Sauté mushroom pieces in 6 Tbsp (100 mL) butter. Remove from pan. Add flour to melted butter, stir until smooth. Add milk, salt, pepper, sautéed mushroom pieces and spinach. Blend sour cream, lemon juice and mayonnaise and pour over casserole. Sauté whole mushrooms in 1 Tbsp (15 mL) butter. Sprinkle over casserole. Bake at 350°F (180°C) 30 minutes. Freezes well without sour cream sauce.

Can freeze   **Serves: 6 to 8**

Baked Curried Zucchini

1	egg	1
1 cup	all purpose flour	250 mL
1 tsp	salt	5 mL
1 tsp	curry powder	5 mL
1 tsp	pepper	5 mL
3	medium zucchini, cut crosswise into ¼ inch (5 mm) slices	3
	olive oil	
	additional curry powder (optional)	

Preheat oven to 400°F (200°C). Generously grease a baking sheet. In a small bowl, beat egg and set aside. Combine flour, salt, curry powder and pepper in shallow dish. Dip zucchini in beaten egg, then roll in seasoned flour, covering completely. Arrange zucchini on prepared sheet. Sprinkle with olive oil and additional curry powder if desired. Bake at 400°F (200°C) 20 minutes until crisp and golden brown, turning once. Drain any excess liquid and serve immediately.

Serves: 4 to 6

Swiss Zucchini Puff
Deliciously different and attractive to serve

2½ lbs	zucchini, washed and cut into chunks	1.25 kg
1 tsp	salt	5 mL
⅓ cup	all purpose flour	75 mL
4	large eggs	4
1 cup	whipping cream	250 mL
1 cup	grated Swiss cheese	250 mL
1 tsp	salt	5 mL
½ tsp	freshly ground pepper	2 mL

Preheat oven to 350°F (180°C). Place zucchini and salt in a saucepan and add water to barely cover. Bring to boil and cook 6 to 8 minutes or until tender. Drain well. In a food processor purée the zucchini until smooth. Transfer mixture to a mixing bowl, sprinkle flour on top and beat with electric mixer. Add the remaining ingredients and mix well. Butter a 6 cup (1.5 L) gratin dish approximately 1½ inches (4 cm) deep and pour in zucchini mixture. Place in oven and bake 45 minutes. If the top has not browned by this time, place dish under broiler for a minute or until browned. Let the gratin "rest" for at least 10 minutes before serving.

Serves: 8

Tomatoes Florentine

6	medium to large tomatoes	6
1 Tbsp	granulated sugar	15 mL
1 tsp	salt	5 mL
⅛ tsp	pepper	0.5 mL
2 pkg	(10 oz/284 g each) spinach	2
4	slices bacon, diced	4
2	large cloves garlic, chopped	2
2	eggs	2
½ cup	whipping cream	125 mL
⅔ cup	freshly grated Parmesan cheese	150 mL

Preheat oven to 325°F (160°C). Slice off top ½ inch (1 cm) of each tomato and discard or save for a soup or sauce. Scoop out seeds and pulp. Discard or save, as above. Lightly sprinkle inside of shells with sugar, salt and pepper. Invert on towel and drain for 30 minutes. Wash and cook spinach in large quantity of boiling water for 6 minutes. Rinse under cold water. Drain and squeeze dry. Chop finely. In frying pan cook bacon until crisp. Remove and blot on paper towel. To remaining bacon fat, add spinach and garlic. Stir and cook for 2 minutes. Remove from pan. Beat eggs with cream and ½ cup (125 mL) of cheese until blended. Stir in spinach mixture and bacon. Season to taste. Sprinkle inside of each tomato with 1 tsp (5 mL) Parmesan cheese. Fill with spinach mixture and lightly sprinkle with remaining cheese. Place in shallow baking dish and bake at 325°F (160°C) 30 minutes.

Serves: 6

Mushroom Onion Casserole 🍒
Excellent with steak or roast beef

1	large Spanish onion, sliced	1
1½ lb	mushrooms, sliced	750 g
2 Tbsp	butter	25 mL
2 Tbsp	white wine	25 mL
1 can	(10 oz/284 mL) golden mushroom soup	1
1 tsp	garlic salt	5 mL
	buttered bread crumbs	

Preheat oven to 350°F (180°C). In skillet, sauté onion and mushrooms in butter. Add wine, soup, garlic, salt and mix together. Place in 8 inch (20 cm) square baking dish. Sprinkle buttered bread crumbs to cover. Bake at 350°F (180°C) 20 minutes.

Serves: 6 to 8

Stuffed Zucchini

4	medium zucchini	4
2 Tbsp	butter	25 mL
4	medium tomatoes, chopped	4
1 Tbsp	chopped green onion	15 mL
1	small clove garlic, chopped salt and pepper to taste	1

SAUCE		
2 Tbsp	butter	25 mL
2 Tbsp	all purpose flour	25 mL
1¼ cups	light cream or milk	300 mL
¼ cup	Parmesan cheese	50 mL
½ tsp	Dijon mustard	2 mL
2 Tbsp	Parmesan cheese	25 mL

Preheat oven to 425°F (220°C). Blanch whole zucchini in boiling salted water 5 minutes. Refresh in cold water. Cut in half lengthwise and scoop out flesh. Chop and place in sieve to drain. Invert zucchini shells on paper towel to drain. In skillet, melt butter and cook chopped zucchini with tomatoes, onion and garlic 2 to 3 minutes. Add salt and pepper to taste. Spoon filling into shells. Place filled shells in flat baking dish.
SAUCE: Melt butter, add flour and slowly stir in cream. Cook until thick, stirring constantly. Add ¼ cup (50 mL) cheese and mustard. Pour sauce over stuffed zucchini shells. Sprinkle with remaining cheese. Bake at 425°F (220°C) 10 minutes or until slightly browned.

Can make ahead   **Serves: 8**

Turnip Puff

3 cups	cooked, mashed turnip	750 mL
3 Tbsp	butter	50 mL
3	eggs, separated salt and pepper to taste	3
1 Tbsp	light brown sugar	15 mL

Preheat oven to 400°F (200°C). Put turnip and butter in a large bowl. Beat egg yolks and add to turnip. Season with salt and pepper. Beat egg whites until stiff. Fold into turnip. Pour into greased soufflé dish and sprinkle with brown sugar. Bake at 400°F (200°C) 12 minutes.

Serves: 4

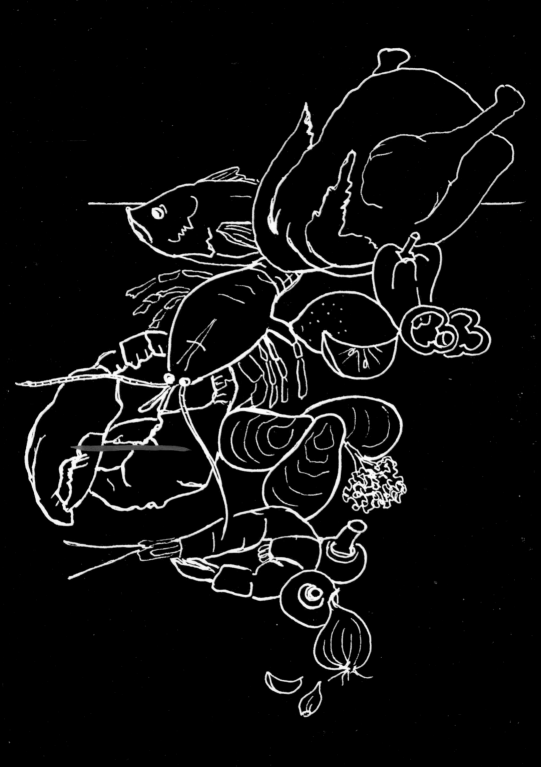

Fish

Aquarian Gratin Lobster or Sole	133
Ceviche	132
East Indian Sole	136
Fresh Halibut in Lemon Cream	130
Sole and Spinach Casserole	135
Sour Cream Tomato Fillets	133

Seafood

Aquarian Gratin Lobster or Sole	133
Broiled Shrimp	126
Carpaccio Di Gamberoni, Il Posto	125
Ceviche	132
Elegant Scallop and Dill Stir Fry	131
Greek Shrimp	129
Hot Lobster or Crab Soufflé	126
Hot Seafood Salad	134
Maritime Seafood Casserole	130
Moules Marinière	137
Scallops in Cream Sauce	134
Seafood Supreme	127
Shrimp and Crabmeat in Patty Shells	128
Shrimp Creole	129

Poultry

Apricot Chicken Curry	145
Buffet Chicken	146
Chicken à la Cerise	144
Chicken Almond Supreme	149
Chicken Artichoke Casserole	146
Chicken Breasts and Almonds	147
Chicken Pineapple	142
Chinese Chicken Wings	140
Company Chicken	140
Coronada Casserole	148
Crab Stuffed Chicken	143
Ghanian Chicken Stew	145
Hawaiian Chicken	150
Honey Glazed Chicken	148
Japanese Chicken	151
Marinated Chicken Breasts	151
Personalized Shake and Bake	149
Poultry Marinade	152
Sauces for Fowl	152
Stir Fry Chicken with Cashew Nuts	141
Telfer's Breast of Chicken with Wild Rice Stuffing	138

🍒 ...designates "Company in a Minute"

IL POSTO RESTAURANT
148 Yorkville Ave., York Square, Toronto

Il Posto's Carpaccio Di Gamberoni

8	jumbo shrimp, deveined	8
	juice of ½ lemon	
2 Tbsp	endive (rugola), finely chopped	25 mL
2	stalks celery, finely chopped	2
	Parmesan cheese, thin strips	

DRESSING

3-4 Tbsp	olive oil	50 mL
	juice of ½ lemon	
pinch	mustard	pinch
	salt and pepper, to taste	

Boil shrimp in salted water and juice of half lemon for about 5 to 8 minutes, depending on size. Drain water and let cool at room temperature. Arrange shrimp on serving platter and sprinkle with finely chopped endive and celery. Place thin strips of Parmesan cheese (do not grate) on top of shrimp. Top with dressing of olive oil, lemon juice, mustard, salt and pepper. Marinate the above for ½ hour.

Must make ahead   **Serves: 2**

Hot Lobster or Crab Soufflé
An old fashioned Nova Scotia recipe

8	slices white bread	8
4 cans	(5oz/142 g each) crab meat or lobster	4
½ cup	mayonnaise	125 mL
1	onion, finely chopped	1
1	green pepper, chopped	1
1 cup	chopped celery	250 mL
3 cups	milk	750 mL
4	eggs	4
2 cans	(10 oz/284 mL each) cream of mushroom soup	2
2 Tbsp	grated Parmesan cheese	25 mL
½ tsp	paprika	2 mL

Cut 4 slices of bread into cubes. Place in bottom of greased casserole dish. In bowl, mix crab meat or lobster, mayonnaise, onion, green pepper and celery. Spread evenly over bread cubes. Trim crusts from remaining 4 slices of bread and place slices over seafood mixture. In a bowl, mix eggs and milk together and pour over bread and seafood in casserole. Refrigerate overnight. Next day, preheat oven to 325°F (160°C). Bake casserole at 325°F (160°C) 15 minutes. Remove from oven and spoon soup over top. Sprinkle Parmesan cheese and paprika over all. Return to oven and bake 1½ hours until golden brown.

Must make ahead   **Serves: 12**

Broiled Shrimp

2 lb	large shrimp	1 kg
½ cup	olive oil	125 mL
2 tsp	finely chopped garlic	10 mL
2 tsp	finely chopped parsley	10 mL
⅛ tsp	crushed red pepper flakes	0.5 mL
½ tsp	dried oregano leaves	2 mL
2 Tbsp	fine, fresh bread crumbs	25 mL
	salt and freshly ground pepper to taste	

Peel and devein shrimp. Rinse and pat dry. In a mixing bowl, mix all remaining ingredients. Add shrimp and toss to coat evenly. Line a shallow baking dish with foil. Arrange shrimp on foil. Place under broiler 3 to 4 inches (8 to 10 cm) from heat. Broil 5 to 6 minutes. It is not necessary to turn shrimp. Serve on a bed of rice.

Serves: 4

Seafood Supreme

1 can	(5 oz/142 g) lobster meat, drained	1
1 can	(5 oz/142 g) crab meat, drained	1
1 can	(6.5 oz/184 g) flakes of chicken	1
½ lb	fresh or frozen scallops or shrimp thawed, if frozen	250 g
½ cup	butter	125 mL
½ cup	flour	125 mL
¼ tsp	dry mustard	1 mL
½ tsp	salt	2 mL
2 cups	milk	500 mL
1 cup	sour cream	250 mL
½ cup	dry sherry or white wine	125 mL
2 Tbsp	butter	25 mL
1 cup	soft bread crumbs	250 mL
½ cup	grated Parmesan or sharp white Cheddar cheese	125 mL

Preheat oven to 350°F (180°C). Mix fish and chicken lightly, breaking into chunks. Melt ½ cup (125 mL) butter, stir in flour, mustard and salt. Add milk and cook over medium heat, stirring slowly, until just boiling. Add sour cream and sherry. Pour over seafood, mix gently and put into a 2½ qt (2.5 L) casserole. Melt 2 Tbsp (25 mL) butter and add bread crumbs. Top seafood mixture with crumbs and sprinkle cheese over all. Bake, uncovered at 350°F (180°C) 20 to 30 minutes.

Can make ahead   **Serves: 10 to 12**

Shrimp and Crab Meat in Patty Shells

½ cup	chopped green pepper	125 mL
1 cup	chopped onions	250 mL
¼ cup	butter	50 mL
¼ cup	all purpose flour	50 mL
3½ cups	evaporated milk	875 mL
2 Tbsp	tomato paste	25 mL
1 tsp	salt	5 mL
¼ tsp	pepper	1 mL
¼ tsp	mace	1 mL
¼ tsp	ginger	1 mL
1 tsp	Worcestershire sauce	5 mL
1 tsp	lemon juice	5 mL
2 cups	crab meat or tuna	500 mL
3½ cups	shrimp, cooked and drained	875 mL
½ cup	canned whole mushrooms, drained	125 mL
6-8	patty shells	6-8

In large fry pan, sauté green pepper and onions in butter. Stir in flour. Gradually stir in evaporated milk and cook over low heat until thickened. Add tomato paste, salt, pepper, mace, ginger, Worcestershire sauce, lemon juice, seafood and mushrooms. Continue to cook about 15 minutes, stirring constantly until heated completely. Place in patty shells and garnish with parsley.

Can make ahead   **Serves: 6 to 8**

Greek Shrimp

¼ cup	butter	50 mL
1	large green pepper, chopped	1
1	large onion, chopped	1
1 can	(28 oz/796 mL) stewed tomatoes	1
2 cans	(6.5 oz/175 g each) minced clams	2
1½ cups	dry white wine	375 mL
1 tsp	Worcestershire sauce	5 mL
1 cup	white or brown rice	250 mL
1½ lb	shrimp, cooked and shelled	750 g
1½ cups	Feta cheese, crumbled	375 mL

Melt butter in large skillet. Add green pepper and onion and sauté until crisp tender, about 5 minutes. Add tomatoes, clam broth (from the 2 cans of clams), white wine, Worcestershire sauce and rice. Increase heat to medium high and boil 25 to 30 minutes. Add shrimp and drained clams. Simmer 3 minutes. Transfer to serving dish and liberally sprinkle with Feta cheese.

Can make ahead **Serves: 6**

Shrimp Creole

1½ lb	jumbo shrimp, raw	750 g
3 Tbsp	butter	50 mL
1	garlic clove, chopped	1
½ cup	white wine	125 mL
1	small green pepper, cut in strips	1
¾ lb	fresh mushrooms, sliced	375 g
1	onion, sliced and separated in rings	1
¾ cup	sour cream	175 mL
1½ cups	whipping cream	375 mL
2 Tbsp	tomato paste	25 mL
	salt	
¼ tsp	cayenne	1 mL
½ tsp	chili powder	2 mL
1 jar	(4½ oz/125 mL) pimento, chopped	1

Sauté shrimp in butter until lightly browned. Add garlic and sauté with shrimp 2 minutes. Add wine and simmer until wine evaporates. Remove from heat. In a separate pan, sauté green pepper, mushrooms and onion. In small bowl, mix sour cream, whipping cream, tomato paste, salt, cayenne and chili powder. Blend into shrimp. Add vegetables and heat. Stir in pimento and serve over rice.

Serves: 4 to 6

Fresh Halibut in Lemon Cream
Fast, easy, tasty

2 lb	halibut fillets or steaks	1 kg
1 cup	18% cream	250 mL
1 Tbsp	finely chopped onion	15 mL
1 tsp	grated lemon rind	5 mL
4 tsp	fresh lemon juice	20 mL
	freshly ground white pepper	

GARNISH   thin lemon slices

Preheat oven to 400°F (200°C). Arrange fish in single layer in flat buttered baking dish. Combine cream, onion, lemon rind, and juice. Pour over fish. Bake uncovered at 400°F (200°C) for 20 minutes. Sprinkle with pepper and garnish with lemon slices. Serve immediately.

Serves: 4

Maritime Seafood Casserole

1½ lb	sole fillets	750 g
1 cup	fresh shrimp	250 mL
½ lb	scallops, halved	250 g
¼ cup	butter	50 mL
¼ cup	all purpose flour	50 mL
¾ cup	milk	175 mL
¾ cup	10% cream	175 mL
2 Tbsp	mayonnaise	25 mL
3 Tbsp	sherry	50 mL
2 Tbsp	chopped parsley	25 mL
1 Tbsp	grated lemon peel	15 mL
	salt, pepper and paprika to taste	

Preheat oven to 300°F (150°C). Arrange fillets in single layer in bottom of dish along with scallops and shrimp. In a saucepan melt butter, stir in flour, add milk and cream and cook until thickened. Blend in mayonnaise and sherry. Add parsley, lemon peel, salt and pepper. Pour sauce over seafood. Dust with paprika. Bake at 300°F (150°C) 30 minutes. Serve on rice. If prepared ahead, refrigerate until baking time.

Can make ahead   **Serves: 4 to 6**

Elegant Scallop and Dill Stir Fry
Serve with rice for delicious fare

¼ lb	fresh mushrooms	125 g
1	green or red pepper	1
	(or substitute ⅓ lb/150 g snow peas)	
1 Tbsp	freshly squeezed lemon juice	15 mL
	(or 2 Tbsp/25 mL dry white wine)	
1	clove garlic, chopped	1
¼ tsp	dried dill weed	1 mL
	freshly grated nutmeg	
pinch	salt and white pepper	pinch
½ lb	fresh or frozen scallops	250 g
1 Tbsp	vegetable oil	15 mL

Prepare and measure all ingredients before proceeding to cook. Thickly slice mushrooms. Cut pepper into 1 inch (2 cm) chunks. Squeeze lemon juice and stir together with garlic, dill weed, a generous sprinkling of nutmeg, salt and pepper. If using frozen scallops, place in sieve and rinse with cold water, until no ice crystals remain and the scallops are separated. Heat oil in a large wok over medium high heat. When piping hot, add mushrooms and stir fry for 1 minute. Immediately add pepper chunks, lemon juice mixture, and then scallops. Continue to stir fry over medium high heat for 2 minutes if using fresh scallops, or 3 to 4 minutes for frozen scallops. Taste and add more nutmeg if desired. Serve with rice.

Serves: 2

Ceviche
Acapulco style

1 lb	haddock or sole fillets or scallops	500 g
5	lemons (or 8 limes), squeezed	5
½ lb	tomatoes	250 g
4	pickled "Serrano" chilies (small green chilies), sliced	4
¼ cup	vegetable oil	50 mL
1 Tbsp	white vinegar	15 mL
½ tsp	dried oregano leaves	2 mL
	salt and pepper to taste	
	shredded lettuce	
1	onion, sliced	1
2	avocados	2

Wash fish fillets, skin and cut into small squares. Place in china or glass dish. Pour juice from lemons or limes over fish and let stand for 3 hours. Turn from time to time with a wooden spoon. Lemon or lime juice "cooks" the fish. Drain. Peel and dice tomatoes and add to fish. Add chilies, oil, vinegar, oregano, salt and pepper. Chill. Serve in sherbet glasses or seafood shells on a bed of shredded lettuce, garnished with onion slices and avocado wedges.

Must make ahead   **Serves: 6**

Aquarian Gratin Lobster or Sole 🍒
Very elegant yet simple

½ lb	cooked lobster meat	250 g
	(or 4 sole fillets, 1 lb/500 g)	
½ cup	mayonnaise	125 mL
2 Tbsp	sherry	25 mL
1 tsp	Worcestershire sauce	5 mL
1 Tbsp	minced onion	15 mL
¼ cup	10% cream	50 mL
	salt and pepper to taste	
	grated Parmesan cheese	
GARNISH	lemon slices or parsley	

Preheat oven to 375°F (190°C). Slice lobster meat or fillets and place in shallow oven proof dish. Bake at 375°F (190°C) for 5 to 6 minutes and drain off liquid. Combine mayonnaise, sherry, Worcestershire sauce, onion, cream, salt and pepper. Pour over lobster or sole. Sprinkle with Parmesan cheese. Place under broiler 5 inches (13 cm) from heat, until browned to your taste. Watch sauce does not curdle. Garnish with lemon slices or parsley. Serve immediately. Frozen fillets can be microwaved according to package directions.

Serves: 2 to 3

Sour Cream Tomato Fillets
A quick and easy way to serve frozen fish fillets

1	medium onion, chopped	1
1 Tbsp	butter	15 mL
4	medium tomatoes, sliced or 1 can	4
	(14 oz/398 mL) tomatoes	
	salt and pepper to taste	
1 lb	frozen fish fillets, thawed	500 g
2 Tbsp	butter	25 mL
1 cup	sour cream	250 mL
GARNISH	parsley	

Sauté onion in butter until soft. Spread tomato slices on bottom of flat casserole dish. Place onion, then fillets on top. Salt and pepper to taste. Dot with butter. Place under broiler for 6 to 7 minutes, until fish flakes. Watch carefully. Remove from oven and spread fish with sour cream. Return to broiler for approximately 2 minutes. Garnish with parsley and serve.

Serves: 4

Hot Seafood Salad 🍒

Use as appetizer or buffet dish

1 cup	shrimp, fresh or canned	250 mL
1 cup	canned crab meat, flaked	250 mL
½ cup	chopped green onion	125 mL
1 cup	thinly sliced celery	250 mL
½ cup	chopped onion	125 mL
1 cup	mayonnaise	250 mL
1 tsp	Worcestershire sauce	5 mL
½ tsp	salt	2 mL
¼ tsp	pepper	1 mL
½ cup	fine dry bread crumbs	125 mL
1 Tbsp	butter, melted	15 mL

Preheat oven to 350°F (180°C). In a 1½ qt (1.5 L) casserole dish, combine all ingredients except bread crumbs and butter. Combine bread crumbs and melted butter. Sprinkle on top. Bake at 350°F (180°C) 20 to 30 minutes until browned. Serve in seafood shells.

Can make ahead   **Serves: 4**

Scallops in Cream Sauce 🍒

½ cup	white wine	125 mL
½ tsp	lemon juice	2 mL
1 lb	scallops	500 g
1 Tbsp	butter	15 mL
2 Tbsp	flour	25 mL
⅔ cup	light cream	150 mL
¼ tsp	salt	1 mL
¼ tsp	pepper	1 mL
⅛ tsp	cayenne pepper	0.5 mL
¼ cup	grated Gruyère cheese	50 mL

In saucepan, bring wine and lemon juice to boiling point. Reduce heat, add scallops and poach 8 to 10 minutes, or until firm. Remove from heat and cool. Strain, reserving liquid. In separate saucepan, melt butter. Stir in flour. Gradually add reserved liquid, stirring constantly. Cook 3 to 4 minutes. Stir in cream, salt, pepper and cayenne. Cook 2 minutes longer and then add scallops. Spoon into seafood shells and sprinkle with cheese. Brown under broiler 4 to 5 minutes or until cheese is browned and sauce is bubbly. Shrimp may be substituted for scallops.

**Serves: 6 as an appetizer
4 as a main course**

Sole and Spinach Casserole

1 pkg	(10 oz/300 g) frozen, chopped spinach	1
2 cups	cooked rice	500 mL
4	eggs, hard-boiled and chopped	4
4	green onions, chopped	4
¼ cup	chopped parsley	50 mL
2 Tbsp	mayonnaise	25 mL
6	medium sole fillets	6
1 can	(10 oz/284 mL) cream of shrimp soup	1
½ cup	sherry	125 mL
¾ cup	10% cream	175 mL
	salt and pepper to taste	

Preheat oven to 350°F (180°C). Thaw spinach and squeeze out as much moisture as possible. Combine spinach and rice and arrange on bottom of a greased 9 x 13 inch (23 x 33 cm) casserole. In a small bowl, mix together eggs, onions, parsley and mayonnaise. Spread mixture on each of the fillets, dividing it equally. Roll up each fillet to enclose filling. Set rolls, seam side down, on rice layer. In a bowl, combine soup, sherry, cream, salt and pepper. Pour over fillets. Bake covered at 350°F (180°C) 45 minutes or until fish flakes easily with a fork.

NOTE: This dish can be made early in the day, covered with foil and refrigerated until baking time.

Can make ahead **Serves: 6**

East Indian Sole
Crisp green vegetables can accompany this dish

6	fillets of sole	6
	salt and pepper	
1 tsp	curry powder	5 mL
3 Tbsp	butter	50 mL
¾ cup	dry white wine	175 mL
SAUCE		
2 Tbsp	butter	25 mL
2 Tbsp	all purpose flour	25 mL
¼ cup	milk	50 mL
¼ cup	cream	50 mL
¼ lb	fresh mushrooms, sliced	125 g
1	small green onion, chopped	1

Preheat oven to 350°F (180°C). Season fillets with salt, pepper and curry powder. Melt butter in fry pan. Add seasoned fish and wine. Cook slowly for 5 minutes or until fillets are white. Transfer carefully to a casserole dish. Reserve ½ cup (125 mL) wine for sauce.

SAUCE: Melt 2 Tbsp (25 mL) butter in fry pan. Stir in flour, reserved wine, milk and cream. Cook over medium heat, stirring constantly until thickened. Pour over fillets. Sprinkle mushrooms and onion over top. Bake at 350°F (180°C) 20 minutes.

Serves: 6

Moules Marinière 🍒

¼ cup	butter	50 mL
2	onions, chopped	2
5	cloves garlic, finely chopped	5
1 cup	white wine	250 mL
¼ cup	chopped fresh parsley	50 mL
¼ cup	chopped celery leaves	50 mL
3 lb	mussels	1.5 kg
1 cup	whipping cream	250 mL
2	egg yolks, beaten	2
2 Tbsp	tomato paste	25 mL

Melt butter in large fry pan. Add onions and garlic and sauté until onions are transparent. Add wine, parsley and celery leaves. Bring to a boil. Add well cleaned mussels. Cover and cook 5 minutes until mussels have opened. Throw away any unopened shells. Remove mussels with slotted spoon and keep warm. Strain cooking liquid, return to pan and reduce by one half. Add ¾ cup (175 mL) whipping cream and reduce slightly. Add yolks to remaining cream and stir in a little of the hot sauce. Beat back into pan. Season with tomato paste before serving. Place mussels on a plate or in a bowl and pour sauce over them.

Serves: 6

TELFER'S RESTAURANT
212 King St. W., Toronto

Telfer's Breast of Chicken with Wild Rice Stuffing

1 cup	wild rice, uncooked	250 mL
1 cup	spinach, steamed and squeezed dry	250 mL
1 cup	leeks, whites only (approximately 1 medium)	250 mL
2 Tbsp	butter	25 mL
½ cup	peeled, seeded, chopped tomato	125 mL
½ cup	finely chopped red pepper	125 mL
3 Tbsp	Pernod	50 mL
1 Tbsp	lemon juice	15 mL
½ tsp	salt	2 mL
¼ tsp	black pepper	1 mL
¼ lb	Feta cheese	125 g
15	Ritz crackers, crushed	15
4	boneless chicken breasts	4

Cook rice in 8 cups (2 L) of rapidly boiling water for 60 minutes. Strain through a sieve, and run under cold water until cooled. While rice is cooking, steam spinach until just cooked, and cool under running cold water. Squeeze out excess moisture. Finely dice leek. Preheat oven to 350°F (180°C).

Sauté leeks in butter just until soft. Add tomatoes and peppers, Pernod, lemon juice, salt and pepper. Allow to simmer over medium-high heat until liquid has evaporated and mixture is fairly dry. Remove from heat and mix with wild rice, spinach, Feta cheese that has been crumbled, and cracker crumbs. Allow mixture to cool. With a sharp knife, cut a pocket into the chicken breasts, inserting the knife at the broad end of the breast, and taking care not to puncture the other side. Fill the pocket generously with the cooled stuffing. Brush the outside of the breasts with melted butter, season with salt and pepper and bake at 350°F (180°C) 20 minutes on a baking sheet.

Serve with White Wine Tarragon Glaze.

TELFER'S RESTAURANT
212 King St. W., Toronto

White Wine Tarragon Glaze

1 Tbsp	finely chopped shallots	15 mL
1	small clove garlic, finely chopped	1
2 Tbsp	butter	25 mL
2 cups	chicken stock	500 mL
1 cup	white wine	250 mL
1 cup	apple juice	250 mL
1 tsp	lemon juice	5 mL
3 Tbsp	fresh chopped tarragon leaves or	50 mL
	2 Tbsp (25 mL) dried tarragon leaves, crumbled	
1½ tsp	salt	7 mL
⅛ tsp	black pepper	0.5 mL
3 Tbsp	Pernod	50 mL
2 Tbsp	cornstarch, slightly heaping, diluted with ¼ cup (50 mL) apple juice	25 mL

Sauté shallots and garlic in butter in a medium saucepan until just soft. Add stock, wine, apple juice, lemon juice, tarragon, salt and pepper. Allow to simmer over medium heat for 5 minutes. Add Pernod. Bring back to a simmer, and carefully whisk in cornstarch and apple juice mixture. Leave on heat until mixture has thickened and is fairly clear. Pour over finished chicken breasts.

Serves: 4

Company Chicken
Easily doubled or tripled for large crowds

6	whole chicken breasts, split, boned and skinned	6
½ cup	flour	125 mL
2 tsp	curry powder	10 mL
½ tsp	salt	2 mL
½ tsp	pepper	2 mL
½ tsp	garlic powder or one clove, chopped	2 mL
½ cup	butter	125 mL
1 cup	sliced onions	250 mL
1 cup	ketchup	250 mL
1 cup	water	250 mL
¼ cup	raisins	50 mL
1 cup	green pepper, chopped (optional)	250 mL
½ cup	toasted almonds	125 mL

Combine flour, curry, salt, pepper and garlic in plastic bag. Add chicken and shake well to coat. Reserve remaining flour mixture. Melt butter in frying pan and sauté chicken until just brown. Remove chicken. Sauté onions in remaining butter until transparent. Add 1 Tbsp (15 mL) reserved flour mixture and stir to form paste. Add ketchup, water and raisins. Mix well. Return chicken to pan, cover and simmer 45 minutes. Add green pepper, if desired, and cook another 10 minutes. Sprinkle with almonds and serve with rice and green salad.

Can freeze   **Serves: 6 to 8**

Chinese Chicken Wings

2 lb	chicken wings	1 kg
1	garlic clove, chopped	1
3 Tbsp	soy sauce	50 mL
2 Tbsp	brown sugar	25 mL
2 Tbsp	dry sherry	25 mL
1 cup	chicken stock	250 mL

Place chicken wings in wok or fry pan. Mix remaining ingredients. Add to chicken. Bring to boil, reduce heat and simmer, covered, until wings are tender, 20 to 30 minutes. Remove lid and boil hard until sauce is reduced to about ½ cup (125 mL). May be served hot or at room temperature.

Can make ahead   **Serves: 4**

Stir Fry Chicken With Cashew Nuts

2	whole, large chicken breasts, split, boned and skinned	2

MARINADE

2 Tbsp	dry sherry	25 mL
½ tsp	salt	2 mL
½ tsp	soy sauce	2 mL
2 tsp	cornstarch	10 mL
2 Tbsp	water	25 mL

VEGETABLES

1 cup	cashew nuts	250 mL
1 cup	vegetable oil	250 mL
8	slices ginger root	8
1 cup	bamboo shoots	250 mL
2	medium, sweet red or green peppers, diced	2
½ tsp	salt	5 mL

SAUCE

2 tsp	soy sauce	10 mL
⅛ tsp	salt	0.5 mL
½ tsp	sugar	2 mL
½ tsp	sesame oil	2 mL
1 tsp	cornstarch	5 mL
½ cup	water	125 mL
dash	white pepper	dash

Cut chicken into ½ inch (1 cm) cubes. Mix chicken well with marinade ingredients. Set aside for 30 minutes or longer. Place cashew nuts in 1 cup (250 mL) oil in a wok or fry pan. Fry nuts over low heat until light brown. Remove and drain on paper towel. Leave oil in wok. Heat oil again over high heat until hot. Add chicken. Stir quickly, separating pieces. When all meat has turned white, remove with slotted spoon and drain. Remove all but 2 Tbsp (25 mL) oil from wok. Add ginger. Stir fry for 1 minute. Add bamboo shoots, green peppers and salt. Stir fry 1 minute. Return chicken to wok, stir together for 1 minute more. Add sauce ingredients. Keep stirring until sauce thickens. Add cashew nuts. Transfer to serving platter and serve immediately.

Serves: 6

Chicken Pineapple
For a crowd

18	whole chicken breasts, split and boned	18
	salt, pepper and paprika	
1 tsp	salt	5 mL
¾ cup	honey	175 mL
½ cup	soy sauce	125 mL
1	chicken bouillon cube, dissolved in ½ cup (125 mL) water	1
½ cup	vegetable oil	125 mL
½ cup	sherry	125 mL
2 tsp	ground ginger	10 mL
3 cans	(10 oz/284 mL each) pineapple tidbits	3
¾ cup	sugar	175 mL
¼ cup	cornstarch	50 mL
¾ cup	cold water	175 mL

Preheat oven to 325°F (160°C). Wash and dry chicken. Season with salt, pepper and paprika. Roll into small, tight "rolls", tucking in side edges. Put skin side up, in 2 casseroles 8 x 12 inch (20 x 30 cm). Roast uncovered at 325°F (160°C) for 1 hour. Meanwhile, combine salt, honey, soy sauce, bouillon, vegetable oil, sherry, ginger and juice from pineapple tidbits in a saucepan. Heat over medium heat. Mix sugar, cornstarch and cold water; add to hot mixture and cook until clear and thick. Add pineapple. Drain most of the juice from roasting pan and pour pineapple sauce over chicken. Bake 15 minutes longer. Serve with rice.

NOTE: Chicken may be frozen after roasting. Thaw before putting sauce on. Final heating will take longer than 15 minutes indicated above. Sauce may be prepared up to 5 days in advance and stored in refrigerator. Do not freeze.

Serves: 25

Crab Stuffed Chicken

4	whole chicken breasts, split boned and skinned	4
3 Tbsp	butter	50 mL
¼ cup	all purpose flour	50 mL
¾ cup	milk	175 mL
⅓ cup	dry white wine	75 mL
¾ cup	chicken stock	175 mL
¼ cup	chopped onion	50 mL
1 cup	chopped mushrooms	250 mL
1 Tbsp	butter	15 mL
6 oz	crabmeat	175 g
½ cup	coarsely crumbled crackers	125 mL
2 Tbsp	chopped parsley	25 mL
½ tsp	salt	2 mL
pinch	pepper	pinch
1 cup	grated Jarlsberg or white Cheddar cheese	250 mL
½ tsp	paprika	2 mL

Preheat oven to 350°F (180°C). Pound chicken between 2 pieces of plastic wrap until very thin. Chill until ready to use. Melt butter in saucepan, blend in flour and cook gently 1 to 2 minutes. Add milk, wine and chicken stock. Cook over medium high heat, stirring, until mixture comes to a boil and thickens. Set aside. Sauté onions and mushrooms in 1 Tbsp (15 mL) butter until liquid evaporates. Stir in crabmeat, crackers, parsley, salt, pepper and 2 Tbsp (25 mL) of prepared sauce. Place stuffing on lower third of each chicken breast. Roll, jelly roll fashion, turning in edges. Place in casserole, seam side down. Pour sauce over chicken. Bake at 350°F (180°C) 1 hour. Just before serving, sprinkle with cheese and paprika. Bake 2 minutes more, or put under broiler to brown lightly.

Can make ahead **Serves: 8**

143

Chicken à La Cerise

6	whole chicken breasts, split, boned and skinned	6
	salt and pepper	
2 Tbsp	butter	25 mL
½ lb	mushrooms, finely chopped	250 g
1 can	(4½ oz/128 g) devilled ham	1
pinch	dried tarragon leaves	pinch
3 Tbsp	all purpose flour	50 mL
½ tsp	paprika	2 mL
¼ cup	butter	50 mL
1 cup	chicken stock	250 mL
SAUCE		
1 cup	port	250 mL
1 can	(14 oz/398 mL) pitted cherries	1
2 Tbsp	cold water	25 mL
2-3 tsp	cornstarch	10-15 mL

Preheat oven to 350°F (180°C).
Pound chicken breasts between two pieces of plastic wrap until flat. Sprinkle with salt and pepper. Heat 2 Tbsp (25 mL) butter in a fry pan, add chopped mushrooms and cook 5 minutes. Transfer to a bowl and cool. Add ham and tarragon. Spread ham mixture evenly among the chicken breasts. Roll up and secure with string. Combine flour and paprika and coat chicken rolls. Heat ¼ cup (50 mL) butter in fry pan and brown chicken rolls. Transfer to a 9 x 13 inch (22 x 33 cm) baking dish. May refrigerate or freeze at this point. Add stock, cover with foil, and bake at 350°F (180°C) 45 minutes. Uncover and bake 10 minutes longer.
SAUCE: Boil port in saucepan until reduced by half. Add cherries and juice, cover and simmer. Combine water and cornstarch and pour gradually into sauce. Cook until thickened, stirring constantly. To serve, remove string from chicken breasts and pass the sauce separately.

Can make ahead   **Can freeze**   **Serves: 6 to 8**

Apricot Chicken Curry 🍒

3	whole chicken breasts, split, boned and skinned	3
3 Tbsp	all purpose flour	50 mL
1 Tbsp	curry powder	15 mL
¼ cup	oil	50 mL
2	beef bouillon cubes	2
2 Tbsp	soy sauce	25 mL
2 Tbsp	lemon juice	25 mL
1 can	(14 oz/398 mL) apricots including juice	1

Preheat oven to 350°F (180°C). Cut chicken into bite-sized pieces. Place flour and curry in bag, add chicken and shake until evenly coated. Brown in oil and place in baking dish. Add bouillon cubes, soy sauce, lemon juice and apricots to oil in frypan and heat until cubes are dissolved. Pour over chicken. If preparing ahead, refrigerate until ½ hour before baking. Bake at 350°F (180°C) 35 to 45 minutes, or until bubbly.

Can make ahead **Serves: 6**

Ghanaian Chicken Stew
Unusual and tasty

3 lb	chicken pieces	1.5 kg
	salt and pepper to taste	
3	medium onions, chopped	3
5	medium tomatoes, peeled and chopped	5
2 Tbsp	oil	25 mL
6 cups	water	1.5 L
3	chicken bouillon cubes	3
1 cup	chunky peanut butter	250 mL
1 Tbsp	tomato paste	15 mL

Season chicken with salt and pepper. Sauté chicken, onions and tomatoes gently in oil in a Dutch oven or large frying pan for 20 minutes. Dissolve bouillon cubes in 5 cups (1.25 L) hot water and add to chicken and vegetables. Simmer 5 minutes. Mix peanut butter, tomato paste and remaining 1 cup (250 mL) water. Add to chicken mixture. Cook, stirring frequently, until mixture comes to a boil. Simmer until chicken is cooked. Serve over rice. This is a heavy rich meal and is traditionally served with a tossed salad, sweet potatoes and lima beans. Beef may be substituted for chicken.

Serves: 6

Buffet Chicken 🍒

4	whole chicken breasts, split, boned and skinned	4
¼ cup	butter	50 mL
¼ cup	Dijon mustard	50 mL
2 Tbsp	prepared mustard	25 mL
½ cup	honey	125 mL
2 tsp	curry powder	10 mL
2 tsp	lemon or lime juice	10 mL
1 tsp	salt	5 mL
⅛ tsp	garlic powder, or 1 small garlic clove, chopped	0.5 mL

Preheat oven to 350°F (180°C). Place chicken in baking pan in a single layer. Melt butter in a saucepan and add remaining ingredients. Stir until smooth. Pour over chicken and bake uncovered at 350°F (180°C) 45 minutes, basting occasionally, until tender and golden. Garnish with watercress or parsley. May be served hot or cold.

Serves: 6

Chicken Artichoke Casserole

3	whole chicken breasts, split, boned and skinned	3
1½ tsp	salt	7 mL
¼ tsp	pepper	1 mL
½ tsp	paprika	2 mL
⅓ cup	butter	75 mL
1 can	(14 oz/398 mL) artichoke hearts, drained	1
¼ lb	mushrooms, sliced	125 g
2 Tbsp	all purpose flour	25 mL
⅔ cup	chicken stock	150 mL
3 Tbsp	sherry	50 mL
¼ tsp	rosemary	1 mL

Preheat oven to 375°F (190°C). Sprinkle salt, pepper and paprika over chicken. Brown chicken in butter and transfer to a 2 qt (2 L) casserole dish. Arrange artichoke hearts between chicken pieces. Sauté mushrooms in remaining butter in pan, until just tender. Sprinkle flour over mushrooms and stir in stock, sherry and rosemary. Cook stirring until slightly thickened and pour over chicken. Cover and bake at 375°F (190°C) for 40 minutes or until tender.

Can make ahead   **Serves: 4 to 6**

Chicken Breasts and Almonds
Attractive, inexpensive dish

3	whole chicken breasts, split	3
½ lb	mushrooms	250 g
¼ cup	butter or margarine	50 mL
4	slices bacon, diced	4
⅓ cup	flour, seasoned with salt and pepper	75 mL
2	scallions, thinly sliced	2
1 can	(10 oz/284 mL) chicken gravy	1
¼ cup	vermouth, chicken stock or cream	50 mL
¼ cup	slivered almonds, toasted	50 mL
	pepper to taste	

Preheat oven to 350°F (180°C). Wash and dry chicken breasts. Set aside. Melt 2 Tbsp (25 mL) butter in a large fry pan and add mushrooms. Sauté gently until they begin to brown. Remove mushrooms. Add bacon and cook until crisp. Remove bacon and pour off fat. Add 2 Tbsp (25 mL) butter to pan and melt. Toss chicken pieces (one at a time) in a bag with seasoned flour. Put in pan and cook until browned on both sides. Place chicken in oven-proof dish. Sprinkle mushrooms, bacon and scallions over chicken. Pour off any fat left in frying pan. Gently warm gravy in frying pan, scraping off bits on pan bottom. Add vermouth, broth or cream to gravy. Pour over chicken. Season with a little pepper. Bake covered at 350°F (180°C) 1 hour. Sprinkle with almonds before serving.

Can make ahead   **Serves: 6**

Coronada Casserole

1 can	(14 oz/398 mL) tomato sauce	1
½ cup	chicken stock	125 mL
1 cup	chopped onions	250 mL
1 can	(4 oz/114 mL) green chilies, drained and chopped	1
2 tsp	salt	10 mL
½ tsp	dried oregano leaves	2 mL
2½ cups	diced cooked chicken	625 mL
2½ cups	cooked rice	625 mL
1 cup	sour cream	250 mL
2 cups	grated Cheddar cheese	500 mL
1½ cups	crushed corn chips	375 mL

Preheat oven to 350°F (180°C). Combine tomato sauce, stock, onions, chilies and seasonings. Cook over low heat about 10 minutes. Add chicken and set aside. Mix rice and sour cream and spoon into buttered 8 cup (2 L) casserole. Sprinkle with 1 cup (250 mL) cheese. Pour chicken mixture over all. Top with remaining cheese. Sprinkle with corn chips. Bake at 350°F (180°C) 30 minutes.

Can make ahead　　**Can freeze**　　**Serves: 4 to 6**

Honey Glazed Chicken

6	chicken pieces (approximately 3 lb/1.5 kg)	6
2 Tbsp	butter or margarine	25 mL
⅓ cup	finely chopped onion	75 mL
⅔ cup	chicken stock	150 mL
⅓ cup	honey	75 mL
¼ cup	lemon juice	50 mL
2 Tbsp	soy or teriyaki sauce	25 mL

Rinse and dry chicken. Melt butter in Dutch oven or frying pan large enough to hold chicken in a single layer. Add chicken and brown on both sides. Combine remaining ingredients in saucepan and heat to boiling point. Pour over chicken, cover and cook at a gentle simmer for 45 minutes turning and basting chicken every 15 minutes, or until chicken is tender. If sauce is too thin, thicken with cornstarch, or remove chicken to hot platter and reduce sauce over high heat until desired consistency. Sauce should be very dark. Serve on a bed of rice.

Can make ahead　　**Serves: 4 to 6**

Chicken Almond Supreme
Expands for crowds!

1 cup	thinly sliced mushrooms	250 mL
2 tsp	butter	10 mL
2 cups	cooked, diced chicken	500 mL
1 cup	sliced water chestnuts	250 mL
2 Tbsp	butter	25 mL
3 Tbsp	flour	50 mL
2 cups	chicken stock	500 mL
⅔ cup	18% cream	150 mL
	salt and pepper to taste	
1 cup	almonds, slivered	250 mL

Preheat oven to 375°F (190°C). Sauté mushrooms in butter until just tender. Put ½ of the chicken in shallow 1½ qt (1.5 L) casserole. Add ½ mushrooms, then ½ water chestnuts. Repeat layers. Set aside. Melt 2 Tbsp (25 mL) butter, add flour and stir until smooth. Slowly add chicken stock and cream. Season to taste. Cook and stir constantly over medium high heat, until thickened. Pour sauce over chicken. Top with almonds. Bake at 375°F (190°C) until hot and bubbly and almonds are slightly browned, 20 to 30 minutes. Serve with rice or noodles.

Can make ahead   **Serves: 4 to 6**

Personalized Shake and Bake
You'll never buy it again

4 cups	dry bread crumbs	1 L
1 Tbsp	celery salt	15 mL
1 Tbsp	garlic salt	15 mL
1 Tbsp	paprika	15 mL
1 tsp	pepper	5 mL
½ cup	salad oil	125 mL

In a large bowl, thoroughly blend all ingredients. Refrigerate or freeze in plastic bag until needed.

NOTE: You may add one or more of the following seasonings depending on flavour and effect desired: dried oregano, dried parsley, poppy seeds, dried grated orange rind, sesame seeds or dried sweet basil.

Can freeze   **Yield: 4 cups (1 L)**

Hawaiian Chicken

4	whole chicken breasts, split, boned and skinned	4
1 tsp	salt	5 mL
1	egg, slightly beaten	1
1 cup	fine dry bread crumbs	250 mL
¼ inch	oil in fry pan	½ cm

SAUCE		
2½ cups	pineapple juice	625 mL
½ cup	lemon juice	125 mL
¼ cup	corn starch	50 mL
1½-2 tsp	curry powder	7-10 mL
¼ cup	sugar	

GARNISH	toasted almonds

Sprinkle chicken breasts with salt. Dip chicken breasts in egg and then in bread crumbs. Sauté in hot oil until lightly browned. Place chicken pieces in 9 x 13 inch (23 x 33 cm) baking pan.

SAUCE: In saucepan, combine pineapple juice and lemon juice. Combine corn starch, curry powder and sugar and stir into juices. Heat, over low heat, stirring constantly until thickened. Pour sauce over chicken and allow to stand for at least one hour to absorb flavour. Bake at 350°F (180°C) 1 hour. Sprinkle with toasted almonds to serve.

Must make ahead   **Serves: 8**

Japanese Chicken

6	whole chicken breasts, split, boned and skinned	6

MARINADE

6 Tbsp	soy sauce	100 mL
4	cloves garlic, chopped	4
¼ cup	sugar	50 mL
6 Tbsp	water	100 mL
¼ cup	sherry	50 mL
¼ cup	vinegar	50 mL
2	green onions, chopped	2
1	piece (2 inch/5 cm) ginger root, peeled and sliced	1

Combine all ingredients for marinade. Simmer 15 to 20 minutes. Pour over uncooked chicken in shallow baking dish. Marinate 3 to 4 hours turning each hour.
Preheat oven to 350°F (180°C). Remove ginger root. Bake, covered, at 350°F (180°C) 1 hour. Turn once during baking.

Must make ahead   **Serves: 8 to 10**

Marinated Chicken Breasts

2 cups	sour cream	500 mL
1	clove garlic, chopped	1
1 Tbsp	Worcestershire sauce	15 mL
1 tsp	Tabasco	5 mL
2 tsp	salt	10 mL
1½ tsp	paprika	7 mL
5	whole chicken breasts, split, boned and skinned	5
1½ cups	fresh bread crumbs	375 mL

GARNISH   **mushrooms and watercress**

Mix sour cream, garlic, Worcestershire sauce, Tabasco, salt and paprika. Coat each chicken piece with sauce. Place in shallow glass baking dish. Pour remaining sauce over chicken. Refrigerate overnight. Next day, roll chicken breasts in bread crumbs and place in buttered shallow baking pan, one layer deep. Cover and refrigerate at least 1½ hours. Preheat oven to 325°F (160°C). Bake uncovered for 1¼ hours. Garnish with mushrooms and watercress.

Must make ahead   **Serves: 8 to 10**

151

Sauces For Fowl

DARK MEAT (Duck, Pheasant, Partridge)

1 jar	(8 oz/250mL) red currant jelly	1
¼ lb	butter	125 g
½ cup	red wine	125 mL

WHITE MEAT

1 jar	(8 oz/250 mL) apple jelly	1
¼ lb .	butter	125 g
½ cup	white wine	125 mL

Combine jelly, butter and wine and heat. Serve in gravy boat.

Yield: 2 cups

Poultry Marinade

2 tsp	dried basil leaves	10 mL
1 tsp	paprika	5 mL
1 cup	oil	250 mL
½ cup	lemon juice	125 mL
1 Tbsp	salt	15 mL
	pepper to taste	
½ tsp	dried thyme leaves	2 mL
2 tsp	onion powder	10 mL
½ tsp	garlic powder	2 mL

Mix all ingredients. Place poultry and marinade in non-metal, shallow container. Refrigerate overnight, or at room temperature for 2-3 hours. HELPFUL HINT: Put poultry and marinade in tightly sealed plastic bag. Put in freezer. When defrosted—ready to cook.

Must make ahead   **Can freeze**   **Yield: 4 to 6 servings**

...designates "Company in a Minute"

UNIONVILLE HOUSE RESTAURANT
187 Main St., Unionville

Pork With Dijon Cream

6 oz	pork tenderloin	175 g
	clarified butter	
1 Tbsp	brandy	15 mL
1 Tbsp	dry white wine	15 mL
4 Tbsp	35% cream	50 mL
1 Tbsp	Dijon mustard	15 mL
	freshly ground pepper	

GARNISH   finely chopped fresh parsley

Divide pork into two medallions (flatten with heavy knife or side of wine bottle). Sauté pork in small amount of clarified butter using heavy pan. Once cooked, remove pork and hold in warm oven. Drain off excess butter. Deglaze pan with brandy and wine and reduce by half. Add cream and Dijon mustard. Whisk ingredients together until smooth. Reduce until sauce coats back of spoon and then remove from heat. Add ground pepper to taste. Serve Dijon sauce over the pork medallions and garnish with chopped parsley.

Serves: 1 to 2

B.B.Q. Spareribs

2 lb	spareribs (side ribs)	1 kg
2 tsp	sugar	10 mL
½ tsp	salt	2 mL
1	clove garlic, chopped	1
½ tsp	ground ginger	2 mL
2 Tbsp	soy sauce	25 mL
2 Tbsp	white wine	25 mL
1 Tbsp	Chinese hoisin sauce	15 mL
2 Tbsp	ketchup	25 mL
¼ cup	honey	50 mL

Place spareribs in large pan. Combine sugar, salt, garlic, ginger, soy sauce, wine, hoisin sauce and ketchup. Spread over spareribs and marinate 1 hour, or overnight, if preferred.

BARBECUE METHOD: Cook ribs on both sides. When almost done, baste with honey and cook for 2 to 3 more minutes on each side.

OVEN METHOD: Preheat oven to 350°F (180°C). Place ribs on rack in roasting pan, and bake 25 minutes. Turn ribs and bake 15 to 20 minutes more. Turn oven to broil, baste with honey and broil 2 to 3 minutes on each side. Can serve hot or cold. Try with chicken.

Must make ahead   **Serves: 4**

Luau Ribs

4 lb	spareribs	2 kg
	salt and pepper	
1 jar	(7½ oz/213 mL) junior apricots or peaches	1
⅓ cup	vinegar	75 mL
2 Tbsp	soy sauce	25 mL
⅓ cup	ketchup	75 mL
½ cup	brown sugar	125 mL
2	cloves garlic, chopped	2
2 tsp	ground ginger	10 mL

Preheat oven to 450°F (230°C). Cut ribs into serving portions and place meaty side up in foil-lined shallow pan. Salt and pepper lightly. Bake in preheated oven for 15 minutes. Spoon off fat. Reduce heat to 350°F (180°C). Mix together remaining ingredients to make sauce. Brush ⅓ of sauce over ribs and bake for 20 minutes. Turn ribs and brush with ⅓ more of sauce. Bake 20 minutes. Turn ribs again and brush with remaining sauce. Cook for further 20 minutes and serve.

Serves: 4 to 6

Pork Chops With Sour Cream
Your family will love these!

6	loin pork chops, trimmed	6
	salt and pepper to taste	
	flour for dredging	
2 Tbsp	vegetable oil	25 mL
½ cup	water	125 mL
1	bay leaf	1
2 Tbsp	wine vinegar	25 mL
1 Tbsp	brown sugar	15 mL
½ cup	sour cream or yogurt	125 mL
	paprika	

Preheat oven to 350°F (180°C). Season chops with salt and pepper and dredge lightly with flour. Brown on both sides in oil in fry pan. Transfer to greased 9 x 13 inch (22 x 33 cm) baking pan. Combine remaining ingredients and pour over chops. Cover with lid or foil (shiny side down) and bake at 350°F (180°C) 1¼ hours. Sprinkle with paprika.

Serves: 4 to 6

Sweet and Sour Spareribs
Easy and can do ahead!

3 lb	spareribs	2.5 kg
	salt and pepper to taste	
¾ cup	water	175 mL
1¼ cups	tomato juice	300 mL
½ cup	vinegar	125 mL
½ cup	white sugar	125 mL
½ pkg	dry onion soup mix	½
½ tsp	ground thyme	2 mL
1 tsp	dry mustard	5 mL
2 Tbsp	soy sauce	25 mL
1 Tbsp	Worcestershire sauce	15 mL

Preheat oven to 350°F (180°C). Layer spareribs in small roasting pan. Sprinkle with salt and pepper. Combine remaining ingredients and pour over ribs. Cover and braise in oven at 350°F (180°C) 2 hours. Remove spareribs to warm platter. Skim excess fat from sauce and if desired, thicken with a little cornstarch mixed with water. Serve sauce in a gravy boat.

Can make ahead   **Serves: 4**

Crown Roast of Pork with Sausage and Raisin Stuffing
A dramatic presentation!

1	**crown roast of pork, 16 chops**	1
	salt and pepper to taste	
	thyme to taste	

Preheat oven to 400°F (200°C). Have the butcher prepare the crown roast of pork, leaving a 2½ inch (6 cm) cavity. Sprinkle the pork well with salt, pepper and thyme. Fit an empty tin can (soup size), top and bottom lids removed, into the hollow centre. (It will help the inner part of the roast to brown.) Cover the rib ends of the chops with foil. Place roast in a pan just large enough to hold it and roast at 400°F (200°C) for 20 minutes. Reduce the heat to 325°F (160°C) and roast the pork for 40 minutes more. Take the pork from oven and remove the tin can. Return pork to oven and roast for 1 hour and 20 minutes more or until meat thermometer registers 175°F (85°C). Transfer the roast to a warm, round serving platter and place stuffing in cavity. Remove the foil from the rib ends of the chops and replace it with paper frills. Keep the roast warm until serving.

SAUSAGE AND RAISIN STUFFING

2 cups	**fresh bread, cubed**	500 mL
⅓ cup	**milk**	75 mL
½ cup	**minced onion**	125 mL
2 Tbsp	**butter**	25 mL
½ lb	**pork sausage meat**	250 g
¾ cup	**chopped celery**	175 mL
¼ cup	**raisins**	50 mL
¼ cup	**chopped raw cranberries**	50 mL
2	**tart apples, peeled and diced**	2
	salt, pepper, sage and thyme to taste	

In a small bowl, moisten the fresh bread cubes with milk. Squeeze dry. In a skillet, sauté the minced onion in butter until soft but not coloured. Add sausage meat and sauté until lightly brown. Add celery, raisins, cranberries and apples and cook the mixture for 5 minutes. Transfer the contents of the skillet to a large bowl. Add the bread cubes and mix well. Season with salt, pepper, sage and thyme to taste. Fill cavity of warm roast with stuffing.

Yield: 4 cups (1 L)

ALTERNATE PRESENTATION: Cook the crown roast as directed. When roast is finished, remove foil from the rib ends of chops. Fill the cavity with watercress or parsley and place a crabapple on the end of each chop. Decorate the platter with watercress or parsley and more crabapples.

Serves: 8

Apricot Stuffed Pork Tenderloin

½ cup	dried apricots, chopped finely	125 mL
	cold water to cover	
3 Tbsp	butter or margarine	50 mL
2 Tbsp	finely chopped onion	25 mL
1½ cups	soft white bread crumbs	375 mL
1 tsp	dried parsley	5 mL
¼ tsp	salt	1 mL
¼ tsp	ground thyme	1 mL
2	pork tenderloin (approximately ¾ lb/375 g each)	2
	soft butter or margarine	
	salt and pepper to taste	

Preheat oven to 325°F (160°C). Cover apricots with cold water. Heat until boiling. Cover and reduce heat. Simmer until tender 5 to 10 minutes. Drain. Sauté onion in (3 Tbsp/50 mL) butter until soft. Add crumbs, parsley, salt and thyme. Toss lightly to combine and mix in cooled apricots. Slit tenderloins lengthwise, not quite through. Lay tenderloins flat and spread each one with half the apricot mixture. Roll lengthwise; like a jelly roll. Tie to secure. (If preferred, place stuffing between two tenderloins and tie securely.) Place on rack in small pan and spread with butter or margarine. Sprinkle with salt and pepper. Bake at 325°F (160°C) 1 to 1¼ hours, basting occasionally. Garnish with spiced crabapples and watercress or parsley.

Can make ahead   **Serves: 4**

Barbecue Sauce

Perfect complement for ribs, chicken, steak or roast

½ cup	brown sugar, packed	125 mL
1 Tbsp	corn starch	15 mL
1 tsp	chili powder	5 mL
1 can	(7½ oz/213 mL) tomato sauce	1
½ cup	vinegar	125 mL
½ cup	ketchup	125 mL
½ cup	dark corn syrup	125 mL
½ cup	water	125 mL
¼ cup	orange liqueur	50 mL

In a saucepan, combine brown sugar, corn starch and chili powder. Stir in tomato sauce, vinegar, ketchup, corn syrup and water. Bring mixture to boil and reduce heat. Simmer uncovered for 30 minutes. Stir in orange liqueur. Simmer uncovered 5 minutes more.
For best results, partially barbeque meat before basting. Dilute a little sauce with some water for the first basting so the meat will not burn. Baste meat several times. Heat some extra sauce to spoon over each portion.

Can make ahead   **Yield: 3 cups (750 mL)**

Veal Marsala

Great for unexpected guests

½ lb	veal scallops	250 g
	salt and pepper	
	flour for dredging	
2 Tbsp	butter	25 mL
3 Tbsp	olive oil	50 mL
½ cup	Marsala wine	125 mL
½ cup	chicken stock	125 mL
2 Tbsp	soft butter	25 mL

Preheat oven to 350°F (180°C). Season veal with salt and pepper. Dredge with flour. Fry in 2 Tbsp (25 mL) butter and oil until brown, approximately 3 minutes on each side. Remove veal and transfer to casserole. Add wine and stock to fry pan. Boil 2 minutes, scraping bits from bottom of pan. Return veal to pan and simmer 10 to 15 minutes. Remove veal again and boil sauce until reduced by half. Add 2 Tbsp (25 mL) butter to sauce and pour over veal. Can be made day ahead and reheated in oven at serving time at 350°F (180°C) for ½ hour.

Can make ahead   **Serves: 4**

Vitello Alla Parmigiana
Veal Parmesan

¼ cup	butter	50 mL
¼ cup	finely chopped onion	50 mL
¼ cup	olive oil	50 mL
2	cloves garlic, chopped	2
3 cans	(7½ oz/213 mL, each) tomato sauce	3
1 lb	thinly sliced veal scallops	500 g
⅔ cup	fine bread crumbs	150 mL
⅔ cup	grated Parmesan cheese	150 mL
¼ cup	all purpose flour	50 mL
2	eggs, slightly beaten	2
8-12 slices	Mozzarella cheese	8-12
	parsley	

Preheat oven to 350°F (180°C). Heat 2 Tbsp (25 mL) each of butter and oil in fry pan. Sauté onions and garlic for 5 minutes. Add tomato sauce. Cover and simmer 10 to 15 minutes, stirring occasionally. Set aside. Cut veal into medallions. Combine bread crumbs and grated cheese. Set aside. Dip veal pieces in flour, then egg, then breadcrumb-cheese mixture. Pan fry in remaining 2 Tbsp (25 mL) each of butter and oil until golden brown. Arrange overlapping pieces of veal and Mozzarella cheese in 9 x 13 inch (23 x 33 cm) baking dish. Pour tomato sauce over top. (If making ahead, refrigerate at this point until ready to bake.) Cover with foil and bake at 350°F (180°C) until bubbly, about 25 minutes. Remove foil, bake 5 minutes longer. Garnish with parsley and pass additional Parmesan cheese.

Can make ahead   **Serves: 4 to 6**

Veal in Yogurt

½ cup	olive oil	125 mL
4	large veal scallops	4
	flour for dredging	
	salt and pepper	
1 cup	beef stock	250 mL
½ cup	dry white wine	125 mL
¼ cup	chopped parsley	50 mL
3	garlic cloves, chopped	3
2 Tbsp	red wine vinegar	25 mL
¼ tsp	dried marjoram leaves	1 mL
¼ tsp	dried thyme leaves	1 mL
½ cup	yogurt	125 mL
2 Tbsp	all purpose flour	25 mL

Preheat oven to 300°F (150°C). Heat olive oil in fry pan until hot. Combine flour, salt and pepper. Dredge scallops in flour and fry 2 minutes on each side until brown. Transfer meat to casserole. Add beef stock, wine, parsley, garlic, vinegar, marjoram and thyme to fry pan. Bring to boil, remove from heat and stir in yogurt combined with 2 Tbsp (25 mL) flour. Pour over veal and bake 1 hour.

Serves: 4

Veal Capriccio

12	veal scallops, very thin	12
12	slices prosciutto ham, very thin	12
	flour	
¼ cup	butter, clarified	50 mL
2 cups	sliced mushrooms	500 mL
pinch	paprika	pinch
	salt and pepper	
2½ cups	Marsala wine	625 mL
12	thin slices Mozarella cheese	12

GARNISH

12	pimento strips	12
	chopped parsley	

Place a slice of prosciutto on each veal scallop and pound between sheets of waxed paper. Dust with flour and sauté in clarified butter in large skillet, prosciutto side down. Turn and brown other side and transfer to a heated dish to keep warm. In same skillet, sauté mushrooms until brown, adding more butter if necessary. Add paprika, salt and pepper to taste and pour in wine. Bring to boil and reduce over high heat for 15 minutes. Transfer sauce to a large serving dish and arrange scallops, prosciutto side up, on top of sauce. Place cheese slice on each scallop. (May be prepared up to this point the day before. Bring to room temperature before broiling.) Broil until cheese is melted. Garnish with a strip of pimento and sprinkling of parsley. Excellent served with buttered green noodles and carrots. NOTE: Marsala wine sweetness best about #8.

Can make ahead   **Serves: 6**

The Honourable Steak

6 lb	sirloin steak (2 inch/5 cm) thick	2.75 kg
¼ cup	prepared or Dijon mustard	50 mL
1	medium Spanish onion, sliced	1
1 lb	mushrooms, sliced	500 g
½ cup	chili sauce	125 mL
1 Tbsp	Worcestershire sauce	15 mL
1 tsp	paprika	5 mL
½ tsp	salt	2 mL
⅛ tsp	pepper	0.5 mL
2 Tbsp	butter	25 mL
6	green pepper rings	6

Preheat oven to 400°F (200°C). Spread both sides of meat with mustard. Place in shallow roasting pan. Put onions and mushrooms on top. Add sauces, paprika, salt pepper and dot with butter. Bake at 400°F (200°C) 50 minutes for rare, 60 minutes for medium rare. Add green peppers 10 minutes before cooking time is completed. To serve, slice on an angle against the grain.

Serves: 6 to 8

Chinese Steak

2 cups	long grain rice, uncooked	500 mL
3 lb	ground beef	1.5 kg
2	large onions, chopped	2
3	green peppers, chopped	3
3 cans	(10 oz/284 mL each) sliced mushrooms	3
½ cup	soy sauce	125 mL
2 cans	(10 oz/284 mL each) consommé (undiluted)	2
3 Tbsp	plum sauce	50 mL
½ cup	sliced almonds, toasted	125 mL

Preheat oven to 350°F (180°C). Cook rice according to package directions. Brown beef, remove from skillet. Sauté onions, green peppers and mushrooms in beef fat. Combine vegetables, soy sauce, consommé, plum sauce, beef and cooked rice in a large casserole. Bake, uncovered, at 350°F (180°C) ½ hour. Sprinkle almonds on top.

Can make ahead   **Can freeze**   **Serves: 14**

Beef Steak and Kidney Pie
A good old Maritime recipe!

1	fresh kidney	1
¼ cup	vegetable oil	50 mL
2	medium onions, chopped	2
2	cloves garlic, chopped	2
2 lb	stewing beef, cut in ¾ inch (1 cm) cubes	1 kg
3¼ cups	boiling water	800 mL
3 Tbsp	Worcestershire sauce	50 mL
½ tsp	each dried thyme and oregano leaves	2 mL
2	bay leaves	2
	salt and pepper to taste	
3 Tbsp	all purpose flour	50 mL
3 Tbsp	butter, softened	50 mL
	puff pastry (frozen variety can be used) for crust	

Simmer kidney in saucepan with small quantity of water for 30 minutes. Drain, cool and cut off outside membrane. Cut into cubes, discarding all fat and tough sections. In Dutch oven, sauté onions and garlic in oil until soft. Remove from pan. Brown beef cubes in same pan and remove. Brown kidney cubes and remove. To the drippings in the pan, add 3¼ cups (800 mL) boiling water, Worcestershire sauce, thyme, oregano, bay leaves, salt and pepper. Add meats, onion and garlic. Cover pot with tight fitting lid and simmer 1½ to 2 hours until meat is very tender. Add more water if necessary. Remove bay leaves. Blend flour and butter. Stir into meat mixture to thicken. Pour mixture into a deep dish casserole. Can make ahead to this point. Top with puff pastry. Bake at 400°F (200°C) or until pastry is browned.

Can make ahead   **Serves: 6**

Brisket in Beer

3-4 lb	beef brisket	1.5-2 kg
	salt and pepper to taste	
1	onion, sliced	1
¼ cup	chili sauce	50 mL
2 Tbsp	brown sugar	25 mL
1	clove garlic, chopped	1
1½ cups	beer	375 mL
2 Tbsp	flour	25 mL
½ cup	water	125 mL

Preheat oven to 350°F (180°C). Season brisket with salt and pepper and place in 9 x 13 inch (23 x 33 cm) baking pan. Cover with onion slices. In bowl, combine chili sauce, brown sugar, garlic and beer. Pour over meat and cover with foil. Bake at 350°F (180°C) 3½ hours. Uncover and bake 30 minutes longer, basting occasionally. Remove meat to platter and skim excess fat from drippings. Measure drippings and add water to make 1 cup (250 mL). Blend flour with ½ cup (125 mL) water and combine with pan drippings. Cook, stirring constantly over medium heat until thickened and bubbly. To serve, slice meat across grain and serve with gravy.

Serves: 8

All Day Beef Roast
Serves a family or a crowd!

6-20 lb	sirloin or rump roast of beef	3-9 kg
	seasonings to taste	

Preheat oven to 375°F (190°C). Place beef in oven and roast 1 hour. Turn off heat and leave beef in oven all day or until oven is completely cool, approximately 4 hours. Remove. One hour before serving, preheat oven to 375°F (190°C). Place meat in oven again and roast 35 minutes for medium rare, 45 minutes for well done.

Sauerbraten
Red cabbage and potato dumplings complete this dish

4 lb	rump roast of beef	2 kg
MARINADE		
2 tsp	salt	10 mL
½ tsp	pepper	2 mL
¼ cup	brown sugar	50 mL
1	medium onion, sliced	1
3	bay leaves	3
1 tsp	peppercorns	5 mL
1 cup	water	250 mL
1 cup	vinegar	250 mL
1 Tbsp	butter	15 mL
SAUCE		
¼ cup	brown sugar	50 mL
¼ cup	seedless raisins	50 mL
6	ginger snaps, crushed	6
1 cup	sour cream	250 mL

Combine marinade ingredients in saucepan and bring to boil. Place roast in a glass dish. Pour marinade over meat and refrigerate 36 to 48 hours, turning several times. Reserve marinade. In large sauce pan or Dutch oven, brown meat. Pour in marinade and simmer covered, for 2 to 2½ hours, until meat is tender. Remove meat, strain marinade into saucepan and add remaining sauce ingredients, stirring in sour cream last. Pour over meat to serve.

Can make ahead   **Serves: 8 to 10**

Whole Beef Tenderloin
A foolproof method

Preheat oven to 500°F (260°C). Place roast in oven for 5 minutes. Turn heat off and leave in oven for ½ hour for medium rare.

Beef Rouladen

8 pieces	beef rouladen, flank or inside round steak (2 to 3 lbs/1 to 1.5 kg)	8
	Dijon mustard	
	salt and pepper	
8	slices bacon	8
1	onion, chopped	1
	dill pickles, thinly sliced	
2 Tbsp	vegetable oil	25 mL
2	onions, sliced	2
3 Tbsp	sour cream	50 mL
½ cup	sliced mushrooms	125 mL

Preheat oven to 350°F (180°C). Flatten each piece of steak, using a mallet and spread with mustard, salt and pepper. Place one strip of bacon, a few onions and a slice of dill pickle on each steak. Roll up and skewer each steak with toothpicks. Place oil and sliced onions in an oven-proof casserole and add rouladen in single layer. Cover pan and bake at 350°F (180°C) for 1 hour. Add sour cream and mushrooms and reduce heat to 300°F (150°C) for another half hour. For additional gravy, add a little water at intervals during cooking.

Serves: 4

Fast and Easy Meat Loaf

1 lb	medium ground beef	500 g
1 lb	lean ground pork	500 g
1 pkg	(35 g) onion soup mix	1
1	egg, beaten	1
	salt and pepper to taste	
2 cups	sour cream	500 mL

Preheat oven to 350°F (180°C). Mix together all ingredients and bake exactly one hour. Good hot or cold.

Can make ahead   **Can freeze**   **Serves: 6**

Spiced Beef

9-10 lb	sirloin tip or round steak roast	4-5 kg
6 Tbsp	saltpetre	75 mL
¾ cup	brown sugar	175 mL
4 Tbsp	ground cloves	50 mL
1 bottle	(1¼ oz/44 g) ground allspice	1
2	whole nutmegs, grated	2
½ cup	salt	125 mL

Mix spices together. Place meat in covered roasting pan or crock. Rub meat with spices, cover and store in a cool spot for 3 weeks, occasionally turning meat and basting with accumulated juices and spices.

COOKING METHOD 1: Roast, uncovered at 350°F (180°C) approximately 2½ to 3 hours or until meat thermometer registers 140°F (60°C) for rare meat.

COOKING METHOD 2: Using a deep pot, cover meat with water and bring to a boil, covered. Boil 5 to 10 minutes. Turn off heat and leave overnight.

NOTE: Saltpetre may be purchased at a drug store.

Must make ahead   **Serves: 20-25**

Mustard Sauce
Serve either hot or cold with ham

5 Tbsp	white sugar	75 mL
2 tsp	mustard powder	10 mL
2	egg yolks	2
5 Tbsp	cider vinegar	75 mL
2 Tbsp	butter	25 mL

In top of small double boiler, mix sugar and mustard. Whisk in egg yolks. Add vinegar and mix thoroughly. Place over boiling water. Add the butter and whisk constantly until butter is melted and sauce is thickened, approximately 10 minutes. Recipe can be doubled or tripled.

Yield: 1 cup (250 mL)

Beef and Wild Rice Casserole

1 cup	wild rice	250 mL
3 cups	boiling water	750 mL
2 Tbsp	oil	25 mL
1½ lb	ground beef	750 g
1	medium onion, chopped	1
1 can	(10 oz/284 mL) cream of mushroom soup	1
1 can	(10 oz/284 mL) cream of chicken soup	1
1 can	(10 oz/284 mL) consommé	1
1 cup	water	250 mL
½ tsp	salt	2 mL
½ tsp	pepper	2 mL
¼ tsp	celery salt	1 mL
¼ tsp	garlic powder	1 mL
¼ tsp	paprika	1 mL
1 Tbsp	poultry seasoning	15 mL
2 Tbsp	chopped parsley	25 mL
½ cup	toasted almonds	125 mL

Preheat oven to 325°F (160°C). Pour boiling water over rice and let stand 25 minutes. Drain. Brown beef and onion in oil. Drain well. Mix together all remaining ingredients except almonds. Combine with meat, onion and rice and put in large (3 qt/3 L) greased casserole. Cover and bake at 325°F (160°C) 2½ to 3 hours. Sprinkle with almonds last 10 minutes of baking.

VARIATIONS: This recipe can be made without meat by substituting 1 lb (500 g) sliced mushrooms for beef. Serve mushroom-wild rice casserole with chicken or duck.

Can make ahead   **Can freeze**   **Serves: 6 to 8**

Fast Fabulous Beef Curry
A recipe from the Far East

1½ lb	round steak, trimmed and cubed	750 g
1	medium onion, chopped	1
2 Tbsp	butter	25 mL
2 cups	water	500 mL
1 Tbsp	sugar	15 mL
1 tsp	salt	5 mL
2-3 Tbsp	grated coconut	25-50 mL
1 Tbsp	curry powder	15 mL
2 Tbsp	flour	25 mL
¼ cup	water	50 mL

GARNISH:	grated sharp Cheddar cheese
	chutney
	coconut
	grape jelly
	ground salted peanuts
	currants (soaked in warm water to soften)

In large skillet or electric frypan, brown steak and onion in butter. Add water, sugar, salt, coconut and curry. Cover and simmer one hour. Mix flour and water together and add to frypan. Mix in well and bring back to boil allowing sauce to thicken. Serve with rice and a salad and all or some of the above condiments.

Can make ahead   **Serves: 4 to 6**

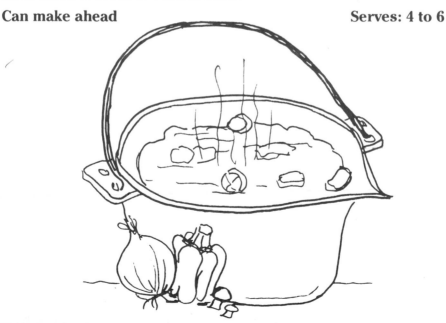

Steak Au Poivre 🍒

4	New York strip steaks, 1¼ inch (3 cm) thick	4
2 Tbsp	black peppercorns, crushed	25 mL
	salt to taste	
¼ cup	butter	50 mL
¼ cup	dry red wine	50 mL
¼ cup	Cognac	50 mL
½ cup	beef stock	125 mL
¼ cup	whipping cream	50 mL

Press crushed peppercorns and a pinch of salt into each side of steak. Melt butter in a hot pan and brown steaks quickly on both sides. Continue cooking until medium rare or desired degree of doneness. Remove to heated platter. Add wine and Cognac to pan juices and simmer 2 minutes, stirring constantly. Add stock and simmer 2 minutes longer. Blend in cream and simmer to desired consistency. Pour over steaks and serve.

BARBECUE METHOD: Barbecue steaks over hot coals to medium rare. Simmer wine, Cognac and stock over low heat, uncovered, 5 minutes. Add 1 tsp (5 mL) crushed peppercorns, if desired. Blend in cream and simmer until sauce is desired consistency. Pour over steaks and serve.

Serves: 4

Unusual Mint Sauce

2	green peppers, chopped	2
6	large onions, chopped	6
2 lb	apples, chopped	1 kg
¾ lb	Sultana raisins	375 g
1 oz	mustard seed	28 g
1¼ cups	chopped mint	300 mL
2 Tbsp	salt	25 mL
2½ lb	sugar	1.25 kg
1 qt	malt vinegar	1 L

In large crock or bowl, place green peppers, onions, apples, raisins, mustard seed and mint. Mix together salt, sugar and vinegar. Pour over fruit and vegetable mixture. Cover and let stand 1 week. Bottle in sterilized jars.

Yield: 6 cups (1.5 L)

Barbecued Leg of Lamb
Tomato sauce makes this interesting

2 Tbsp	Dijon mustard	25 mL
2 Tbsp	tarragon vinegar	25 mL
2 Tbsp	olive oil	25 mL
7 lb	leg of lamb, trimmed, boned and butterflied	3.5 kg
	salt and pepper to taste	

BASTING SAUCE

4 cups	tomato sauce	1 L
2 Tbsp	Worcestershire sauce	25 mL
¼ tsp	celery salt	1 mL
1	garlic clove, chopped	1
1	small onion, chopped	1
2 Tbsp	medium dry sherry	25 mL
2 Tbsp	red wine vinegar	25 mL
1 Tbsp	olive oil	15 mL
	salt and pepper to taste	

Combine mustard, vinegar and oil. Place the lamb, boned side up, in a glass baking dish just large enough to hold it. Season with salt and pepper. Spread with mustard mixture and marinate, covered, at room temperature for several hours or in refrigerator overnight. Combine ingredients for the basting sauce. Grill lamb, basting liberally with sauce. Turn every 10 minutes, for 45 minutes, or until meat thermometer registers 140°F (65°C) for medium-rare meat. Transfer lamb to a cutting board. Let rest 10 minutes. Carve across the grain. Serve with remaining basting sauce.

Serves: 10

Stuffed Leg of Lamb
An elegant company main course

10 oz	fresh leaf spinach (or 1-10 oz/284 g bag)	284 g
¼ cup	firmly packed parsley leaves	50 mL
2	medium garlic cloves	2
2 oz	proscuitto, cut in ½ inch chunks	60 g
2-3	slices fresh white bread, torn in pieces	2-3
¼ cup	olive oil	50 mL
¼ tsp	each dried marjoram, savory, rosemary, thyme crushed	1 mL
	salt and freshly ground pepper to taste	
5-7 lb	leg of lamb, boned, butterflied and trimmed (boned weight about 4 lb/ 2 kg.)	2.3-3 kg

Preheat oven to 425°F (220°C). Cook spinach stirring frequently, over medium heat in a 4 qt (4 L) Dutch oven until spinach wilts, about 5 minutes. Drain. Rinse spinach with cold water and squeeze very dry with your hands. Insert metal knife blade in food processor container. Process parsley 20 seconds, add garlic cloves and continue processing until both are finely chopped; scrape down container side. Add proscuitto and partially chop with 6 to 8 two second pulses. Add bread and chop with 6 one second pulses. Add spinach and chop with 8 to 10 one second pulses. Add 2 Tbsp (25 mL) oil, herbs, salt and pepper to taste. Rub lamb inside and out with remaining oil. Sprinkle inside lightly with salt and pepper. Put stuffing into space taken up by bone. Roll up leg so it resumes its shape and tie securely with kitchen twine. If desired, refrigerate 24 to 48 hours before cooking. Remove from refrigerator one hour before cooking. Adjust oven rack to lowest position, and roast, fat side up at 425°F (220°C) 10 minutes. Turn lamb over and roast 10 minutes more. Reduce oven to 325°F (160°C). Continue roasting 50 minutes. Meat thermometer should register 125°F to 130°F (55°C) for medium rare. Remove lamb from oven and cover pan tightly with foil. Set aside 15 minutes to rest before removing strings and slicing.

Can make ahead   **Serves: 6 to 8**

Lamb Chops with Orange Mustard Butter 🍒
Use the butter with vegetables for a nice change

8	loin lamb chops, ¾ inch (2 cm) thick	8
2 Tbsp	vegetable oil	25 mL
	freshly ground pepper	
1 Tbsp	dried rosemary leaves, divided	15 mL

ORANGE MUSTARD BUTTER

¼ cup	butter, room temperature	50 mL
2 Tbsp	Dijon mustard	25 mL
	grated rind of 1 orange	

Brush oil on both sides of chops. Sprinkle with pepper. Set aside ½ tsp (2 mL) rosemary for butter. Sprinkle remaining rosemary on chops. Place chops on broiler pan. Broil 6 inch (15 cm) from broiler 3 to 4 minutes per side depending on thickness. Meanwhile, stir together butter, mustard, orange rind and reserved ½ tsp (2 mL) rosemary. Place about 1 Tbsp (15 mL) butter mixture on top of each chop after broiling. Serve immediately.

Serves: 4

Lamb Shish Kebab

1	leg of lamb, boned and cubed	1

MARINADE

½ cup	water	125 mL
½ cup	vinegar	125 mL
3	garlic cloves, chopped	3
1	large onion, chopped	1
1 tsp	pepper	5 mL
1 Tbsp	salt	15 mL
	mushrooms	
	green pepper	
	onions	
	zucchini	
	cherry tomatoes	

Mix marinade ingredients. Pour over lamb cubes and marinate for 48 hours, turning several times. Thread skewers, alternating vegetables and lamb. Barbecue approximately 15 minutes or to desired doneness.

Serves: 8

Liver and Onions Supreme

½ lb	bacon	250 g
¼ cup	all purpose flour	50 mL
1 tsp	dry mustard	5 mL
	salt, pepper and Accent	
1 lb	liver, thinly sliced	500 g
1	large onion, chopped or sliced	1

Preheat oven to 325°F (160°C). Fry bacon until crisp. Drain on paper towel. Reserve bacon fat. Mix flour, mustard, salt, pepper and Accent in a small bag. Shake liver in bag, one piece at a time, until well coated. Sauté liver quickly on each side in hot bacon fat, turning just as it starts to brown, but do not cook through. When lightly browned place pieces in 5 x 9 inch (13 x 23 cm) baking dish. Sauté onion in remaining fat until it begins to brown. Spoon onions and all remaining juices over liver. Cover tightly (may use tin foil) and bake at 325°F (160°C) 1 hour. Remove cover for the last 10 minutes and lay bacon on top to heat.

Serves: 3 to 4

Liver with Fresh Herbs

1½ lb	calves or baby beef liver	750 g
1	onion, thinly sliced	1
2 Tbsp	vegetable oil	25 mL
2 Tbsp	butter	25 mL
½ inch	piece ginger root, thinly sliced	1.3 cm
1 Tbsp	finely chopped shallots or green onions	15 mL
1	sweet red pepper, julienned	1
1	green pepper, julienned	1
1 Tbsp	fresh, chopped rosemary	15 mL
2 tsp	fresh chopped savory or sage	10 mL
	generous pinch of salt and cayenne pepper	
½	lemon	½

Slice liver into strips (½ x 2 inch/1 x 5 cm). Set aside. Separate onion into rings. Heat oil and butter in wok, add onion, ginger and shallots. Stir fry over medium-low heat 5 minutes. Turn heat to high, add liver strips, peppers, herbs and seasonings. Stir fry about 2 to 3 minutes until liver is cooked. Squeeze lemon juice over all and serve immediately with rice and a salad.

Serves: 4

...designates "Company in a Minute"

OLIVER'S OLD FASHIONED BAKERY
2433 Yonge St., Toronto

Oliver's Awesome Cookies

1 cup	unsalted butter	250 mL
1 cup	chunky peanut butter	250 mL
1 cup	brown sugar	250 mL
1 cup	white sugar	250 mL
½ cup	corn syrup	125 mL
2	eggs	2
1½ tsp	almond extract	7 mL
3½ cups	all purpose flour	875 mL
1 tsp	baking soda	5 mL
1 tsp	salt	5 mL
1 pkg	(12 oz/350 mL) chocolate chips	1
1 cup	unsalted peanuts, coarsely chopped	250 mL

Preheat oven to 350°F (180°C). Cream unsalted butter, peanut butter, brown sugar and white sugar. Add corn syrup, eggs and almond, and beat until light. Add dry ingredients and blend well. Mix in chocolate and peanuts. Drop by heaping tablespoonsful onto baking sheet. Bake at 350°F (180°C) 10 minutes.

Yield: 36 awesome cookies

Lace Cookies

2¼ cups	quick-cooking rolled oats	550 mL
2½ cups	brown sugar	625 mL
3 Tbsp	flour	50 mL
1 tsp	salt	5 mL
1 cup	melted butter	250 mL
1	egg, lightly beaten	1
1 tsp	vanilla	5 mL

Preheat oven to 375°F (190°C). Mix rolled oats, brown sugar, flour and salt. Add butter, egg and vanilla and mix well. Drop from a teaspoon onto ungreased teflon cookie sheet leaving large spaces between each cookie as they spread during baking. Bake at 375°F (190°C) 7 minutes. Let stand 1 to 2 minutes until cookies begin to harden. Remove from pan.

Can freeze   **Yield: 5 to 6 dozen**

Almond Cookies

1 cup	butter	250 mL
½ cup	brown sugar	125 mL
½ cup	white sugar	125 mL
1	egg	1
1 Tbsp	almond extract	15 mL
2 cups	all purpose flour	500 mL
½ tsp	baking soda	2 mL
2 tsp	cream of tartar	10 mL
¾ cup	ground almonds	175 mL

Preheat oven to 375°F (190°C). Cream butter and sugars together until soft. Add egg and almond extract. Mix well and add flour, baking soda, cream of tartar and ground almonds. Roll into small balls and place on ungreased cookie sheet. Press lightly with fork. Bake at 375°F (190°C) 8 to 10 minutes until golden.

Can freeze   **Yield: 3 to 4 dozen**

Chocolate Covered Cherry Cookies
A cookie with a hidden treat!

1½ cups	all purpose flour	375 mL
½ cup	cocoa	125 mL
¼ tsp	salt	1 mL
¼ tsp	baking powder	1 mL
¼ tsp	baking soda	1 mL
½ cup	butter, softened	125 mL
1 cup	sugar	250 mL
1	egg	1
1½ tsp	vanilla	2 mL
24	maraschino cherries	24
1 pkg	(6 oz/175 g) chocolate chips	1
½ cup	sweetened condensed milk	125 mL
4 tsp	maraschino cherry juice	20 mL

Preheat oven to 350°F (180°C). Sift together flour, cocoa, salt, baking powder and baking soda. Set aside. In large bowl, cream butter and sugar. Add egg and vanilla. Mix in dry ingredients, combining well. Shape dough into 1 inch (2.5 cm) balls and place on ungreased cookie sheet. Press down centre of each ball with your thumb and place half a cherry in each centre. In small saucepan over medium heat combine chocolate chips and condensed milk, stirring frequently until chocolate has melted. Stir in cherry juice. Spoon 1 tsp (5 mL) chocolate frosting over each cherry, covering cherry completely. If frosting seems too thick, add more cherry juice. Bake at 350°F (180°C) 10 minutes. Remove to wire rack and cool.

Can make ahead   **Yield: 4 dozen**

Corn Flake Toffee Balls
For the Christmas cookie platter

5 Tbsp	butter, softened	75 mL
2½ cups	icing sugar	625 mL
2 bars	(2 oz/56 g each) Macintosh toffee	2
¼ cup	cream	50 mL
2 cups	crushed corn flakes	500 mL

Cream butter. Add up to 2½ cups icing sugar. Form into very small balls and refrigerate. Melt toffee in double boiler and add cream. Dip chilled balls into warm toffee and roll in crushed corn flakes to coat.

Can make ahead   **Can freeze**   **Yield: 4 to 5 dozen**

Chocolate Chocolate Chip Cookies
For the chocoholic

2 squares	(2 oz/60 g) unsweetened chocolate	2
6 squares	(6 oz/180 g) semi-sweet chocolate	6
2 Tbsp	butter	25 mL
¼ cup	sifted all purpose flour	50 mL
¼ tsp	baking powder	1 mL
⅛ tsp	salt	0.5 mL
2	eggs	2
¾ cup	sugar	175 mL
½ tsp	vanilla	2 mL
1 cup	chocolate chips	250 mL
8 oz	chopped pecans (optional)	250 g

Preheat oven to 350°F (180°C). Place oven rack one-third of the way down in oven. Melt chocolate squares and butter over hot water and stir gently. Sift flour, baking powder and salt. Beat together eggs, sugar and vanilla. Add melted chocolate and sifted ingredients to egg mixture. Add chocolate chips and nuts. Mixture will look too runny for a cookie mixture but when baked will be perfect. Cover cookie sheets with aluminum foil, shiny side down. Drop cookie mixture from teaspoon, one dozen on each sheet. Bake at 350°F (180°C) 10 minutes. Remove from oven and let cool before removing cookies from foil.

Can freeze **Yield: 3 dozen**

Oatmeal Cookies

1 cup	butter or margarine	250 mL
½ cup	brown sugar	125 mL
1 tsp	vanilla	5 mL
1 cup	all purpose flour	250 mL
½ tsp	baking soda	2 mL
2 cups	quick cooking rolled oats	500 mL

Preheat oven to 350°F (180°C). Combine butter or margarine, brown sugar and vanilla and beat until fluffy. Combine flour and soda and add to first mixture. Add rolled oats. Drop from a teaspoon onto ungreased cookie sheets. Flatten with a fork. Bake in 350°F (180°C) oven 8 to 10 minutes.

Can freeze **Yield: 3½ dozen**

Ginger Shortbread
A delightful change from plain shortbread

1 cup	butter, room temperature	250 mL
½ cup	fruit sugar or brown sugar	125 mL
2 cups	all purpose flour	500 mL
⅓ cup	candied ginger, chopped	75 mL

Preheat oven to 325°F (160°C). In mixing bowl, cream butter well. Blend in sugar gradually, beating well. Blend in flour gradually with a wooden spoon. Add candied ginger and mix. Form mixture into a ball and knead on a lightly floured board just until smooth. Pat dough into an ungreased 9 inch (23 cm) round pie plate. Prick surface with fork and mark wedges lightly with knife. Bake at 325°F (160°C) 20 to 25 minutes or until lightly browned. Store in tightly covered cookie tin.

Can freeze **Yield: 16**

Raisin Drop Cookies
These soft cookies are a great favourite

2 cups	raisins	500 mL
1 cup	water	250 mL
1 tsp	baking soda	5 mL
2 cups	sugar	500 mL
1 cup	vegetable oil	250 mL
1 tsp	vanilla	5 mL
3	eggs	3
4 cups	all purpose flour	1 L
1 tsp	salt	5 mL
1 tsp	baking powder	5 mL
1 tsp	ground cinnamon	5 mL
¼ tsp	ground nutmeg	1 mL

Preheat oven to 400°F (200°C). Boil raisins and water together for 5 minutes. Cool and then add baking soda. Mix sugar, oil, vanilla and eggs. Sift dry ingredients and add to egg mixture alternating with raisin mixture. Drop from a teaspoon onto cookie sheet. Bake at 400°F (200°C) 12 minutes.

Can freeze **Yield: 6 dozen**

Coffee Dipped Dainties

1 Tbsp	instant coffee	15 mL
2 tsp	boiling water	10 mL
1 cup	butter, softened	250 mL
1 cup	sugar	250 mL
1	egg	1
2 tsp	lemon juice	10 mL
1 tsp	vanilla	5 mL
2½ cups	sifted all purpose flour	625 mL
½ tsp	baking powder	2 mL
¼ tsp	salt	1 mL
	sugar	

GLAZE

4 Tbsp	instant coffee	50 mL
6 Tbsp	boiling water	100 mL
4 cups	sifted icing sugar	1 L
2 tsp	vanilla	10 mL
1½ cups	ground pecans	375 mL

Preheat oven to 375°F (190°C). Combine coffee and water. Cream butter and sugar. Beat in egg, lemon juice, vanilla and coffee mixture. Combine flour, baking powder and salt, and add to coffee mixture. Roll dough into small balls and place on ungreased cookie sheet. Flatten balls with bottom of glass dipped in sugar. Bake at 375°F (190°C) 5 to 7 minutes. Cool.

GLAZE: Combine coffee, boiling water, icing sugar and vanilla and beat until creamy. Dip baked cookies into glaze so that half the surface is coated. Dip glazed portion into ground pecans to coat. Store in tightly sealed cookie tin.

Yield: 8½ dozen

Filbert Fingers

1 cup	soft butter	250 mL
½ cup	icing sugar	125 mL
2 cups	sifted all purpose flour	500 mL
¼ tsp	salt	1 mL
¾ cup	finely ground filberts (hazelnuts)	175 mL
½ cup	semi-sweet chocolate chips	125 mL
4 tsp	butter	20 mL

Preheat oven to 325°F (160°C). Cream butter and icing sugar. In separate bowl, mix flour, salt and filberts. Add to butter and icing sugar mixture. Roll into small fingers and bake on ungreased cookie sheet 11 minutes or until bottom of cookie is golden brown. Let cookies cool. Melt chocolate chips and butter over hot water. Dip half of cookie in chocolate mixture. Let harden on waxed paper. Store in refrigerator or freezer.

Can freeze   **Yield: 3½ dozen**

"Three Tartes" Butter Tarts

¼ cup	butter	50 mL
1 cup	brown sugar	250 mL
1	egg	1
½ tsp	vanilla	2 mL
1 cup	currants, rinsed well under hot water	250 mL
24	small tart shells	24

Preheat oven to 400°F (200°C). Cream butter and brown sugar together. Beat in egg and vanilla. Add currants. Fill tart shells ¾ full. Bake at 400°F (200°C) 10 to 12 minutes.

Can freeze   **Yield: 24**

Ginger Cookies

¾ cup	butter	175 mL
1 cup	sugar	250 mL
¼ cup	molasses	50 mL
1	egg	1
2 cups	all purpose flour	500 mL
¼ tsp	salt	1 mL
1 tsp	ground cinnamon	5 mL
1 tsp	ground cloves	5 mL
1 tsp	ground ginger	5 mL
	white sugar for coating	
	candied ginger for decoration	

Preheat oven to 375°F (190°C). Cream butter and sugar together until fluffy. Add molasses and egg. Add dry ingredients and mix well. Roll into small balls and coat with white sugar. Bake on ungreased cookie sheet at 375°F (190°C) 10 minutes until golden. If desired, decorate with small pieces of candied ginger while still warm.

Can freeze   **Yield: 4 dozen**

Pecan Delights

1 lb	small pecan pieces	500 g
¾ tsp	salt	3 mL
2 cups	brown sugar, packed	500 mL
1 tsp	vanilla	5 mL
½ cup	egg whites, unbeaten	125 mL

Preheat oven to 325°F (160°C). Blend pecans, salt and brown sugar. Add vanilla and egg whites. Drop batter from a teaspoon on a greased and floured cookie sheet. Bake at 325°F (160°C) until golden brown, about 15 minutes, or until the centre is slightly firm.

Can freeze   **Yield: 3 dozen**

Scrumptious Chocolate Rum Squares
These received a fantastic rating

CHOCOLATE LAYER

8 squares	(8 oz/225 g) semi-sweet chocolate	8
½ cup	water	125 mL
1 cup	sugar	250 mL
1 lb	unsalted butter	500 g
2	eggs	2
⅓ cup	rum	75 mL

COFFEE BISCUIT LAYER

2 Tbsp	instant coffee	25 mL
1 Tbsp	boiling water	15 mL
2 Tbsp	sugar	25 mL
⅓ cup	milk	75 mL
⅓ cup	rum	75 mL
1½ lb box	social tea or petit beurre biscuits	750 g
⅓ cup	orange marmalade (optional) cookie crumbs	75 mL

CHOCOLATE LAYER: Melt chocolate with water, sugar and butter in small saucepan. Remove from heat. When mixture is cool, add eggs one at a time, blending thoroughly. Add rum. Cool mixture in refrigerator, stirring occasionally. Leave until thickened.

COFFEE BISCUIT LAYER: Mix coffee, boiling water and sugar; add milk and rum. Dip biscuits into coffee mixture and line bottom of 9 x 13 inch (23 x 33 cm) pan with ⅕th of cookies. Spread ⅕th of the chocolate mixture evenly over cookies. Repeat cookie layer dipped in coffee mixture, then repeat chocolate layer. After third layer, spread orange marmalade over cookies, if desired. Fill in corners of rows with pieces of cookie. Repeat layers until there are 5 layers of cookies and chocolate, ending with chocolate mixture. Sprinkle cookie crumbs on top to decorate. Cover and chill overnight. Cut into small squares. Store in container in refrigerator.

Must make ahead   **Yield: 3 dozen**

Showcase Squares

CRUST

1 cup	all purpose flour	250 mL
¼ cup	brown sugar, packed	50 mL
1 cup	pecans, finely chopped	250 mL
½ cup	butter, melted	125 mL

FILLING

1 lb	cream cheese	500 g
1 cup	sugar	250 mL
1 tsp	vanilla	5 mL
3	eggs	3

GLAZE

2 cups	sour cream	500 mL
6 Tbsp	sugar	100 mL
1 tsp	vanilla	5 mL

Preheat oven to 350°F (180°C).

CRUST: Mix flour, brown sugar, pecans and butter. Press firmly into bottom of 9 x 13 inch (23 x 33 cm) baking pan. Bake at 350°F (180°C) 10 to 15 minutes or until browned.

FILLING: Beat cheese, sugar and vanilla. Add eggs and beat well. Pour over crust. Return to oven for 20 minutes.

GLAZE: Mix sour cream, sugar and vanilla. Pour over baked filling. Bake at same temperature 3 to 5 minutes. Cool and refrigerate before cutting into small squares.

Can freeze   **Yield: 4 dozen**

Apricot Squares

FILLING

1 cup	dried apricots, cut in pieces	250 mL
½ cup	sugar	125 mL
1 cup	water	250 mL

CRUST

1 cup	all purpose flour	250 mL
¼ cup	sugar	50 mL
¼ tsp	salt	1 mL
½ cup	softened butter	125 mL
2	egg yolks	2

MERINGUE

2	egg whites	2
¾ cup	brown sugar	175 mL
½ cup	coconut (optional)	125 mL
1 tsp	vanilla	5 mL

Preheat oven to 325°F (160°C).

FILLING: In small saucepan, combine apricots, ½ cup (125 mL) sugar and water. Simmer together until apricots are soft, up to 20 minutes. Cool.

CRUST: Into mixing bowl, sift flour, ¼ cup (50 mL) sugar and salt. Cut butter into mixture until crumbly. Add egg yolks, mixing well. Press into 8 inch (20 cm) square pan. Bake at 325°F (160°C) 10 minutes. Remove from oven and cool. Cover crust with apricot mixture. Increase oven temperature to 350°F (180°C).

MERINGUE: Beat egg whites until they form soft peaks. Add brown sugar gradually, continuing to beat until stiff. Fold in coconut and vanilla. Spoon over apricot mixture. Bake for 25 to 30 minutes. Cut into squares.

Yield: 16

Butter Mallow Brownies
A rich treat!

¾ cup	all purpose flour	175 mL
1 tsp	baking powder	5 mL
¼ tsp	salt	1 mL
⅓ cup	butter, melted	75 mL
1 cup	brown sugar, lightly packed	250 mL
1	egg	1
1 tsp	vanilla	5 mL
25	marshmallows	25

TOPPING

1½ cups	brown sugar	375 mL
¼ cup	butter	50 mL
⅓ cup	18% cream	75 mL
pinch	salt	pinch
1 tsp	vanilla	5 mL

Preheat oven to 350°F (180°C). Sift dry ingredients together. Combine melted butter, brown sugar, egg and vanilla. Stir dry ingredients into butter mixture. Spread batter into greased 8 inch (20 cm) square pan. Bake at 350°F (180°C) 25 minutes. Cut marshmallows in half. Place cut side down on top of hot cake. Press down gently. You may return to oven to melt slightly.

TOPPING: Combine brown sugar, butter, cream and salt in small saucepan. Cover and bring to a boil. Remove cover and continue cooking until mixture reaches 238°F (117°C) on candy thermometer or soft ball stage. Cool 5 minutes without stirring. Beat in vanilla and continue beating until good spreading consistency. Spread icing over marshmallows. Cut into small squares.

Yield: 24

Walnut Squares
Often requested

1 cup	all purpose flour	250 mL
½ cup	butter or margarine	125 mL
½ cup	brown sugar	125 mL
2	eggs	2
1 cup	brown sugar	250 mL
2 Tbsp	all purpose flour	25 mL
½ tsp	baking powder	2 mL
1 cup	chopped walnuts	250 mL
½ cup	coconut	125 mL
1 tsp	vanilla	5 mL

Preheat oven to 350°F (180°C). Combine 1 cup (250 mL) flour, butter and ½ cup (125 mL) brown sugar to make crumbly dough. Press into 8 inch (20 cm) square pan. Bake at 350°F (180°C) 10 minutes. Mix eggs, 1 cup (250 mL) brown sugar, 2 Tbsp (25 mL) flour, baking powder, walnuts, coconut and vanilla, and pour on top of base. Bake at same temperature 20 to 25 minutes until set and lightly browned. Cut into squares.

Can make ahead   **Yield: 16**

Toffee Bars

1 cup	butter	250 mL
1 cup	brown sugar, firmly packed	250 mL
1 tsp	vanilla extract	5 mL
1 cup	sifted all purpose flour	250 mL
dash	salt	dash
1 pkg	(6 oz/175 g) semi-sweet chocolate chips	1
1 cup	chopped walnuts or pecans	250 mL

Preheat oven to 350°F (180°C). Cream butter, sugar, and vanilla until light and fluffy. Add flour and salt, mix well. Stir in chocolate chips and nuts and spread mixture on a jelly-roll pan. Bake at 350° F (180°C) 20 minutes. Remove from oven, cut into squares immediately, and let cool in pan.

Can freeze   **Yield: 4 dozen**

Apple Squares

1 cup	all purpose flour	250 mL
1 Tbsp	baking powder	15 mL
¼ tsp	salt	1 mL
¼ tsp	ground cinnamon	1 mL
¼ cup	butter or margarine	50 mL
½ cup	brown sugar, firmly packed	125 mL
½ cup	white sugar	125 mL
1	egg	1
½ cup	finely chopped apple	125 mL
½ cup	finely chopped nuts	125 mL
1 tsp	vanilla	5 mL
¼ cup	white sugar	50 mL
½ tsp	ground cinnamon	2 mL

Preheat oven to 350°F (180°C). Sift together flour, baking powder, salt and ¼ tsp (1 mL) cinnamon. Melt butter, remove from heat, beat in brown sugar, white sugar and egg, until smooth. Stir in dry ingredients, apple, nuts and vanilla. Batter will be stiff. Spread in greased 8 inch square (20 cm) cake pan. Mix together remaining ¼ cup (50 mL) sugar and ½ tsp (2 mL) cinnamon and sprinkle on top of batter. Bake at 350°F (180°C) 30 minutes.

Can freeze   **Yield: 16**

Chocolate Raisin Brownies

2 squares	(2 oz/60 g) bitter chocolate	2
¼ lb	butter	125 g
1 cup	sugar	250 mL
½ cup	all purpose flour	125 mL
2	eggs	2
1 tsp	vanilla	5 mL
1 cup	raisins	250 mL
½ cup	nuts (optional)	125 mL

Preheat oven to 350°F (180°C). Melt chocolate and butter in double boiler. Add remaining ingredients. Mix well. Pour into greased 8 inch (20 cm) square pan. Bake at 350°F (180°C) 25 to 30 minutes. When cool, brownies may be iced with chocolate butter icing. Cut into squares.

Can freeze   **Yield: 24**

Maple Coconut Chews
A tasty square that cuts well

CRUST

1 cup	brown sugar	250 mL
¼ cup	butter	50 mL
1	egg	1
1 cup	flour	250 mL
1 tsp	baking powder	5 mL
¼ tsp	salt	1 mL
1 tsp	vanilla	5 mL
¾ cup	coconut	175 mL

ICING

¼ cup	butter	50 mL
½ cup	brown sugar	125 mL
2 Tbsp	milk	25 mL
1 cup	icing sugar	250 mL

Preheat oven to 350°F (180°C)

CRUST: In bowl cream brown sugar and butter. Beat in egg. Blend flour, baking powder and salt and add to mixture. Add vanilla and coconut and blend. Press into an 8 inch (20 cm) square pan and bake at 350°F (180°C) exactly 22 minutes. Cool.

ICING: Melt butter in saucepan and stir in brown sugar. Stir over low heat for 2 minutes. Add milk and bring to a boil. Remove from heat and beat in icing sugar until thick. Ice the cooled squares.

Yield: 16

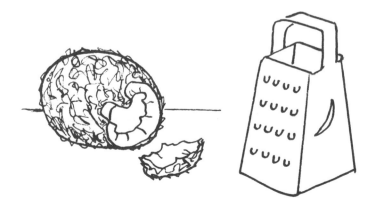

189

Almond Squares

½ cup	butter	125 mL
1 cup	sugar	250 mL
2	egg yolks	2
1½ cups	all purpose flour	375 mL
1 tsp	baking powder	5 mL
½ tsp	almond extract	2 mL
pinch	salt	pinch

TOPPING

2	egg whites	2
1 cup	brown sugar	250 mL
1 cup	minced, blanched almonds	250 mL

Preheat oven to 350°F (180°C). Cream butter and sugar. Add egg yolks, flour, baking powder, almond extract and salt. Mix well and pat into 8 inch (20 cm) square pan. Bake for 20 minutes.
TOPPING: Beat egg whites until stiff peaks form. Fold in brown sugar and almonds. Spread over crust. Bake at 250°F (120°C) 45 minutes or until topping is well done. Cool completely before cutting.

Can freeze   Yield: 1½ to 2 dozen

Cherry Coconut Bars
Great Christmas bars!

1 cup	sifted all purpose flour	250 mL
½ cup	butter or margarine	125 mL
3 Tbsp	icing sugar	50 mL
2	eggs, slightly beaten	2
1 cup	sugar	250 mL
⅓ cup	all purpose flour	75 mL
½ tsp	baking powder	2 mL
¼ tsp	salt	1 mL
1 tsp	vanilla	5 mL
¾ cup	chopped nuts	175 mL
½ cup	coconut	125 mL
½ cup	maraschino cherries, quartered	125 mL

Preheat oven to 350°F (180°C). Mix first three ingredients with pastry blender or two knives until crumbly. Press into 8 inch (20 cm) square pan. Bake 20 to 25 minutes until golden. Stir remaining ingredients into eggs. Spread over base, no need to cool. Return to oven and bake 25 minutes. Cut into bars when cool.

Can freeze   Yield: 18 to 20

Butter Tart Squares
A "no fuss" treat for butter tart lovers!

CRUST

1¼ cups	all purpose flour	300 mL
½ cup	butter	125 mL
¼ cup	brown sugar	50 mL

FILLING

⅓ cup	butter	75 mL
2 Tbsp	cream	25 mL
1 tsp	vanilla	5 mL
1 cup	raisins	250 mL
1 cup	brown sugar	250 mL
1	egg, beaten	1
1 Tbsp	all purpose flour	15 mL

Preheat oven to 350°F (180°C).
CRUST: In bowl combine all crust ingredients. Press into 9 inch (23 cm) square pan and bake at 350°F (180°C) 15 minutes.
FILLING: In bowl combine all filling ingredients. Spread over partially baked crust. Return to oven and continue baking 20 to 30 minutes or until golden brown. Cut into squares.

Yield: 20

Mincemeat Squares

1½ cups	all purpose flour	375 mL
¼ tsp	soda	1 mL
¼ tsp	salt	1 mL
1 cup	brown sugar, firmly packed	250 mL
1½ cups	quick cooking rolled oats	375 mL
¾ cup	butter	175 mL
1⅔ cups	mincemeat	400 mL

Preheat oven to 375°F (190°C). Sift flour, soda and salt into a large mixing bowl. Mix in brown sugar and rolled oats. Cut butter into dry mixture with a pastry blender or two knives, until mixture is crumbly. Press half this mixture into the bottom of a 9 inch (23 cm) square pan. Spread mincemeat on top. Then lightly press remaining flour mixture over all. Bake at 375°F (190°C) 40 to 45 minutes until browned. When cool cut into squares.

Yield: 16

Three-Step Chocolate Squares

2 squares	(2 oz/60 g) unsweetened chocolate	2
½ cup	margarine	125 mL
1 cup	sugar	250 mL
½ cup	all purpose flour	125 mL
2	eggs	2
½ cup	chopped walnuts	125 mL

FILLING

¼ cup	margarine	50 mL
2 Tbsp	evaporated milk	25 mL
2 cups	icing sugar	500 mL
½ tsp	vanilla	2 mL

TOPPING

2 squares	(2 oz/60 g) semi-sweet chocolate	2
2 Tbsp	margarine	25 mL

Preheat oven to 350°F (180°C). Melt chocolate and margarine together. Combine with sugar, flour, eggs and walnuts. Spread in 9 inch (23 cm) square baking pan, and bake at 350°F (180°C) 15 to 20 minutes.

FILLING: Melt margarine and combine with remaining ingredients. Spread over crust and refrigerate for 10 minutes.

TOPPING: Melt chocolate and margarine together. Spread over filling and refrigerate 10 to 15 minutes.

Can freeze   **Yield: 25 squares**

...designates "Company in a Minute"

TRAPPER'S RESTAURANT
3479 Yonge St., North York

Trapper's Deep Dish Apricot and Pear Pie

8	Northern Spy or Granny Smith Apples	8
3	ripe pears	3
½ cup	dried apricots, coarsely chopped	125 mL
¼ cup	raisins	50 mL
1 tsp	grated orange zest	5 mL
1 tsp	grated lemon zest	5 mL
¼ cup	apple juice	50 mL
1 cup	sugar	250 mL
1 Tbsp	cornstarch	15 mL
1 tsp	ground cinnamon	5 mL
½ tsp	ground nutmeg	2 mL
¼ tsp	ground ginger or candied ginger finely chopped	1 mL
pinch	ground cloves	pinch
1 egg		1
1 Tbsp	water	15 mL

Peel, core and slice apples and pears, and place in a large bowl with apricots, raisins and apple juice. Toss fruit in apple juice to discourage discolouring. Combine dry ingredients in a small bowl and mix thoroughly. Add the dry ingredients to the fruit and toss until fruit is coated. Place in ungreased 9 x 13 inch (23 x 33 cm) pan, roll out pastry, (recipe follows) and place over filling. Trim edges and brush with egg wash. (1 egg and 1 Tbsp./15 mL water, lightly beaten) Cut several small slashes in pastry. Bake in 400°F (200°C) over for 50-60 minutes or until pastry is golden brown and filling is bubbling.

Pastry

2	cups all purpose flour	500 mL
1 tsp	salt	5 mL
¾ cup	chilled lard or shortening	175 mL
¼ tsp	white vinegar	1 mL
5-6 Tbsp	cold water	75-90 mL

Sift flour and salt. Cut in lard/shortening until it resembles coarse meal. Mix vinegar with water, make a well in centre of flour. Add water all at once. Mix only until dough holds together. Form into ball, refrigerate for one hour before using dough.

Frozen Banana Meringue

Keeps in freezer for 3 months— always ready for company

MERINGUE

3	egg whites	3
¾ cup	sugar	175 mL
½ tsp	vanilla	2 mL
¼ tsp	vinegar	1 mL

FILLING

1 cup	mashed ripe bananas	250 mL
¼ tsp	salt	1 mL
2 Tbsp	lemon juice, fresh or bottled	25 mL
1 cup	whipping cream, whipped	250 mL
¼ cup	icing sugar	50 mL
	sliced strawberries or raspberries	

SAUCE (optional)

4 squares	(4 oz/120 g) semi-sweet chocolate	4
2 Tbsp	butter	25 mL
¼ cup	corn syrup	50 mL
⅓ cup	Kahlua	75 mL
¼ cup	whipping cream	50 mL

Preheat oven to 275°F (140°C)

MERINGUE: Beat egg whites until stiff. Gradually beat in sugar, then add vanilla and vinegar. Cut two pieces of waxed paper, 8 x 5 inch (20 x 13 cm) and place on baking sheet. Divide egg white mixture equally between them. Spread to almost cover paper to edges. Bake at 275°F (140°C) 45 to 55 minutes, or until well cooked. Let cool to tepid. To remove wax paper from meringue: place meringue on top of damp towel, wait a few minutes, them remove meringue from paper. Let meringue stand until completely cooled.

BANANA FILLING: In a small bowl, combine filling ingredients. Place one meringue on serving plate, cover with banana filling and top with the second meringue. Wrap in foil. Freeze at least 3 hours or until banana filling is as set as ice cream. To serve, remove from freezer 15 minutes ahead and garnish with sliced strawberries or raspberries. For a change, serve with hot chocolate sauce.

CHOCOLATE SAUCE: Combine all ingredients in sauce pan and simmer gently for 20 minutes. This will keep in refrigerator and can be rewarmed.

Must freeze   **Serves: 6 to 8**

Frozen Café Praline Mousse
Looks complicated, but worth it for special friends!

½ cup	slivered almonds	125 mL
⅓ cup	sugar	75 mL
3 Tbsp	water	50 mL
4	eggs, separated	4
¼ cup	sugar	50 mL
1 Tbsp	instant coffee	15 mL
2 Tbsp	sugar	25 mL
1 cup	whipping cream	250 mL
½ tsp	vanilla	2 mL
2 Tbsp	sifted icing sugar	25 mL

GARNISH	chocolate curls

Warm (not brown) nuts in 350°F (180°C) oven or at minimum heat in fry pan. While nuts heat, boil ⅓ cup (75 mL) sugar and water in sauce pan, until mixture forms a light caramel syrup, 248°F (120°C) on a candy thermometer. Add warm nuts and stir until nuts are well coated with syrup. Pour onto an oiled pan and spread apart with fork. Freeze until hardened, then chop coarsely. Set aside. Place egg yolks in top of double boiler. Beat with ¼ cup (50 mL) sugar until light and creamy. Place over boiling water and continue to beat until thickened, about 5 minutes. Add coffee granules and stir until dissolved. Remove from heat, add praline mixture and cool. In medium bowl, beat egg whites until frothy. Beat in 2 Tbsp (25 mL) sugar and continue beating until soft peaks form. Set aside. In large bowl, whip cream with vanilla and icing sugar until thick. Set aside. Fold one-third egg whites into praline mixture and then fold back into remaining egg whites, blending well. Fold into whipped cream. Spoon into serving dish and freeze at least 3 hours or overnight. Just before serving, decorate with chocolate curls.

Must freeze　　　　　　**Serves: 6 to 8**

Frozen Grand Marnier Soufflé
Well worth the effort!

6	shortbread cookies or 8 lady fingers, crumbled	6
½ cup	Grand Marnier, divided	125 mL
6	egg yolks	6
1 cup	sugar	250 mL
1 Tbsp	finely grated orange peel	15 mL
⅓ cup	orange juice	75 mL
2½ cups	whipping cream	625 mL

GARNISH   chocolate curls

Spread cookie crumbs on a cookie sheet and sprinkle with 4 Tbsp (50 mL) of Grand Marnier and set aside. Beat egg yolks until thick and lemon coloured. Pour sugar, orange peel and orange juice in a sauce pan and bring to a boil. Boil briskly until mixture reaches 230°F (110°C) on a candy thermometer. Immediately pour into egg yolks in a steady stream, while beating constantly. Continue beating for 10 to 15 minutes until smooth and thick. Beat in remaining Grand Marnier. Set aside. Beat whipping cream until soft peaks form. Gently fold into egg mixture until there is no white showing. Fill serving bowl with ⅓ egg mixture and then ½ crumbs. Repeat. Top with final ⅓ egg mixture. Freeze. Ten minutes before serving transfer to refrigerator. Garnish with chocolate curls.

Must freeze   **Serves: 10 to 12**

Fresh Lemon Ice Cream
Quick and easy!

2 cups	half and half cream	500 mL
1 cup	sugar	250 mL
2 Tbsp	grated lemon rind	25 mL
⅓ cup	fresh lemon juice	75 mL

In a large bowl, stir together cream and sugar until sugar dissolves. Mix in lemon rind and juice. Pour into 8 inch (20 cm) square pan or sherbet dishes. Freeze until firm. If you desire a creamier texture beat again before mixture is completely frozen. To add a "party pretty" look, serve in scooped-out lemon shells.

Must freeze   **Serves: 6 to 8**

Frozen Cappuccino

3	eggs, separated	3
1 Tbsp	sugar	15 mL
2 tsp	instant coffee granules	10 mL
¼ cup	boiling water	50 mL
½ oz	unsweetened chocolate, chopped	15 g
1 tsp	brandy	5 mL
⅛ tsp	cinnamon	0.5 mL
1 cup	whipping cream, divided	250 mL
¼ tsp	cream of tartar	1 mL
¼ cup	sugar	50 mL

GARNISH cinnamon

Cook egg yolks with 1 Tbsp (15 mL) sugar over moderately low heat, whisking constantly until mixture is hot. Dissolve coffee in boiling water and add to egg mixture, continually whisking until thickened. DO NOT LET IT BOIL. Remove from heat and add chocolate, brandy, and cinnamon. Whisk until chocolate is melted. Transfer to a large bowl. Beat half the whipping cream until it holds stiff peaks. Fold into coffee mixture. Beat egg whites until foamy. Add cream of tartar and beat until egg whites hold soft peaks. Gradually add remaining ¼ cup (50 mL) sugar and beat until peaks are glossy and stiff. Fold egg whites into coffee mixture. Spoon into dessert glasses or serving bowl and freeze one hour or until firm, NOT hard. Before serving, whip remaining cream for topping and sprinkle with cinnamon.

Must freeze **Serves: 4**

Frozen Maple Cream

1 pkg	(1 Tbsp/7 g) unflavoured gelatine	1
2 Tbsp	water	30 mL
1 cup	maple syrup, at room temperature	250 mL
2 cups	whipping cream, whipped	500 mL
½ cup	chopped walnuts	125 mL

Mix gelatine in water in pyrex measuring cup. Place cup in pot of simmering water until gelatine dissolves. Combine maple syrup and gelatine. Cool mixture in refrigerator until it begins to thicken. Fold into whipped cream. Pour into serving bowl and top with nuts. Freeze.

Must freeze **Serves: 6**

Blender Raspberry Sorbet
A light refreshing end to a meal

3 pkg.	(14 oz/425 g each) frozen raspberries	3
1 cup	icing sugar	250 mL
	juice of 3 lemons	

GARNISH   whipped cream, berries, mint leaves

Place undrained berries in blender. Blend until puréed. Spoon in icing sugar and lemon juice. Blend for 2 minutes. Press pulp through a sieve to remove seeds. Freeze for 2 hours. Remove from freezer and beat with a whisk to dissolve ice crystals. Return to freezer. Transfer sorbet from freezer to refrigerator 20 minutes before serving. Spoon into individual dishes and garnish with whipped cream, berries or fresh mint.

Must freeze   **Serves: 6 to 8**

Tropical Ice

	juice and rind of 1 lemon	
	juice of 1 orange	
1	banana, mashed	1
1	egg	1
¾ cup	sugar	175 mL
1 cup	water	250 mL

In a medium bowl using an electric mixer, beat together all ingredients. Place bowl in freezer and freeze until firm. Break up frozen mixture with a fork and beat again, not allowing mixture to thaw completely. Refreeze. Serve in sherbet glasses and garnish with fresh fruit in season or well-drained mandarin oranges. Sherbet may also be frozen in a mold and turned out for serving.

Must freeze   **Serves: 6**

Brandy Freeze

½ gal.	vanilla ice cream	2 L
1 cup	brandy	250 mL
1 cup	Kahlua	250 mL

Allow ice cream to soften slightly. Add liqueurs and mix well. Pour into wine glasses or brandy snifters and freeze. Remove from freezer 10 minutes before serving, stir gently. Mixture will be crystalized but not frozen solid. May be served with a spoon or guests may 'drink' the dessert. Variations: vanilla ice cream and Crème de Menthe; orange sherbet and Cointreau.

Must freeze   **Serves: 8**

Café Liegeois
An instant winner!

¼ cup	instant coffee	50 mL
¼ cup	water	50 mL
6 scoops	chocolate ice cream	6
6 Tbsp	Kahlua, divided	90 mL
½ cup	whipping cream, whipped	125 mL

| GARNISH | maraschino cherries |

Mix coffee and water. Divide evenly among 6 wine glasses. Place a scoop of ice cream in each glass and top with 1 Tbsp (15 mL) Kahlua and a dollop of whipped cream. Garnish with a cherry.

Serves: 6

Strawberries in Sherry Cream

5	egg yolks	5
1 cup	sugar	250 mL
1 cup	sherry	250 mL
1 cup	whipping cream, whipped	250 mL
3 cups	strawberries, washed and hulled	750 mL

Put egg yolks in top of double broiler. Beat until thick and lemon coloured. Beat in sugar and sherry. Cook and stir constantly over hot water until thick. Cool. Just before serving, fold in whipped cream and strawberries. Garnish with extra berries.

Can make ahead   **Serves: 6 to 8**

199

Cantaloupe Supreme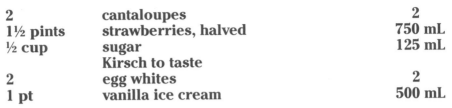

2	cantaloupes	2
1½ pints	strawberries, halved	750 mL
½ cup	sugar	125 mL
	Kirsch to taste	
2	egg whites	2
1 pt	vanilla ice cream	500 mL

Cut melons in half and seed. Cut bottoms off melons so they sit straight on cookie sheet. Remove melon from skins, cut into pieces and put back in rind. Slice berries and add enough sugar to sweeten (¼ cup/50 mL, approximately). Place on top of melon pieces. Sprinkle with Kirsch. At this point they may be covered with plastic wrap and kept refrigerated until serving time. Beat egg whites until foamy, add remaining sugar slowly, beating until stiff peaks form. Put one scoop of ice cream in centre of melon, cover top with egg whites and set under broiler until brown.

Can make ahead   **Serves: 4**

Fruit Brulée

	fresh fruit selection (eg: strawberries, blueberries, peaches, melons, bananas, pineapple, grapes)	
2 cups	whipping cream, whipped	500 mL
	brown sugar to cover	

Arrange any combination of fruit, cut in pieces in 9 x 13 inch (23 x 33 cm) baking dish. Spread whipped cream thickly and evenly over the fruit. Refrigerate all day (4 hours minimum). Top with a quarter inch layer of brown sugar and place in top third of oven under broiler for 2 to 3 minutes or until carmelized. Watch carefully. Return to refrigerator for 1 hour.
NOTE: If using banana, use sparingly as it will overpower the flavour.

Must make ahead   **Serves: 6 to 8**

Hot Strawberries
A "unique" summer recipe

¼ cup	butter or margarine	50 mL
1 cup	cubed crouton size, day old, white bread	250 mL
¼ cup	brown sugar	50 mL
½ tsp	cinnamon	2 mL
2 cups	small fresh strawberries	500 mL
	vanilla ice cream	

Melt butter in heavy frying pan. Add bread cubes and cook gently, stirring constantly until cubes are golden. CAN BE MADE AHEAD to this point. Add brown sugar and cinnamon. Cook and stir until bread is crisp. Add strawberries and cook gently, stirring constantly for 2 minutes. Serve immediately over ice cream.

Serves: 4

Cherries Jubilation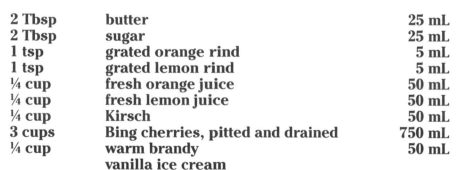

2 Tbsp	butter	25 mL
2 Tbsp	sugar	25 mL
1 tsp	grated orange rind	5 mL
1 tsp	grated lemon rind	5 mL
¼ cup	fresh orange juice	50 mL
¼ cup	fresh lemon juice	50 mL
¼ cup	Kirsch	50 mL
3 cups	Bing cherries, pitted and drained	750 mL
¼ cup	warm brandy	50 mL
	vanilla ice cream	

Melt butter in skillet, blend in sugar and heat mixture until it bubbles. Stir in orange and lemon rind and simmer until mixture is light brown. Stir in fruit juices and cook until mixture bubbles. Add Kirsch and cherries. Stir gently until cherries are well saturated. May make ahead to this point, then reheat. Pour in warm brandy, ignite and stir sauce until flames die away. Serve over vanilla ice cream.

Can make ahead   **Serves: 6**

Orange Soufflé

1 pkg	(1 Tbsp/7 g) unflavoured gelatine	1
¼ cup	water	50 mL
3	eggs, separated	3
	juice of 3 oranges	
	grated rind of 2 oranges	
	juice of 1 lemon	
1 cup	sugar	250 mL
1 cup	whipping cream, whipped	250 mL

In a small bowl, soften gelatine in water. Place egg yolks, orange juice and rind, lemon juice and sugar in top of double boiler. Cook over simmering water, stirring constantly, until slightly thickened. Fold in softened gelatine and stir until thoroughly dissolved. Remove from heat and cool. Fold cooled mixture into whipped cream. Beat egg whites until stiff, fold into orange mixture. Spoon mixture into sherbet glasses or serving dish. Chill.

Serves: 4 to 6

Very Berry Fruit Sauce

1 pkg	(14 oz/425 g) frozen raspberries	1
	in heavy syrup, thawed	
2 cups	fresh or frozen blueberries	500 mL
4 cups	fresh strawberries, sliced	1 L

Purée raspberries with syrup in blender. Add purée to blueberries and sliced strawberries. Chill. Serve over ricotta cheese, ice cream or pound cake.

Yield: 7 cups (1.75 L)

Summer Fruit Sauce

1½ cups	sour cream	375 mL
½ cup	brown sugar	125 mL
1 Tbsp	white sugar	15 mL
¼ cup	rum	50 mL

Combine sour cream and sugars together. Fold in rum. Refrigerate 2 hours. Serve over any mixture of fresh fruit.

Must make ahead   **Serves: 6 to 8**

Mint Dip for Strawberries

1 cup	whipping cream	250 mL
2 Tbsp	green Crème de Menthe	25 mL
2 Tbsp	brown sugar	25 mL

Whip cream in a medium bowl, until it holds stiff peaks. In a small dish blend Crème de Menthe and sugar and fold the mixture into whipped cream. Chill

Yield: 1½ cups (375 mL)

Georgeous Grapes
A taste sensation

> seedless green grapes
> sour cream or unsweetened whipped
> cream or yogurt
> peanut brittle

Combine grapes with sour cream, whipped cream or yogurt. Mix or top with peanut brittle. May be served immediately or chilled.

Café Santos Parfait
Out of this world!

6	egg yolks	6
1¼ cups	icing sugar	300 mL
1 Tbsp	instant coffee	15 mL
1 Tbsp	Crème de Cacao	15 mL
2 cups	whipping cream	500 mL
6 Tbsp	coffee liqueur	100 mL
18	coffee beans	18

Beat egg yolks with sugar. Add coffee granules and Crème de Cacao. Beat cream until stiff then fold into egg mixture. Pour into 6 parfait glasses and freeze. Remove from refrigerator 15 minutes before serving. Pour 1 Tbsp (15 mL) coffee liqueur over each parfait and decorate with 3 coffee beans.

Must freeze   **Serves: 6**

Velvet Cream Pudding
Everyone will want the recipe—and it's so easy!

1 cup	sugar	250 mL
1 pkg	(1 Tbsp/15mL) unflavoured gelatine	1
2 cups	whipping cream	500 mL
2 cups	sour cream	500 mL
1 tsp	vanilla	5 mL
	frozen raspberries or strawberries	

Combine sugar and gelatine in a saucepan and stir in whipping cream. Let stand 5 minutes. Stir over medium heat until gelatine and sugar are dissolved (mixture should be hot but not boiling). Chill one hour. Using a wire whisk stir in sour cream and vanilla and transfer to serving bowl. Chill overnight or up to two days. Serve with thawed raspberries or strawberries over top of each serving.

Must make ahead   **Serves: 8**

Lemon Cream
Could become addictive!

1 cup	sugar	250 mL
2 Tbsp	cornstarch	25 mL
pinch	salt (optional)	pinch
1 cup	water	250 mL
¼ cup	fresh lemon juice, strained	50 mL
1	egg	1
1 tsp	grated lemon rind	5 mL
1 tsp	vanilla	5 mL
1 cup	whipping cream, whipped	250 mL

GARNISH   strawberries

Combine sugar, cornstarch and salt in top of double boiler. Gradually stir in water. Cook over hot water, stirring constantly, until thickened (approximately 15 minutes). Stir in lemon juice, and reheat until rethickened. Mix a little of the hot sauce with the lightly beaten egg, then return to remaining hot sauce. Cook, stirring constantly, one or two minutes over very low heat. Remove from heat and add lemon rind and vanilla. Cool. Just before serving fold in whipped cream. Serve in sherbet glasses garnished with strawberries.

Can make ahead   **Serves: 6**

Pot de Crème 🍒
So simple! So rich! So chocolaty!

1 pkg	(6 oz/175 g) semi-sweet chocolate chips	1
2	egg yolks	2
3 Tbsp	hot coffee	50 mL
2 Tbsp	rum	25 mL
½ tsp	vanilla	2 mL
¾ cup	milk, scalded	175 mL

GARNISH   whipped cream

Place all ingredients in blender. Mix 3 minutes on high. Pour into Pot de Crème pots or parfait glasses. Chill. Top with whipped cream.

Can make ahead   **Serves: 4 to 6**

Daiquiri Soufflé
Easy, light and delightful

10	eggs, separated	10
2 cups	sugar, divided	500 mL
½ cup	lime juice	125 mL
½ cup	lemon juice	125 mL
	grated rind of 1 lime	
	grated rind of 1 lemon	
½ tsp	salt	2 mL
2 pkg	(2 Tbsp/14 g) unflavoured gelatine	2
¾ cup	white rum	175 mL
2 cups	whipping cream	500 mL

Beat egg yolks until light and fluffy. Add 1 cup (250 mL) sugar gradually. Beat until smooth and light in colour. Add juices, rinds and salt. Mix until blended. Stir over low heat until thick and custard coats a spoon. Soak gelatine in rum 5 minutes and stir into hot custard until dissolved. Cool. Oil 6 cup (1.5 L) souffle dish and wrap an oiled collar around the top. Beat egg whites until stiff. Gradually beat in remaining 1 cup (250 mL) sugar, 2 Tbsp (25 mL) at a time. Beat until stiff peaks form and fold into custard. Whip cream until stiff and fold into mixture. Pour into souffle dish and chill. Top may be decorated with lemon or lime slices or grated rind. Serve next day.

Must make ahead   **Serves: 12 to 14**

Danish Rum Soufflé

4	eggs, separated	4
1 cup	sugar	250 mL
¼ cup	light rum	50 mL
1 pkg	(1 Tbsp/7 g) unflavoured gelatine	1
¼ cup	cold water	50 mL
1 cup	whipping cream	250 mL

GARNISH   **unsweetened chocolate curls**

Beat 4 egg yolks and ½ cup (125 mL) sugar until lemon coloured. Add rum. In top of double boiler, over boiling water dissolve gelatine in water. Add to yolk-rum mixture. Beat whipping cream until stiff. Fold into yolk-rum mixture. Beat egg whites until stiff. Gradually beat in ½ cup (125 mL) sugar. Fold egg whites into yolk-rum mixture. Chill in serving bowl at least 6 hours. Garnish with chocolate curls.

Must make ahead   **Serves: 6**

Mocha Praline Chocolate Torte

MERINGUE

6	egg whites	6
¼ tsp	salt	1 mL
¼ tsp	cream of tartar	1 mL
1½ cups	sugar	375 mL
½ tsp	almond extract	2 mL

PRALINE

½ cup	whole almonds	125 mL
¼ cup	sugar	50 mL

FILLING

2 cups	whipping cream	500 mL
1 tsp	instant coffee	5 mL
1 Tbsp	sugar	15 mL
2 squares	(2 oz/60 g) semi-sweet chocolate	2

Preheat oven to 275°F (140°C).

MERINGUE: Line 2 cookie sheets with foil. Lightly butter, then flour. Trace a 9 inch (23 cm) circle with your finger on each. In large bowl, beat egg whites with salt and cream of tartar until soft peaks form. Continue beating and gradually add sugar. Add almond extract and beat until stiff peaks form. Spread mixture into circles. Bake at 275°F (140°C) 1 hour. Turn oven off and leave meringues in oven overnight or reduce heat to 200°F (100°C) and bake for an additional 1¼ hours. Remove and let cool. When cool, meringues may be frozen.

PRALINE: In small heavy saucepan, cook almonds and sugar over medium-low heat, stirring until sugar melts and almonds start to crackle. When sugar is caramel colour, pour mixture onto buttered baking sheet. When cooled, crush coarsely with mallet or in food processor. (Store at room temperature in air-tight container.)

FILLING: In large bowl whip cream and coffee granules until thick. Beat in sugar. Fold in crushed praline. Make chocolate shavings from squares of chocolate using grater or vegetable peeler.

To assemble place a meringue on serving plate. Cover with half the cream filling and sprinkle with half the chocolate. Place second meringue on top and cover with remaining cream and chocolate. Refrigerate at least 5 hours or overnight.

NOTE: Crispy Crunch Chocolate bars or Old English Toffee can be substituted for praline.

Must make ahead   **Serves: 8 to 10**

Chocolate Mousse Torte
Spectacular!

MERINGUE

5	egg whites	5
pinch	cream of tartar	pinch
¾ cup	sugar	175 mL
1¾ cups	icing sugar	425 mL
⅓ cup	unsweetened cocoa	75 mL

CHOCOLATE MOUSSE

13 oz	semi-sweet chocolate	364 g
7	egg whites	7
¼ tsp	cream of tartar	1 mL
3 cups	whipping cream	750 mL
1½ tsp	vanilla	7 mL

Preheat oven to 275°F (140°C)

MERINGUE: In a large bowl, beat egg whites and cream of tartar until they hold soft peaks. Beat in sugar, 2 Tbsp (25 mL) at a time until meringue holds stiff peaks. Sift together icing sugar and cocoa and fold into meringue. Using an 8 inch (20 cm) square cake pan as a guide, trace three squares onto parchment paper set on baking sheets. Divide the meringue among the squares spreading it evenly to the edges. Bake at 275°F (140°C) for 1 to 1¼ hours. Alternate the baking sheets if necessary for even baking. Turn the oven off and leave meringues inside to cool for two hours. Transfer to racks and peel off parchment paper.

CHOCOLATE MOUSSE: In a double broiler over hot water, melt semi-sweet chocolate. Let it cool until lukewarm. In a large bowl beat egg whites and cream of tartar until stiff peaks form. In another bowl beat whipping cream with vanilla until stiff. Fold chocolate into egg whites and then fold in whipped cream.

TO ASSEMBLE: Put one meringue on a cake plate and spread thickly with one-third of the chocolate mousse. Repeat layers and top with the remaining meringue. Transfer the remaining mousse to a pastry bag fitted with a decorative tip and decorate the top with overlapping figure eights. Chill, lightly covered, for 4 hours or overnight.

Must make ahead   **Serves: 9 to 12**

Forgotten Meringue

MERINGUE

6	egg whites	6
¼ tsp	salt	1 mL
½ tsp	cream of tartar	2 mL
1½ cups	sugar	375 mL
1 tsp	almond extract	5 mL

SAUCE

4	egg yolks, well beaten	4
1 cup	sugar	250 mL
1 cup	sherry	250 mL
1 cup	whipping cream, whipped	250 mL
	fresh fruit: peaches, blueberries, strawberries	

Preheat oven to 400°F (200°C)

MERINGUE: Butter bottom (not sides) of angel cake pan. Beat egg whites until soft peaks form. Add salt and cream of tartar. Gradually add sugar and continue beating until stiff peaks form. Spread in prepared pan. Turn oven off. Put meringue in oven and "forget" about it for 4 hours or overnight. Remove from pan and chill. Meringue will be soft and moist.

SAUCE: Beat egg yolks gently and add sugar and sherry. Place over hot water in double boiler. Stir and cook over medium heat until thick and coats silver spoon (custard test). Before serving, fold in whipped cream. To serve, place meringue on large platter and place fresh fruit in centre and around sides. Serve sauce in bowl at side.

NOTE: Sauce is wonderful by itself with any fresh fruit.

Must make ahead   **Serves: 8 to 10**

Strawberry-Chocolate Meringue Torte
A fabulous dessert for entertaining

MERINGUE

6	egg whites, room temperature	6
pinch	salt	pinch
¼ tsp	cream of tartar	1 mL
1½ cups	sugar	375 mL

FILLING

8 squares	(8 oz/250 g) semi-sweet chocolate	8
3 Tbsp	water	50 mL
3 cups	whipping cream	750 mL
½ cup	white sugar	125 mL
1 qt	strawberries	1 L

Preheat oven to 250°F (120°C.)

MERINGUE:Beat egg whites, salt and cream of tartar until soft peaks form. Beat in sugar gradually until meringue is very stiff. Trace three 9 inch (23 cm) circles on sheets of waxed paper or tin foil and arrange the paper on cookie sheets. Spread meringue evenly within each circle and bake at 250°F (120°C) 35 to 45 minutes until dry and lightly coloured. Remove from oven and carefully peel paper from bottom. Put meringues on cake racks to cool.

FILLING: In the top of a double boiler over hot water, melt chocolate and water. Cool slightly and spread a thin layer over two of the meringue layers. Beat whipping cream until it holds soft peaks. Beat in sugar and continue to beat until stiff. Hull, wash, dry and slice strawberries reserving some for garnish. Spread a ¾ inch (2 cm) layer of whipped cream on top of one chocolate covered meringue and top this with half the strawberries. Put the second chocolate covered meringue on top and repeat. Top with remaining meringue round. Frost top and sides with remaining whipped cream. Decorate top with reserved strawberries and drizzle with chocolate if desired. Chill for 4 hours.

Must make ahead   **Serves: 8 to 10**

Vacherin au Café
Always creates a sensation!

MERINGUE

4	egg whites	4
3 Tbsp	fruit sugar	50 mL
1½ cups	brown sugar, loosely packed	375 mL

FILLING

1 cup	whipping cream	250 mL
1 tsp	instant coffee	5 mL
	sugar to taste	

GARNISH

3 Tbsp	sifted icing sugar	50 mL
½ cup	whipping cream, whipped (optional)	125 mL

Preheat oven to 275°F (140°C).

MERINGUE: Line 2 cookie sheets with parchment paper. Draw an 8 inch (20 cm) circle on each sheet of paper. Beat egg whites in a bowl until stiff. Add fruit sugar and continue beating for 10 seconds. Gradually fold in brown sugar. Divide mixture in half and spread onto circles or use a pastry bag with a plain ½ inch (1 cm) tip and pipe the meringue in a spiral pattern, to cover each circle. Bake at 275°F (140°C) 30 to 50 minutes until dry and slightly browned. Cool on wire rack. When almost cold, peel off paper.

FILLING: Whip cream until it holds peaks and flavour with coffee granules moistened with a little water. Sweeten lightly with sugar. Spread cream filling on one meringue then place second meringue on top. Using a sieve, dust the top of the vacherin with icing sugar and decorate, if desired, with rosettes of whipped cream. May make meringues days ahead and keep in cool dry place. Assemble about 4 hours before serving.

Can make ahead   **Serves: 6 to 8**

Florentine Tart

CRUST

½ cup	unsalted butter	125 mL
2 Tbsp	sugar	25 mL
1	egg	1
½ tsp	vanilla	2 mL
1½ cups	all purpose flour	375 mL

FILLING

¾ cup	unsalted butter	175 mL
½ cup	sugar	125 mL
4 Tbsp	cream	50 mL
	grated rind of 1 lemon	
	grated rind of 1 orange	
¾ cup	mixed red and green candied cherries, halved	175 mL
½ cup	mixed dark and golden raisins	125 mL
½ cup	almonds, slivered or sliced	125 mL
4 squares	(4 oz/120 g) semi-sweet chocolate	4

Preheat oven to 350°F (180°C).

CRUST: Cream together in a large bowl butter and sugar. Stir in the egg and vanilla, then add the flour and work it in lightly with your fingertips. When the ingredients are smooth enough to pack into a ball, gather the pastry together, wrap in plastic wrap and refrigerate at least 30 minutes. Take the pastry from the refrigerator and leave it at room temperature for a few minutes to facilitate rolling. Roll out the pastry on a lightly floured surface to a 12 inch (30 cm) circle. Transfer the dough to a pizza pan or baking sheet. If the dough cracks a bit, simply pinch it together and piece the edge if necessary. Refrigerate the tart crust 15 minutes, then bake in a preheated 350°F (180°C) oven 10 minutes. Tuck three 3 inch (8 cm) wide strips of aluminum foil under and up around the pastry edge to act as protective barriers when the filling is poured into the crust.

FILLING: Heat the butter and sugar in a small saucepan over medium heat. When the sugar has dissolved and the mixture is at a rolling boil, add the remaining ingredients, except the chocolate. Stir briefly, then remove from heat. Pour the filling over the crust—try to leave a small border free, as the filling will expand outward as it heats. Distribute the fruit evenly over the crust. Bake in a preheated 350°F (180°C) oven about 20 minutes—watch carefully toward the end of baking time. The filling will first bubble up and look as if it has sugared, then it will dissolve into a smooth caramel which will grow darker as it bakes. Remove the tart from the oven when it turns a pleasant gold. Let cool to room temperature (the caramel will solidify), and transfer to a serving platter. Melt the chocolate in a double boiler over hot water until smooth. Let cool briefly, then when it is cool enough to handle, drizzle some in a free-form pattern, over the top of the tart. Spoon the rest into a pastry bag fitted with a small star tube. Border the edge of the tart with a chocolate scallop. Refrigerate. Serve cut into wedges.

Serves: 10 to 12

Marbled Raspberry Mousse

2 pkg	(14 oz/425 g each) frozen raspberries, thawed	2
2 Tbsp	unflavoured gelatine	25 mL
½ cup	water	125 mL
⅓ cup	sugar	75 mL
½ cup	rosé or sweet white wine	125 mL
2 cups	heavy cream	500 mL

Pour raspberries and syrup into food processor or blender, cover and process on high for 30 seconds, or until smooth. Strain into a medium metal bowl. Soften gelatine in water in a small saucepan. Heat slowly, stirring constantly, until gelatine dissolves and liquid is clear. Pour into bowl with raspberry purée. Stir in sugar and wine until sugar dissolves. Cool to room temperature. Make an aluminum foil collar for a 4 cup (1 L) soufflé dish and attach it to dish. Beat cream until stiff in large bowl. Fold into raspberry mixture to give a marbled effect. Spoon into soufflé dish. Refrigerate.

Can make ahead   **Serves: 8**

Mock Milles Feuilles
Children and adults love this; be prepared to serve seconds!

48	whole graham crackers	48
2 pkg	(4 oz/113 g each) vanilla pudding and pie filling	2
3½ cups	milk	875 mL
1½ cups	whipping cream	375 mL
2 Tbsp	sugar	25 mL
1 tsp	vanilla	5 mL
1½ cups	icing sugar, sifted	375 mL
3-4 Tbsp	hot water	50 mL
1 square	(1 oz/28 g) semi-sweet chocolate, melted	1

Butter a 9 x 13 inch (23 x 33 cm) baking pan. Line bottom with whole graham crackers cutting them to fit together and cover the entire bottom. Make vanilla pudding following package directions but using only 3½ cups (875 mL) of milk. Cool. Place plastic wrap on surface of pudding while cooling. Spread pudding over crackers. Whip cream with sugar and vanilla until stiff. Spread on top of pudding. Top with another layer of graham crackers cutting them to cover the entire surface. Combine icing sugar and hot water. Spread over crackers. Melt semi-sweet chocolate and drizzle over glaze. Chill. Can be made early in the day or the day before.

Can make ahead   **Serves: 8 to 10**

Crunchy Topping
Wonderful on ice cream!

1½ cups	wheat or corn cereal flakes	375 mL
½ cup	butter	125 mL
1 cup	brown sugar packed	250 mL

Mix cereal, butter and sugar in frying pan over medium heat until very sticky. Spread on bottom of greased cake pan. Cool thoroughly and then break and crumble. Store in air tight sealer and serve on ice cream topped with Tia Maria.

Yield: 3 cups (750 mL)

Lime Cheesecake
Cool and refreshing for a warm summer night

CRUST
1 cup	shredded coconut	250 mL
2 Tbsp	butter, melted	10 mL
2 Tbsp	flour	10 mL

FILLING
1 pkg	(1 Tbsp/7 g) unflavoured gelatine	1
¼ cup	cold water	50 mL
3	eggs, separated	3
¾ cup	water	175 mL
¾ cup	sugar	175 mL
2 pkg	(8 oz/250 g each) cream cheese, beaten	2
¼ cup	lime juice (1½ limes)	50 mL
2 tsp	grated lime rind	10 mL
few drops	green food colouring	few drops
1 cup	whipping cream	250 mL

GARNISH thin slices of lime and grated lime rind

Preheat oven to 350°F (180°C)

CRUST: Combine coconut, flour and butter. Press into 9 inch (23 cm) springform pan. Bake at 350°F (180°C) 12 to 15 minutes. Remove from oven and cool.

FILLING: Soften gelatine in ¼ cup (50 mL) cold water. Combine egg yolks, ¾ cup (175 mL) water and sugar in saucepan. Stir over moderate heat for 5 minutes. Add gelatine and stir until dissolved. Gradually add gelatine mixture to cream cheese. Beat until blended. Add lime juice, rind and food colouring. Beat cream until stiff, fold into cheese mixture. Beat egg whites until stiff and fold into above. Pour filling over cooled crust and chill overnight or until firm. Remove from pan. Decorate with thin slices of lime (cut to centre and twist) and grated lime rind sprinkled around edge.

Must make ahead   **Serves: 8 to 10**

Cuisine d'or Oreo Cheesecake
A beautiful and impressive company dessert

CRUST

1½ cups	graham cracker crumbs	375 mL
½ cup	butter, melted	125 mL
¼ cup	brown sugar, firmly packed	50 mL
1 tsp	ground cinnamon	5 mL

FILLING

2 lb	cream cheese, room temperature	1 kg
1¼ cups	sugar	300 mL
2 Tbsp	all purpose flour	25 mL
4	extra large eggs	4
2	large egg yolks	2
⅓ cup	whipping cream	75 mL
2 tsp	vanilla	10 mL
1½ cups	coarsely chopped Oreo cookies	375 mL
2 cups	sour cream	500 mL

SWISS FUDGE GLAZE

1 cup	whipping cream	250 mL
8 oz	semi-sweet chocolate, chopped	250 g
1 tsp	vanilla	5 mL
5	Oreo cookies, halved crosswise	5
1	maraschino cherry, halved	1

Preheat oven to 425°F (220°C).

CRUST: Blend together all ingredients and press into bottom and sides of a 9 or 10 inch (23 or 25 cm) spring form pan. Refrigerate until firm, about 30 minutes.

FILLING: Beat cream cheese in large bowl of electric mixer on lowest speed until smooth. Beat in 1¼ cups (300 mL) sugar and flour until well blended. Add eggs and yolks and continue beating until mixture is smooth. Stir in whipping cream and 1 tsp (5 mL) vanilla. Pour half of batter into prepared crust. Sprinkle with chopped Oreo cookies. Pour in remaining batter. Smooth with spatula. Bake at 425°F (220°C) 15 minutes. Reduce oven temperature to 225°F (100°C) and continue baking 50 minutes. If browning too quickly, cover top loosely with foil. Remove from oven. Increase oven temperature to 350°F (180°C). Blend sour cream and remaining 1 tsp (5 mL) of vanilla in small bowl. Spread over cake. Return cake to oven and bake 7 minutes. Cool. Cover cake with plastic wrap and chill overnight in refrigerator.

SWISS FUDGE GLAZE: Scald cream in heavy saucepan over high heat. Watch carefully. Add chocolate and vanilla and stir 1 minute. Remove from heat and stir until all chocolate is melted. Refrigerate glaze 10 minutes.

TO SERVE: Remove cake from spring form pan and set on platter. Pour glaze over top and using a pastry brush, smooth chocolate over the top and sides. Arrange Oreo cookie halves, cut side down, on the top of the cake around the outer edge. Place cherry halves in centre. Refrigerate cake until ready to serve.

Must make ahead   **Serves: 10 to 12**

Angel Cheesecake
Light and airy!

CRUST

1¼ cups	graham cracker crumbs	300 mL
2 Tbsp	sugar	25 mL
2 Tbsp	butter, melted	25 mL

FILLING

2 pkgs	(8 oz/250 g each) cream cheese	2
2 cups	sour cream	500 mL
½ cup	sugar	125 mL
1 Tbsp	lemon rind	15 mL
2 Tbsp	lemon juice	25 mL
1 tsp	vanilla	5 mL
½ tsp	salt	2 mL
5	eggs, separated	5
½ cup	sugar	125 mL

Preheat oven to 300°F (150°C).

CRUST: Combine graham cracker crumbs, sugar and butter. Press into 10 inch (25 cm) spring form pan. Chill for at least 10 minutes.

FILLING: Cream the cheese. Add sour cream, ½ cup (125 mL) sugar, lemon rind, lemon juice, vanilla, salt and egg yolks. Beat well. Beat egg whites, slowly adding ½ cup (125 mL) sugar, until stiff peaks form. Fold into cheese mixture. Pour into prepared crust. Bake at 300°F (150°C) 1 hour. Turn off heat and leave in oven 1 more hour. Remove and cool overnight. Top with fruit, if desired.

Must make ahead   **Serves: 12**

Brandy Alexander Cheesecake

CRUST

3 oz	social teas or vanilla wafers	90 g
¼ cup	hazelnuts	50 mL
¼ cup	butter	50 mL
2 oz	dark chocolate	60 g

FILLING

8 oz	cottage cheese	250 g
8 oz	cream cheese	250 g
½ cup	sugar	125 mL
1 tsp	vanilla	5 mL
2 tsp	unflavoured gelatine	10 mL
2 Tbsp	hot water	25 mL
1 cup	whipping cream	250 mL
2	egg whites	2
1 Tbsp	brandy	15 mL
1 Tbsp	Crème de Cacao	15 mL

TOPPING

1 cup	whipping cream	250 mL
1 tsp	instant coffee	5 mL
1 tsp	brandy	5 mL
1 tsp	Crème de Cacao	5 mL
2 tsp	sugar	10 mL

GARNISH   ground nutmeg

CRUST: Finely crush biscuits in food processor and place in large bowl. Finely chop hazelnuts and add to biscuits. Melt butter over low heat. Add chocolate and stir until melted. Add to biscuit mixture and mix well. Press firmly into 8 inch (20 cm) spring form pan. Refrigerate. FILLING: Press cottage cheese firmly through fine sieve. Put cream cheese and cottage cheese into bowl, beat until light and fluffy. Gradually beat in sugar and vanilla. Dissolve gelatine in hot water; cool. Beat gelatine mixture and unwhipped cream into cheese mixture. Beat egg whites until soft peaks form. Fold into cheese mixture with brandy and Crème de Cacao. Pour over crust and refrigerate. TOPPING: Place whipping cream, instant coffee granules, brandy, Crème de Cacao and sugar in a bowl, mix lightly, and let stand 10 minutes. Beat until soft peaks form, and spoon over top of cheesecake. Sprinkle with nutmeg, and refrigerate 4 to 6 hours.

Must make ahead   **Serves: 12 to 16**

Southern Fruitcake
Makes a delightful light cake for Christmas gift giving!

12 oz	candied citron	375 g
12 oz	candied pineapple	375 g
12 oz	golden raisins	375 g
8 oz	slivered almonds	250 g
8 oz	red candied cherries, halved	250 g
8 oz	green candied cherries, halved	250 g
¾ cup	dessicated coconut	175 mL
2 cups	sifted all purpose flour	500 mL
1 tsp	baking powder	5 mL
½ tsp	salt	2 mL
1 tsp	ground nutmeg	5 mL
1 cup	butter	250 mL
1 cup	sugar	250 mL
4	large eggs	4
½ cup	light medium sherry (not dry)	125 mL
1½ tsp	vanilla	7 mL
½ tsp	almond extract	2 mL
	brandy as required	

Preheat oven to 275°F (140°C). Combine fruit and nuts. Sift flour once before measuring. Use ⅓ cup (75 mL) to coat fruit and nuts. Sift remaining flour with baking powder, salt and nutmeg. Cream butter and gradually blend in sugar. Add eggs one at a time, beating well after each addition until light and fluffy. Mix in dry ingredients alternately with sherry, add flavourings with last of sherry. Mix in fruit and nuts. Grease brown paper or heavy duty foil and line pans. You may use an 8 inch (20 cm) square Christmas cake pan, or two 9 x 5 inch (23 x 13 cm) loaf pans or three small pans. Turn batter into lined pans. Place a pan of hot water in bottom of oven and put cakes on rack above. Bake at 275°F (140°C) 3 hours for large pan. Bake 2 hours for small pans or until cake is firm when pressed. When cool, wrap each cake in brandy-soaked cloth and then in foil. Place in plastic bag and put in cool place. In 10 days, unwrap each loaf and resoak cloth in brandy. Rewrap and store. Repeat every 2 weeks. Cakes should age at least 4 weeks. If kept longer, repeat brandy soaking every 2 weeks.

Must make ahead   **Can freeze**   **Yield: 1 to 3 cakes**

Dark Fruitcake
Rich, moist, chock full of goodies— the ultimate dark fruitcake!
Perfect for the traditional wedding!

MAKE AT LEAST A MONTH IN ADVANCE!

1 lb	blanched sliced almonds	500 g
½ lb	blanched slivered almonds	250 g
1 lb	chopped walnuts	500 g
1 lb	chopped pecans	500 g
2½ lb	raisins	1.25 kg
1½ lb	currants	750 g
1 lb	figs, chopped	500 g
1 lb	dates, chopped	500 g
½ lb	red cherries, quartered	250 g
½ lb	green cherries, quartered	250 g
1 lb	mixed candied fruit	500 g
1 lb	diced candied pineapple	500 g
1 lb	diced citron	500 g
1 lb	mixed orange/lemon peel	500 g
1½ cups	brandy	375 mL
¾ cup	corn syrup	175 mL
1¼ cups	flour, preferably whole wheat	300 mL
1½ lb	butter	750 g
3 cups	brown sugar	750 mL
12	eggs, separated	12
5½ cups	flour, preferably ½ all purpose and ½ whole wheat	1.4 L
1 tsp	salt	5 mL
2 tsp each	ground cinnamon, mace, allspice, nutmeg	10 mL
1 tsp	ground cloves	5 mL
1 Tbsp	baking soda	15 mL
1 cup	grape jelly	250 mL
	brandy for soaking	

NIGHT BEFORE: In large container, mix all fruit and nuts with 1 cup (250 mL) brandy and corn syrup.

BAKING DAY: Start early, as cakes require up to 3½ hours baking at 275°F (140°C). Any combination of pans may be used. All should be lined with foil and greased. One combination of sizes would be:
1   9 x 5 inch (23 x 13 cm) loaf pan
2   8 x 4 inch (20 x 10 cm) loaf pans
2   10 inch (25 cm) tube pans.

Preheat oven to 275°F (140°C). Toss fruit and nuts with 1¼ cups (300 mL) whole wheat flour. Set aside. In large preserving kettle cream together butter and sugar and beat until light and fluffy. In small bowl beat egg yolks until light in colour and using a fork add to creamed mixture. Sift 5½ cups (1.25 L) flour with salt, spices and baking soda. In small bowl mix together ½ cup (125 mL) brandy and 1 cup (250 mL) grape jelly. To creamed mixture, alternately add dry ingredients (½ cup/125 mL at a time) and grape mixture. Add fruit mixture. (Using hands is the easiest method.) Beat 12 egg whites until stiff but not dry. Fold into batter. (Again use hands). Spoon batter into prepared pans, pressing well into all corners. Place shallow pan of water on bottom rack of oven. Place cakes in centre of oven. Baking time varies depending on size of pan and individual oven. As a general rule:
10 inch (25 cm) tube pan—3½ hours
9 x 5 inch (23 x 13 cm) loaf pan—3¼ hours
8 x 4 inch (20 x 10 cm) loaf pan—3 hours

Cake should be firm to touch and tester inserted comes out clean. Cool in tin for 15 minutes and then remove to rack to finish cooling. Using a toothpick, prick holes into the cakes and slowly ladle warmed brandy over top. Wrap cakes in brandy soaked cheese cloth, then foil and then plastic wrap. Keep in a cool place and open every 2nd week to remoisten cloths with brandy. Repeat at least twice before serving. Recipe may easily be halved or quartered.

Must make ahead   **Can freeze**   **Yield: 16 lb (8 kg)**

No Name Cake with Strawberries

This recipe has never had a name—just passed around on the back of an envelope for generations.

½ cup	unsalted butter	125 mL
1½ cups	sugar, white or brown	375 mL
1	egg	1
1 Tbsp	instant coffee	15 mL
1 Tbsp	boiling water	15 mL
2 cups	all purpose flour	500 mL
1 tsp	baking soda	5 mL
1 tsp	baking powder	5 mL
½ cup	cocoa	125 mL
1½ cups	buttermilk	375 mL

FILLING AND FROSTING

1 cup	whipping cream	250 mL
½ cup	sugar	125 mL
1 cup	sour cream	250 mL
2 cups	fresh strawberries	500 mL

Preheat oven to 350°F (180°C). In large mixing bowl, cream together butter, sugar and egg. Dissolve coffee granules in boiling water and add to creamed mixture. Sift together flour, baking soda, baking powder and cocoa. Add dry ingredients to creamed mixture alternately with buttermilk. Pour batter into greased and floured 10 inch (25 cm) spring form pan. Bake at 350°F (180°C) 50 to 60 minutes. Release spring on pan but allow cake to cool in pan. When cool, remove from pan and cut horizontally into 2 layers.

FILLING AND FROSTING: Whip cream with sugar until stiff. Fold in sour cream. Use one-third of cream mixture for filling. Frost sides and top of cake with remaining cream. Mound fresh strawberries in centre. Cake and frosting may be prepared ahead and assembled just before serving.

Can make ahead   **Serves: 12**

California Cake

1	orange	1
1	banana, peeled	1
1 cup	raisins	250 mL
2 cups	sifted cake and pastry flour	500 mL
¾ tsp	baking soda	3 mL
¼ tsp	salt	1 mL
½ cup	butter	125 mL
1 cup	sugar	250 mL
2	eggs	2
½ cup	buttermilk	125 mL
½ tsp	vanilla	2 mL

GLAZE

6 Tbsp	sugar	100 mL
6 Tbsp	orange juice	100 mL
1 Tbsp	rum	15 mL

GARNISH

| 1 cup | whipped cream | 250 mL |

Preheat oven to 350°F (180°C). Cut unpeeled orange into pieces and remove seeds. Chop orange, banana and raisins in food processor. Sift flour, baking soda and salt. In large bowl, cream butter and sugar until fluffy. Add eggs, one at a time, beating well after each addition. Mix in fruit. Combine buttermilk and vanilla. Add dry ingredients to fruit mixture alternately with buttermilk, mixing after each addition. Turn into greased and floured 8 inch (20 cm) square pan. Bake at 350°F (180°C) 55 to 60 minutes or until knife comes out clean.

GLAZE: Stir together sugar, orange juice and rum until sugar is dissolved. Spoon over warm cake and allow to soak in. Serve with whipped cream.

Can freeze   **Serves: 9**

Date and Nut Cake

1 lb	dates, chopped into small pieces	500 g
1 cup	pecans, chopped	250 mL
¾ cup	butter	175 mL
1½ cups	brown sugar, packed	375 mL
1 tsp	baking soda	5 mL
1 cup	boiling water	250 mL
1 cup	sifted all purpose flour	250 mL
2	eggs, beaten	2
⅓ cup	rum	75 mL

ICING

¼ cup	butter	50 mL
2 cups	icing sugar	500 mL
1-2 Tbsp	rum	15-25 mL

Preheat oven to 325°F (160°C). Place dates, nuts, butter and brown sugar in a large bowl. In separate bowl, combine soda with boiling water. (Be careful, it bubbles.) Add to large bowl. Mix well. Add flour, eggs and ⅓ cup (75 mL) rum. Beat until smooth. Spoon into greased and floured 9 x 13 inch (23 x 33 cm) baking pan. Bake at 325°F (160°C) 40 to 50 minutes. Let cool.
NOTE: If freezing, leave uniced.
ICING: Cream butter and icing sugar in a bowl. Add rum to desired consistency.

Can freeze   **Serves: 12 to 15**

Chocolate Buttercream Frosting

1 cup	semi-sweet chocolate chips	250 mL
¼ cup	boiling water or coffee	50 mL
2 Tbsp	icing sugar	25 mL
4	large egg yolks	4
½ cup	butter, cut into 1 inch (2 cm) squares	125 mL
2 Tbsp	rum (optional)	25 mL

Using steel blade of food processor, place chocolate chips in bowl and process on high for 10 seconds. Turn off and scrape sides of bowl. Add boiling water or coffee and process 10 seconds. Add sugar, egg yolks, butter and rum. Blend until smooth, about 30 seconds. Chill until icing is consistency required for spreading.
NOTE: This recipe is ample to frost two 8 inch (20 cm) layers, one 10 inch (25 cm) tube cake, or one 9 x 13 inch (23 x 33 cm) cake.

Yield: 2 cups (500 mL)

Self-Iced Cake

4 tsp	butter	20 mL
1 cup	sugar, divided	250 mL
2	eggs, separated	2
1 cup	all purpose flour	250 mL
1 tsp	baking powder	5 mL
½ tsp	salt	2 mL
½ cup	milk	125 mL
1 cup	shredded coconut	250 mL

Preheat oven to 325°F (160°C). Cream butter and ½ cup (125 mL) sugar. Beat in egg yolks. Sift together flour, baking powder and salt. Add to butter mixture, alternating with milk. Pour into greased and floured 9 inch (23 cm) square baking pan. Beat egg whites until stiff. Gradually add remaining ½ cup (125 mL) sugar and beat for 2 minutes. Stir in coconut and spread on top of batter in pan. Bake at 325°F (160°C) 45 minutes. Good served with ice cream or berries.

Can freeze　　　　　**Serves: 8 to 10**

Pike's Peak Spiked Apple Crisp

5 cups	peeled and sliced apples	1.25 L
½ tsp	sugar cinnamon	2 mL
1 tsp	grated lemon rind	5 mL
1 tsp	grated orange rind	5 mL
2 Tbsp	Grand Marnier	25 mL
2 Tbsp	Amaretto	25 mL
¾ cup	sugar	175 mL
¼ cup	brown sugar, packed	50 mL
¾ cup	all purpose flour	175 mL
¼ tsp	salt	1 mL
½ cup	butter or margarine	125 mL

GARNISH whipped cream or ice cream

Preheat oven to 350°F (180°C). Arrange apple slices in greased 2 qt. (2 L) round casserole. Sprinkle sugar cinnamon, lemon and orange rind and both liqueurs on top of apples. In a separate bowl, mix sugars, flour, salt and butter until crumbly. Spread mixture over top of apples. Bake uncovered at 350°F (180°C) until apples are tender and top is lightly browned, approximately 1 hour. Serve warm with whipped cream or vanilla ice cream.

Can make ahead　　　　　**Serves: 8** 225

Saucy Apple Cake 🍒
Delicious, fast dessert

CAKE

1 cup	sugar	250 mL
¼ cup	butter	50 mL
1	egg	1
2 cups	peeled and chopped apples	500 mL
1 cup	all purpose flour	250 mL
1 tsp	baking soda	5 mL
1 tsp	cinnamon	5 mL
¼ tsp	salt	1 mL
½ cup	chopped walnuts or pecans	125 mL

SAUCE

½ cup	brown sugar	125 mL
½ cup	white sugar	125 mL
¼ cup	butter or margarine	50 mL
½ cup	18% cream	125 mL

Preheat oven to 350°F (180°C)

CAKE: Mix cake ingredients, in order given. Place in greased 9 inch (23 cm) square baking pan. Bake at 350°F (180°C) for 45 minutes or until tester comes out clean.

SAUCE: In saucepan, bring all sauce ingredients to a gentle boil. Serve cake with warm sauce and, if desired, ice cream.

Can freeze   **Serves: 8 to 10**

Raisin Gingerbread
Yummy served warm with homemade applesauce!

1 cup	butter	250 mL
1 cup	black treacle molasses	250 mL
1 cup	cold water	250 mL
1 cup	brown sugar	250 mL
2 cups	all purpose flour	500 mL
1 tsp	ground ginger	5 mL
½ cup	sultana raisins	125 mL
2	eggs, slightly beaten	2
1 tsp	baking soda	5 mL
1 Tbsp	boiling water	15 mL

Preheat oven to 300°F (150°C). Melt butter in molasses and water over gentle heat. Remove from heat. Combine sugar, flour, ginger and raisins. Add molasses mixture, eggs and mix well. Dissolve baking soda in boiling water and add to mixture. Pour into a shallow 9 inch (23 cm) square, greased and floured pan and bake at 300°F (150°C) for 40 to 50 minutes.

Can freeze   **Serves: 12**

Foamy Sauce
Wonderful served over pound cake or ice cream

1 cup	brown sugar	250 mL
1 tsp	vanilla	5 mL
2	eggs, separated	2
2 Tbsp	butter	25 mL
2 Tbsp	hot water	25 mL

Beat together sugar, vanilla, egg yolks, butter and hot water. In a separate bowl beat egg whites until soft peaks form. Fold egg whites into sugar mixture. Serve. If made ahead, sauce will separate but can be rewhipped.

Serves: 4

Valentine Pie
Spectacular

CRUST

1 cup	all purpose flour	250 mL
¼ cup	finely crushed vanilla wafers	50 mL
½ tsp	salt	2 mL
⅓ cup	shortening or lard	75 mL
3 Tbsp	finely chopped pecans	50 mL
3 Tbsp	water	50 mL

FRUIT LAYER

1 pkg	(4 oz/125 g) raspberry flavoured jelly powder	1
¼ cup	sugar	50 mL
1¼ cups	boiling water	300 mL
1 pkg	(14 oz/425 g) frozen raspberries	1
1 Tbsp	lemon juice	15 mL

CHEESE LAYER

1 pkg	(4 oz/125 g) cream cheese	1
⅓ cup	icing sugar	75 mL
1 tsp	vanilla	5 mL
pinch	salt	pinch
1 cup	whipping cream	250 mL

Preheat oven to 450°F (230°C).

CRUST: Combine flour, wafers and salt. Cut in shortening until the size of small peas. Stir in pecans. Sprinkle water over mixture, tossing gently with a fork. Form dough into a ball. On a lightly floured surface, roll dough into a 12 inch (30 cm) circle. Transfer to a 9 inch (23 cm) pie plate. Flute edge and prick bottom with a fork. Bake 10 to 12 minutes until pastry is golden. Cool on wire rack.

FRUIT LAYER: Dissolve jelly powder and sugar in boiling water. Add frozen berries and lemon juice. Chill until partially set.

CHEESE LAYER: Blend cream cheese, sugar, vanilla and salt. Whip cream and fold into cheese mixture. Spread half of cheese mixture over pie shell. Cover with half jelly mixture. Repeat layers. Chill until set.

NOTE: This will also make an excellent pie without the fruit layer. Double the amount of cream cheese and icing sugar, following the above method. Garnish with berries.

Must make ahead   **Serves: 8 to 10**

Amaretto Pie
Crust with a difference!

CRUST

2 cups	finely shredded coconut	500 mL
1 pkg	(6 oz/175 g) semi-sweet chocolate chips	1
4 Tbsp	unsalted butter	50 mL
1½ Tbsp	light corn syrup	25 mL

FILLING

¼ cup	Amaretto	50 mL
2 tsp	unflavoured gelatine	10 mL
½ cup	sour cream	125 mL
1½ cups	whipping cream	375 mL
1 cup	powdered sugar	250 mL
¾ cup	finely chopped almonds, lightly toasted	175 mL

Preheat oven to 200°F (100°C).

CRUST: Lightly grease a 9 or 10 inch (23 or 25 cm) pie plate or deep square serving dish. Warm coconut in oven. Combine chocolate chips, butter and corn syrup in double boiler over hot, NOT simmering water. Stir until melted and smooth. Mix warm coconut with chocolate mixture and press into bottom and sides of pie plate. Chill.

FILLING: Combine Amaretto with gelatine in heat resistant cup. Mix until softened. Place cup in simmering water and heat until gelatine dissolves, 2 to 3 minutes. Transfer to large bowl and add sour cream. Blend well and stir in whipping cream and powdered sugar. Whip until stiff. Fold in ½ cup (125 mL) almonds and spoon into pie shell. Garnish with remaining almonds. Refrigerate at least 2 hours.

Must make ahead   **Serves: 10**

Sour Cream Lemon Pie
The best ever lemon pie!

1	baked 9 inch (23 cm) pie shell	1

FILLING

1 cup	sugar	250 mL
3 Tbsp	cornstarch	50 mL
1 Tbsp	all purpose flour	15 mL
1 Tbsp	grated lemon rind	15 mL
⅓ cup	fresh lemon juice	75 mL
1 cup	light cream	250 mL
¼ cup	butter	50 mL
1 cup	sour cream	250 mL

TOPPING

1 cup	whipping cream	250 mL
2 Tbsp	icing sugar	25 mL
½ cup	sour cream	125 mL
½ tsp	almond extract	2 mL
	grated lemon rind	

GARNISH lemon slices

FILLING: In saucepan, over medium heat, combine sugar, cornstarch, flour, lemon rind and juice and cream. Bring slowly to boil, stirring constantly. Add butter and cook until thick and smooth. Remove from heat and cool. Stir in sour cream and pour filling into pie shell. Refrigrate until ready to serve.

TOPPING: Whip cream and fold in sugar, sour cream and almond extract. Spoon over lemon pie filling. Sprinkle with grated lemon rind and decorate with lemon slices.

Serves: 6 to 8

Topless Blueberry Pie

CRUST

1 cup	all purpose flour	250 mL
2 Tbsp	sugar	25 mL
½ cup	butter	125 mL
1 Tbsp	white vinegar	15 mL

FILLING

2 Tbsp	all purpose flour	25 mL
⅔ cup	sugar	150 mL
pinch	cinnamon	pinch
2½ cups	fresh blueberries, divided	625 mL
	icing sugar to taste	

Preheat oven to 350°F (180°C).
CRUST: Mix flour and sugar. Cut in butter until mixture resembles coarse meal. Stir in vinegar. Pat into 9 inch (23 cm) pie plate. Chill. FILLING: Mix together flour, sugar, cinnamon and 1½ cups (375 mL) blueberries. Pour into crust and bake at 350°F (180°C) 40 minutes. Cool. Cover with remaining blueberries and sprinkle with icing sugar.

Can make ahead   **Serves: 6 to 8**

Sour Cream Raisin Pie

1	unbaked 9 inch (23 cm) pie shell	1

FILLING

1	egg	1
1 cup	sugar	250 mL
1 cup	sour cream	250 mL
1 cup	raisins	250 mL
pinch	salt	pinch
½ tsp	vanilla	2 mL
	whipped cream (optional)	

Preheat oven to 400°F (200°C). Beat egg and sugar together until sugar is partially dissolved. Add sour cream, raisins, salt and vanilla. Blend and pour into unbaked pie shell. Bake at 400°F (200°C) 10 minutes. Reduce temperature to 350°F (180°C) and bake an additional 30 minutes, or until a knife inserted in filling comes out clean. Garnish with whipped cream if desired.

Can make ahead   **Serves: 8 to 10**

Rhubarb Cream Streusel Pie
Always a hit

| 1 | unbaked 10 inch (25 cm) pie shell | |

FILLING

1¼ cups	sugar	300 mL
¼ cup	all purpose flour	50 mL
¾ cup	sour cream	175 mL
1	egg yolk	1
4 cups	rhubarb, cut in ½ inch (1 cm) pieces	1 L

TOPPING

½ cup	flour	125 mL
½ cup	brown sugar	125 mL
¾ tsp	cinnamon	3 mL
¼ cup	butter, cold	50 mL

Preheat oven to 425°F (220°C)

FILLING: Blend sugar, flour, sour cream and egg yolk. Add rhubarb pieces and mix well until rhubarb is thoroughly coated. Pour into pie shell.

TOPPING: Mix flour, brown sugar and cinnamon. Using a pastry blender or two knives, cut in butter until mixture is crumbly. Spoon over rhubarb. Bake at 425°F (220°C) 15 minutes, reduce heat to 350°F (180°C) and bake 30 minutes more. Serve warm.

Can make ahead   **Serves: 6 to 8**

Year Round Fruit Pies
Handy hint for serving fresh fruit year round

Line your pie plate with foil large enough to hang well over edges. Fill plate with fresh fruit and desired amount of sugar and thickening agent. Dot with butter. Fold tin foil tightly over filling and place plate with filling in freezer. The next day, or when fruit is frozen firmly, remove plate and wrap filling with second layer of foil. Put in a plastic bag, label and place back in freezer. When needed place frozen filling into an unbaked pie shell and bake as usual!

Glazed Peach Pie
Great fresh flavour when made the same day as serving

1	baked 10 inch (25 cm) pie shell	1

FILLING

6 cups	fresh peach slices (6 large)	1.5 L
1 cup	sugar	250 mL
¼ cup	cornstarch	50 mL
¼ tsp	cinnamon	1 mL
½ cup	orange juice	125 mL
	whipped cream	

Mash enough peach slices to measure 1 cup (250 mL). Reserve remaining slices. In a saucepan, combine sugar, cornstarch and cinnamon; stir in orange juice and mashed peaches. Cook over medium heat, stirring constantly until mixture boils. Cook and stir 1 minute. Spread half of glaze over bottom and sides of baked pie shell. Cover with reserved peach slices. Pour remaining glaze over fruit. Spread to completely cover peaches. Cover and chill at least 3 hours. Serve with whipped cream.

Must make ahead   **Serves: 8**

Cranberry Pecan Pie
A festive finale!

1	unbaked 8 inch (20 cm) pie shell	1

FILLING

3	eggs, beaten	3
1 cup	dark corn syrup	250 mL
⅔ cup	sugar	150 mL
¼ cup	butter, melted	50 mL
1 cup	fresh cranberries, halved	250 mL
1 cup	pecan halves	250 mL
	whipped cream, sweetened	

Preheat oven to 325°F (160°C). Mix eggs, corn syrup and set aside. In a separate bowl, combine sugar, butter, cranberries and pecans and spoon into pie shell. Carefully pour syrup mixture over filling. Bake at 325°F (160°C) 50 to 55 minutes or until a knife inserted in the centre comes out clean. Cool. Serve topped with whipped cream.

Can make ahead   **Serves: 6**

Banana Cream Pie

1	baked 9 inch (23 cm) pie shell	1
FILLING		
½ cup	sugar	125 mL
2 Tbsp	cornstarch	25 mL
2 Tbsp	flour	25 mL
2 cups	hot milk	500 mL
3	egg yolks	3
1 tsp	vanilla	5 mL
3	bananas	3
MERINGUE		
2	egg whites, room temperature	2
4 Tbsp	sugar	50 mL

Preheat oven to 325°C (160°C).

FILLING: Blend sugar with cornstarch and flour. Add hot milk and cook over low heat stirring constantly until thickened. In small bowl beat egg yolks well. Stir a little of the hot mixture into yolks; then add to hot custard. Cool slightly. Stir in vanilla. Slice bananas into pie shell to cover bottom. Pour in filling and top with meringue.

MERINGUE: Beat egg whites until soft peaks form. Add sugar 1 Tbsp (15 mL) at a time, beating well after each addition. Continue beating until meringue stands in stiff peaks. Top pie with meringue and bake 30 minutes until golden.

Serves: 6 to 8

Chef Alvin's Coconut Cream Pie
A favourite dessert from the Montserrat Springs Hotel, B.W.I.

PASTRY

1 cup	cake and pastry flour	250 mL
1 Tbsp	sugar	15 mL
1 tsp	salt	5 mL
½ cup	shortening	125 mL
¼ cup	ice water	50 mL

FILLING

1⅔ cups	milk	400 mL
1 cup	sugar	250 mL
1 cup	finely shredded coconut	250 mL
1 tsp	ground nutmeg	5 mL
3	egg yolks	3

MERINGUE

3	egg whites	3
½ cup	sugar	125 mL
1 Tbsp	lime juice	15 mL
¼ tsp	almond extract	1 mL

Preheat oven to 350°F (180°C).

PASTRY: Mix flour, sugar and salt. Cut in shortening until crumbly. Add ice water and form into a ball. Roll out to fit an 8 inch (20 cm) pie plate.

FILLING: Place milk, sugar, coconut and nutmeg in a saucepan. Cook over medium heat until sugar is dissolved. Whisk egg yolks until frothy. Pour hot mixture into egg yolks. Return to saucepan and cook just until slightly thick. Add vanilla. Pour filling into pie shell. Bake at 350°F (180°C) 30 minutes. Remove pie from oven. Increase oven temperature to 400°F (200°C).

MERINGUE: Beat egg whites until stiff. Gradually add sugar, lime juice and almond extract. Spread meringue over pie. Bake at 400°F (200°C) 5 minutes or until lightly browned.

Serves: 6 to 8

Quebec Sugar Pie
Tarte au sucre

| 1 | unbaked 10 inch (25 cm) deep dish pie shell | 1 |

FILLING

1½ cups	maple syrup	375 mL
¼ tsp	baking soda	1 mL
½ tsp	vanilla	2 mL
1 cup	all purpose flour	250 mL
1 cup	dark brown sugar	250 mL
pinch	ground nutmeg	pinch
⅓ cup	soft butter	75 mL

GARNISH whipped cream (optional)

Preheat oven to 350°F (180°C). Mix maple syrup, baking soda and vanilla. Pour into pie shell. Blend, in a bowl, flour, brown sugar, nutmeg and butter. Sprinkle evenly on top of syrup. Bake at 350°F (180°C) 30 to 35 minutes until pie crust has browned. Filling will set as it cools. Delicious served with whipped cream.

Serves: 8

Jubilation

...designates "Company in a Minute"

FENTON'S RESTAURANT
2 Gloucester St., Toronto

Fenton's Autumn Conserve

2 medium	lemons, thinly sliced, seeds removed	2
3 medium	oranges, thinly sliced, seeds removed	3
2 large	grapefruit, thinly sliced, seeds removed	2
6 large	pears, peeled, cored and diced	6
1 cup	golden raisins	250 mL
1 cup	pecans, lightly toasted	250 mL
½ cup	pinenuts, lightly toasted	125 mL
6 cups	sugar	1.5 L

Combine the sliced lemons, oranges and grapefruit with the sugar and let stand at room temperature for 8 to 12 hours. Drain off liquid and chop the citrus fruit by hand or pulse in a food processor for a few seconds. In a heavy bottomed large pot, combine the chopped fruit with the liquid and bring to a boil. Let simmer for approximately ½ hour. Add the prepared pears and the raisins and boil for 15 minutes, stirring well to prevent the conserve from scorching. Add the pecans and the pinenuts and cook for another few minutes, just to heat them through. Fill washed and sterilized jars with the conserve and process in a hot water bath (canner) for 10 minutes.

NOTE: This conserve is good served with roasts or to enjoy with toast in the morning.

Yield: 12 (8 oz/250mL) jars

Swiss Truffles

1 lb	Swiss milk chocolate	500 g
½ lb	unsalted butter	250 g
6	egg yolks	6
6 Tbsp	Cointreau	100 mL
1 bar	(13 oz/325 g) bittersweet chocolate	1

Melt milk chocolate and butter together in top of double boiler. In a small bowl, beat egg yolks. Pour a little of the hot chocolate mixture into yolks. Mix well, then pour egg mixture into chocolate. Add Cointreau. Cook in double boiler 10 minutes. Chill mixture several hours to harden. With melon baller, scoop out chocolate balls. Melt bittersweet chocolate; allow chocolate to cool to 89°F (30°C) over cold water, keeping a runny consistency. Dip balls in chocolate using a toothpick. Coat each with the aid of a pastry brush. Let stand on waxed paper until chocolate has hardened.

Can freeze   **Yield: 45**

Chocolate Amaretto Truffles

1 lb	semi-sweet chocolate, divided	500 g
2 Tbsp	boiling water	25 mL
⅛ tsp	almond extract	0.5 mL
½ cup	butter, cut in small pieces	125 mL
¼ cup	Amaretto	50 mL

In top of double boiler, combine 8 oz (250 g) of chocolate with boiling water. Set over hot water and heat until chocolate melts. Remove from heat, stir in almond extract, then butter, a small piece at a time until all is incorporated. Stir in Amaretto and refrigerate 3 hours until hardened. Using a spoon or melon ball cutter, form chocolate mixture into small balls ¾ inch (2 cm) in diameter. If chocolate is hard, first dip spoon in warm water. Freeze balls uncovered on a baking sheet 1 hour. Melt remaining chocolate over hot, not boiling, water and stir until melted. Chill pot over cold water until chocolate is cool but still of runny consistency. Working quickly, coat frozen balls with melted chocolate. Place on greased waxed paper. To store, place truffles in paper candy cups, wrap in foil and refrigerate 1 week or freeze 2 weeks.

VARIATION: Omit Amaretto and almond extract. Add 1 Tbsp (15 mL) instant coffee to boiling water, stir in ¼ cup (50 mL) brandy after butter is incorporated.

Must make ahead   **Can freeze**   **Yield: 36**

Chocolate Rum Truffles
A special treat

1 cup	semi-sweet chocolate chips	250 mL
⅔ cup	butter	150 mL
1	egg yolk	1
1½ cups	icing sugar	375 mL
2 tsp	rum	10 mL
1 tsp	instant coffee	5 mL
⅓ pkg	chocolate wafer biscuits, crumbled	⅓

In double boiler, melt chocolate chips and cool. In a mixing bowl, cream butter and blend in egg yolk, icing sugar, rum and coffee. Add melted chocolate to butter mixture, mixing well. Chill until almost firm. Form into balls and roll in biscuit crumbs. Store in refrigerator or freezer.

Can freeze   **Yield: 4 dozen**

Chocolate Dipped Apricots
Delectable!

8 oz	Turkish dried apricots (top quality)	250 g
4 squares	(4 oz/120 g) semi-sweet chocolate	4

Melt chocolate in top of double boiler over hot water. Dip apricots into chocolate, covering one-half to three-quarters of fruit. Let dry on waxed paper. Strawberries are also superb this way.

Must make ahead   **Serves: 12 to 16**

Sweet Marie Bars 🍒
Little kids and big kids love them!

1 cup	peanut butter	250 mL
1 cup	corn syrup	250 mL
1 cup	brown sugar	250 mL
1 Tbsp	butter	15 mL
1 cup	salted white peanuts	250 mL
3 cups	rice krispies	750 mL
1 pkg	(6 oz/175 g) semi-sweet chocolate chips	1

In heavy saucepan heat peanut butter, corn syrup and brown sugar. Stir constantly until mixture just reaches boiling point. Do not boil. Remove from heat immediately. Add butter, peanuts and rice krispies. Press into 9 x 13 inch (23 x 33 cm) pan. Ice with melted chocolate chips.

Yield: 4 dozen

5 Minute Fudge 🍒
Great for children to make

2 Tbsp	butter	25 mL
⅔ cup	evaporated milk, small can	150 mL
1⅔ cups	sugar	400 mL
½ tsp	salt	2 mL
2 cups	miniature marshmallows	500 mL
1½ cups	semi-sweet chocolate chips	375 mL
1 tsp	vanilla	5 mL
½ cup	chopped nuts	125 mL

Combine butter, evaporated milk, sugar and salt in saucepan. Over medium heat, bring to boil. Stirring constantly, cook 5 minutes. Remove from heat. Stir in marshmallows, chocolate, vanilla, and nuts. Stir vigorously for 1 minute, until marshmallows melt. Pour into 8 inch (20 cm) square buttered pan. Cool and cut into squares.

Yield: 2 lb (1 kg)

Bitter Sweet French Chocolates
Pretty on an assorted cookie platter

2 squares	(2 oz/60g) unsweetened chocolate	2
1 can	(10 oz/300 mL) sweetened condensed milk	1
1 tsp	vanilla	5 mL
1 cup	flaked coconut	250 mL

Melt chocolate slowly in heavy saucepan. Add sweetened condensed milk and boil gently for 5 minutes stirring constantly. Add vanilla. Cool and refrigerate until cold, or overnight. The next day, roll into very small balls with buttered hands. Roll balls in coconut to coat. Store in refrigerator.

Can make ahead   **Yield: 3 to 4 dozen**

Baked Nuts
A lovely hostess gift

1½ cups	sugar	375 mL
½ tsp	salt	2 mL
2 tsp	ground cinnamon	10 mL
2 tsp	ground ginger	10 mL
1 tsp	ground cloves	5 mL
1 tsp	ground allspice	5 mL
4	egg whites	4
3 lb	nuts, whole blanched cashews, pecans and unsalted almonds	1.5 kg

Preheat oven to 200°F (100°C). Mix sugar, salt and spices together and place in 9 x 13 inch (23 x 33 cm) pan. Beat egg whites until just foamy. With slotted spoon dip nuts into egg whites, a few at a time, until moistened. Roll in sugar mixture. Spread on jelly roll pan. Continue until all nuts are coated. Bake at 200°F (100°C) 2½ hours. Stir or break apart every 30 minutes. Cool. Store in air tight container. Will keep for several months.

Yield: 3 lb (1.5 kg)

Green Tomato Chutney
An Old English recipe

5 lb	green tomatoes	2.5 kg
1 lb	onions	500 g
1 Tbsp	peppercorns	15 mL
2 Tbsp	salt	25 mL
2 cups	sugar	500 mL
5 cups	vinegar	1.25 L
1 lb	sultana raisins	500 g

Slice tomatoes, chop onions and mix together in a large bowl with peppercorns and salt. Let stand overnight. Next day, bring sugar and vinegar to the boil and add raisins. Simmer 5 minutes. Add tomatoes and onions. Simmer until thick, stirring occasionally to keep mixture from burning. When thick and brown, seal in hot jars. Wait approximately 2 months before using for best flavour.

Yield: 12 (8 oz/250 mL) jars

Bread and Butter Pickles

12	medium cucumbers, scrubbed and sliced	12
6	onions, sliced	6
1 qt	water	1 L
⅔ cup	coarse salt	150 mL
3 cups	vinegar	750 mL
1 cup	water	250 mL
2 cups	sugar	500 mL
1 Tbsp	mustard seed	15 mL
1 Tbsp	celery seed	15 mL
1 Tbsp	turmeric powder	15 mL
2	sweet red peppers, chopped	2

Let cucumbers and onions stand in salt and water for 12 hours. Drain, rinse with water and drain again. Pour vinegar and water into preserving kettle. Add drained cucumbers and onions along with sugar, mustard seed, celery seed, turmeric and red peppers. Mix well. Bring to boil. Fill hot sterilized jars and seal.

Yield: 20 (8 oz/250 mL) jars

Chili Sauce
An easy and delightful accompaniment for beef

30	tomatoes, cored and peeled	30
6	peaches, peeled and sliced	6
6	medium to large onions, chopped	6
½ cup	salt	125 mL
4½ cups	sugar	1125 mL
2 cups	vinegar	500 mL
3 Tbsp	mustard seed	50 mL
⅛ tsp	cayenne pepper	0.5 mL
4	green peppers, finely chopped	4
1	hot red pepper, finely chopped	1

Prepare tomatoes, peaches and onions. Place in large preserving kettle. Add salt. Let stand overnight. Drain all juice, then add sugar, vinegar, mustard seed, cayenne, green and red peppers. Boil uncovered 15 minutes. Pour into sterile jars and seal with paraffin wax.

Yield: 12 (8 oz/250 mL) jars

Indian Relish

12	ripe tomatoes	12
12	tart apples	12
9	large onions	9
5 cups	cider vinegar	1.25 L
6 cups	sugar	1.5 L
¼ cup	salt	50 mL
1½ tsp	dry mustard	7 mL
1½ tsp	ground ginger	7 mL
1½ tsp	ground cinnamon	7 mL
1½ tsp	ground cloves	7 mL
1½ tsp	pepper	7 mL

Peel and slice tomatoes. Chop apples and onions. Place in large preserving kettle. Add all remaining ingredients. Bring to boil and cook 2 hours over medium heat. Stir often as mixture becomes quite thick in last hour and must be prevented from sticking. Pour hot pickle into 10 to 12 sterilized jars. Seal with paraffin wax.

Yield: 10 to 12 medium jars

Green Tomato Mincemeat

6 cups	chopped green tomatoes	1.5 L
6 cups	chopped apples	1.5 L
3 cups	raisins	750 mL
2 tsp	salt	10 mL
1 cup	butter or margarine	250 mL
¾ cup	vinegar	175 mL
4 cups	brown sugar	1 L
1 tsp	ground cinnamon	5 mL
1 tsp	ground cloves	5 mL
1 tsp	ground allspice	5 mL
1 cup	chopped mixed peel	250 mL

Chop tomatoes, apples and raisins using meat grinder or food processor. Mix all ingredients in large preserving kettle. Bring to boil stirring constantly. Simmer 1 to 2 hours until mixture is thick. Place in hot sterilized jars. Seal with paraffin wax.

Yield: 12 (8 oz/250 mL) jars

Rhubarb Pickle
Quite tart— great with cold meats!

4 lb	rhubarb	2 kg
4 lb	brown sugar	2 kg
1 pint	cider vinegar	500 mL
2 tsp	ground cinnamon	10 mL
1 tsp	ground allspice	5 mL
1 tsp	ground cloves	5 mL

Cut rhubarb in ½ inch (1 cm) pieces. Put in preserving kettle. Add sugar, vinegar and spices. Bring slowly to a boil and boil until thick, allowing about 1 to 1½ hours at low heat to avoid burning. Pour hot into sterilized jars and seal with paraffin wax.

HINT: Ground spices give a deep brown colour. Whole spices tied in a bag give a lighter, more pink colour.

Yield: 6 to 8 medium jars

Pickled Onion Slices
Wonderful with cold roast beef

1	large Spanish onion	1
1 tsp	dill weed	5 mL
½ cup	sugar	125 mL
2 tsp	salt	10 mL
½ cup	vinegar	125 mL
¼ cup	water	50 mL

Thinly slice onion and place in bowl. Sprinkle with dill weed. Combine sugar, salt, vinegar and water. Heat to boiling point. Pour over onion. Cover and chill overnight. Keeps for several weeks in the refrigerator.

Yield: 1 cup (250 mL)

Port Wine Jelly
Great with poultry or crackers and cheese

2 cups	Port wine	500 mL
3 cups	sugar	750 mL
⅛ tsp	ground cinnamon	0.5 mL
⅛ tsp	ground cloves	0.5 mL
½ bottle	Certo liquid fruit pectin	½

In top of double boiler combine wine, sugar, cinnamon and cloves. Place over rapidly boiling water. Stirring constantly, heat 3 minutes. Then over direct heat, bring to full rolling boil. Stir in pectin and again bring to full rolling boil. Boil 1 minute, stirring constantly. Remove pan from heat. Skim off foam and ladle jelly into hot sterilized jars. Seal with paraffin wax.

Yield 4: (8 oz/250 mL) jars

Pepper Jelly

2 cups	chopped red and green peppers, drained	500 mL
1½ cups	cider vinegar	375 mL
7 cups	sugar	1.75 L
1 bottle	Certo liquid fruit pectin	1

In large saucepan place peppers, vinegar and sugar. Mix well. Bring to boil and boil hard 1 minute, stirring constantly. Remove from heat. Stir in pectin. Stir and skim off foam. Cool 5 minutes. Pour into hot sterilized jars. Seal with thin layer of paraffin wax.

Yield: 8 (8 oz/250 mL) jars

Brandied Cranberries
An attractive gift, and the perfect accompaniment to turkey, duck, goose or ham

1½ cups	sugar	375 mL
¼ cup	brandy	50 mL
½ cup	water	125 mL
¼ cup	orange juice	50 mL
2 Tbsp	grated orange rind	25 mL
4 cups	fresh cranberries	1 L
2 cups	red currant jelly	500 mL
1 tsp	ground ginger	5 mL

Combine the sugar, brandy, water, orange juice and rind in a large heavy saucepan. Bring to a boil, stirring until sugar is dissolved. Add the cranberries, and boil, stirring constantly for 5 minutes or until skins pop. Remove from heat and add currant jelly and ginger. Mix well and refrigerate.

Yield: 4 cups (1 L)

Tangerines in Brandy

6	tangerines or clementines	6
9	whole cloves	9
1¼ cups	brandy or cognac	300 mL
3 Tbsp	sugar	50 mL

Sterilize 3 (8 oz/250 mL) preserving jars. Peel tangerines or clementines and rub with linen cloth. Separate into sections. Remove seeds and prick each section with a fork. Place sections in jars and add 3 cloves to each jar. Dissolve sugar in brandy and pour syrup over tangerines. Seal and store for 2 months. Keep tangerines moist by turning jars periodically. Serve with ham or for dessert with ice cream.

Yield: 3 (8 oz/250 mL) jars

Spiced Grapes
Recipe dates from 1870!

2	6 qt (6 L) baskets of Concord grapes	2
15 lb	sugar	7 kg
4 cups	vinegar	1 L
½ lb	pickling spices	250 g

Separate grapes. Put skins in one large pot, pulp in another. Boil pulp for 20 minutes. Put through sieve or colander to remove seeds. Add seedless pulp to skins. Add sugar and vinegar. Place spices in muslin bag. Add to grape mixture. Boil 2 to 2½ hours until mixture begins to jell. Pour into jars and seal. Compliments poultry and meats.

Yield: 12 (8 oz/250 mL) jars

Spicy Honey Spread
Delicious on raisin bread

1 cup	honey	250 mL
¼ cup	soft butter or margarine	50 mL
1 Tbsp	ground cinnamon	15 mL
1 tsp	ground cardamon	5 mL
1 tsp	grated lemon rind	5 mL
¼ tsp	ground cloves	1 mL

Blend above ingredients in food processor. Place in glass jar. Seal well. Refrigerate.

Yield: 1¼ cups (300 mL)

NOTES

(... designates "Company in a Minute"

JUBILATION

The Junior League of Toronto
P.O. Box 1986, Don Mills, Ontario M3C 2E0

NAME _____

ADDRESS _____

CITY _____ PROVINCE _____

POSTAL CODE _____

Please send me _____ copies of JUBILATION AT **$16.95** each _____

Postage and Handling at $2.00 each   _____

TOTAL   _____

CHEQUES PAYABLE TO JUBILATION
Please charge to my VISA CARD NO. ☐☐☐☐☐☐☐☐☐☐☐☐☐☐

Expiry date _____

SIGNATURE OF CARD HOLDER _____

All proceeds realized from the sale of JUBILATION shall be used by the Junior League of Toronto to support community services.

- -

JUBILATION

The Junior League of Toronto
P.O. Box 1986, Don Mills, Ontario M3C 2E0

NAME _____

ADDRESS _____

CITY _____ PROVINCE _____

POSTAL CODE _____

Please send me _____ copies of JUBILATION AT **$16.95** each _____

Postage and Handling at $2.00 each   _____

TOTAL   _____

CHEQUES PAYABLE TO JUBILATION
Please charge to my VISA CARD NO. ☐☐☐☐☐☐☐☐☐☐☐☐☐☐

Expire date _____

SIGNATURE OF CARD HOLDER _____

All proceeds realized from the sale of JUBILATION shall be used by the Junior League of Toronto to support community services.

- -

JUBILATION

The Junior League of Toronto
P.O. Box 1986, Don Mills, Ontario M3C 2E0

NAME _____

ADDRESS _____

CITY _____ PROVINCE _____

POSTAL CODE _____

Please send me _____ copies of JUBILATION AT **$16.95** each _____

Postage and Handling at $2.00 each   _____

TOTAL   _____

CHEQUES PAYABLE TO JUBILATION
Please charge to my VISA CARD NO. ☐☐☐☐☐☐☐☐☐☐☐☐☐☐

Expire date _____

SIGNATURE OF CARD HOLDER _____

All proceeds realized from the sale of JUBILATION shall be used by the Junior League of Toronto to support community services.

JUBILATION   The Junior League of Toronto
                                  P.O. Box 1986, Don Mills, Ontario M3C 2E0

NAME _____

ADDRESS _____

CITY _____ PROVINCE _____

POSTAL CODE _____

Please send me _____ copies of JUBILATION AT **$16.95** each _____

Postage and Handling at $2.00 each   _____

TOTAL   _____

CHEQUES PAYABLE TO JUBILATION   □□□□□□□□□□□□□□□□
Please charge to my VISA CARD NO.

                                   Expiry date _____

SIGNATURE OF CARD HOLDER _____

All proceeds realized from the sale of JUBILATION shall be used by the Junior League of Toronto to support community services.

- -

JUBILATION   The Junior League of Toronto
                                  P.O. Box 1986, Don Mills, Ontario M3C 2E0

NAME _____

ADDRESS _____

CITY _____ PROVINCE _____

POSTAL CODE _____

Please send me _____ copies of JUBILATION AT **$16.95** each _____

Postage and Handling at $2.00 each   _____

TOTAL   _____

CHEQUES PAYABLE TO JUBILATION   □□□□□□□□□□□□□□□□
Please charge to my VISA CARD NO.

                                   Expire date _____

SIGNATURE OF CARD HOLDER _____

All proceeds realized from the sale of JUBILATION shall be used by the Junior League of Toronto to support community services.

- -

JUBILATION   The Junior League of Toronto
                                  P.O. Box 1986, Don Mills, Ontario M3C 2E0

NAME _____

ADDRESS _____

CITY _____ PROVINCE _____

POSTAL CODE _____

Please send me _____ copies of JUBILATION AT **$16.95** each _____

Postage and Handling at $2.00 each   _____

TOTAL   _____

CHEQUES PAYABLE TO JUBILATION   □□□□□□□□□□□□□□□□
Please charge to my VISA CARD NO.

                                   Expire date _____

SIGNATURE OF CARD HOLDER _____

All proceeds realized from the sale of JUBILATION shall be used by the Junior League of Toronto to support community services.

JUBILATION   The Junior League of Toronto
                                   P.O. Box 1986, Don Mills, Ontario M3C 2E0

NAME _____

ADDRESS _____

CITY _____ PROVINCE _____

POSTAL CODE _____

Please send me _____ copies of JUBILATION AT **$16.95** each _____

Postage and Handling at $2.00 each   _____

TOTAL   _____

CHEQUES PAYABLE TO JUBILATION   ☐☐☐☐☐☐☐☐☐☐☐☐☐☐
Please charge to my VISA CARD NO.

                                Expiry date _____

SIGNATURE OF CARD HOLDER _____

All proceeds realized from the sale of JUBILATION shall be used by the
Junior League of Toronto to support community services.

- -

JUBILATION   The Junior League of Toronto
                                   P.O. Box 1986, Don Mills, Ontario M3C 2E0

NAME _____

ADDRESS _____

CITY _____ PROVINCE _____

POSTAL CODE _____

Please send me _____ copies of JUBILATION AT **$16.95** each _____

Postage and Handling at $2.00 each   _____

TOTAL   _____

CHEQUES PAYABLE TO JUBILATION   ☐☐☐☐☐☐☐☐☐☐☐☐☐☐
Please charge to my VISA CARD NO.

                                Expire date _____

SIGNATURE OF CARD HOLDER _____

All proceeds realized from the sale of JUBILATION shall be used by the
Junior League of Toronto to support community services.

- -

JUBILATION   The Junior League of Toronto
                                   P.O. Box 1986, Don Mills, Ontario M3C 2E0

NAME _____

ADDRESS _____

CITY _____ PROVINCE _____

POSTAL CODE _____

Please send me _____ copies of JUBILATION AT **$16.95** each _____

Postage and Handling at $2.00 each   _____

TOTAL   _____

CHEQUES PAYABLE TO JUBILATION   ☐☐☐☐☐☐☐☐☐☐☐☐☐☐
Please charge to my VISA CARD NO.

                                Expire date _____

SIGNATURE OF CARD HOLDER _____

All proceeds realized from the sale of JUBILATION shall be used by the
Junior League of Toronto to support community services.